Offshore Ferry Services

Maritime books by the same author:

Arctic Victory
Battleship *Royal Sovereign*
British Battle Cruisers
Critical Combat
Cruise Ships
Cruisers in Action
Destroyer Action
Destroyer Leader
Eagle's War
Fighting Flotilla
Hard Lying
Heritage of the Sea
HMS *Wild Swan*
Into the Minefields
Midway Dauntless Victory
Naval Warfare in the English Channel 1939–1945
Pedestal: the convoy that saved Malta
Per Mare, Per Terram
Royal Navy Ships' Badges
Sailors in Dock
Task Force 57
The Battle-Cruiser HMS *Renown* 1916–1948

Offshore Ferry Services

A Useful Guide to the Shipping Lines and Routes

Peter C. Smith

Pen & Sword
MARITIME

First published in Great Britain in 2012 by
PEN & SWORD MARITIME
An imprint of
Pen & Sword Books Ltd
47 Church Street
Barnsley
South Yorkshire
S70 2AS

Copyright © Peter C. Smith, 2012.

See all of Peter's books at www.dive-bombers.co.uk

ISBN 978-1-84884-665-4

The right of Peter C. Smith to be identified as the author of this work has been asserted by him in accordance with the Copyright, Designs and Patents Act 1988.

A CIP catalogue record for this book is available from the British Library.

All rights reserved. No part of this book may be reproduced or transmitted in any form or by any means, electronic or mechanical including photocopying, recording or by any information storage and retrieval system, without permission from the Publisher in writing.

Typeset by Concept, Huddersfield, West Yorkshire.
Printed and bound in India by Replika Press Pvt. Ltd.

Pen & Sword Books Ltd incorporates the imprints of Pen & Sword Aviation, Pen & Sword Family History, Pen & Sword Maritime, Pen & Sword Military, Pen & Sword Discovery, Wharncliffe Local History, Wharncliffe True Crime, Wharncliffe Transport, Pen & Sword Select, Pen & Sword Military Classics, Leo Cooper, The Praetorian Press, Remember When, Seaforth Publishing and Frontline Publishing.

For a complete list of Pen & Sword titles please contact
PEN & SWORD BOOKS LIMITED
47 Church Street, Barnsley, South Yorkshire, S70 2AS, England
E-mail: enquiries@pen-and-sword.co.uk
Website: www.pen-and-sword.co.uk

Contents

Introduction vii
Acknowledgements ix
1: Penzance – Scilly Isles 1
2: Plymouth – Roscoff – Santander 9
3: Weymouth – Channel Islands – St. Malo 15
4: Poole – Cherbourg 20
5: Lymington – Yarmouth (IOW) 26
6: Southampton – Cowes 30
7: Portsmouth – St. Malo – Ouistreham (Caen) – Le Havre – Cherbourg 35
8: Portsmouth – Bilbao 47
9: St. Malo – Channel Islands 50
10: Isle of Wight – Wootton Creek and Ryde 56
11: Newhaven – Dieppe 61
12: Dover – Boulogne – Calais – Dunkirk 64
13: Ramsgate – Ostend 79
14: Pembroke – Rosslare 83
15: Harwich – Esbjerg – Hook 86
16: Holyhead – Dún Laoghaire – Dublin 94
17: Birkenhead – Liverpool – Belfast – Dublin 101
18: Douglas IoM – Heysham – Dublin – Belfast – Ardrossan 108
19: Larne – Cairnryan (formerly Stranraer) 114
20: Tynemouth – Amsterdam (Ijmuiden) 119
21: Tarbert – Islay – Jura – North Uist 123
22: Gourock – Dunoon 130
23: Ardrossan – Arran 135
24: Oban – Tiree – Coll – Lochhosidale – Castlebay – Islay – South Uist – Skye – North Uist – Tarbert 140
25: Aberdeen – Shetland Isles – Scrabster – Orkney Islands 169
26: Ullapool – Stornoway, Isle of Lewis 195
27: Hull – Zeebrugge – Rotterdam 198
28: Killingholme – Hoek van Holland – Rotterdam Europoort . . . 203
29: Other Offshore Operators 207
Glossary 212

Vital island ferries continue to work in almost all weather conditions. (© Dave Greer)

Introduction

The United Kingdom is a nation of islands. Just how many is, naturally, hotly disputed and depends on what one terms a 'genuine' island rather than a rocky outcrop, or an 'offshore' island rather than islets in lakes or just rocks above the tide-line. One generally quoted figure lists a total of 6,289 islands, most of them in Scotland, while Northern Ireland is said to have at least fifty-seven offshore islands. Smaller groups are equally diffuse, the Isle of Man has five main islands but many more islets; Guernsey has a total of eight main islands and Jersey six, but again, both have many smaller features.

The UK is also a land of rivers, river estuaries, sounds and straits all of which, down the centuries, have required boats to cross them and at various periods have hosted ferry routes of one kind or another, from coracle to chain ferry.

This present study confines itself to offshore ferry routes that have been established for some time and are currently still in regular usage. A second volume, covering river and inshore crossings is hoped to follow, but of course, some routes could equally qualify for either listing according to whatever classification is adopted. The term 'Salt-water Crossing' is also deemed insufficient as a definition. For example the inter-island ferries of the Hebrides, the Orkney Islands and the Shetland Islands are definitely off-shore, but small enough for some to insist that they be listed as in-shore, which they are definitely not according to the seas and weather conditions they have to face. Here they have been included as off-shore services which some critics will inevitably dispute. However, between the two volumes it is hoped to cover them all.

The routes selected are, almost universally, *passenger* routes first and foremost, although again not exclusively, as many crossings provide isolated communities with essential vehicle, cargo and livestock services without which they could not survive, even should air transport be assumed to be a viable alternative. Years of experience has shown this not to be the case. Therefore in this volume freight-only services are not described in detail at all, although many are mentioned. Equally, the arrival of fixed structures, like the Channel Tunnel or the Skye Bridge, have been widely proclaimed in the popular media to herald the demise of the traditional ferry routes, but, again, time has

Bow view of *Norman Arrow*, a typical High-Speed Catamaran (HSC). (© LD Lines)

proved this not to be the case in many instances. What is most certainly threatening our traditional over-water links and crossings today is not such technological innovations but the perilous and dire state of the economy in these years of financial crisis, which is driving down passenger- and vehicle-numbers and thus risking some wonderful investments in new ships and facilities that many of the ferry companies have bravely taken on in recent years. The operators and investors certainly deserve better, but only time will tell how many will survive the downturn and how many either go to the wall or become part-and-parcel of the increasing number of mergers and take-overs of recent years.

These facts hang heavily over existing ferry services; however, a look at the outline histories of both the routes themselves and some of the many ferry companies that serviced them and have come and gone down the centuries, will quickly show that it was ever thus. Boom and bust, new types of ships, economic good times and soaring tourism have alternated with wars, slumps and tragedies down the years. Ferry operators have come and gone in dizzying succession, trying to match the services they can provide with the shifts in demand, with one always being out of synchronicity with the other, due to the time taken to invest and build the appropriate vessels, against the increasing speed at which change has taken place. So oar gave way to sail, which was ousted by the steam engine and paddle power, which in turn was displaced by the screw, the turbine and the catamaran. The hovercraft had its brief day; it came, conquered and disappeared in a few decades. The high-speed passenger catamarans craft currently in vogue might be the future or just another short-term trend. Who can say? But as long as man wishes to link city with city, port with port and nation with nation across the waters, wide or narrow, shallow or deep, the ferry in some form or other, will surely ever be with us.

VERY IMPORTANT NOTE

Ferries are dependent upon the weather, the sea and the tides. Ferry operators also respond to actual demand, which is never constant. There have always been summer services and winter services for example, and many variations in between the two. While the outline of timetables existent at the time of writing have been included to give a general indication of availability these times are for outline information only and must not be taken as guaranteed on any particular day or period. Similarly, in the present economic climate, services are continually being examined, modified, trimmed and changed, and, almost day-to-day, crossings and timings that exist on one week, may be axed or reduced by the next and companies might vanish overnight due to financial constraints or take-overs.

It is therefore ESSENTIAL that any journeys planned or undertaken that involve any of the ferry routes described in this book are checked and verified with the Ferry Companies themselves in advance of any travel. Each operator's Contact Details are included here, with telephone, fax, email and web site details provided, and it is totally incumbent of each individual to ensure that the most up-to-date information regarding any particular service is totally verified by the company involved. Author and Publisher *cannot accept any responsibility* for any information which proves to be different to that stated due to such a continuous changing circumstances or events that have taken place between the inclusion of data here recorded and any subsequent events.

Acknowledgements

This book could not have been written without the considerable help and input of a great many people concerned with the operations and running of these vital links. My thanks and appreciation then to the following who gave me advice, assistance and permission to quote facts and reproduce their copyright photos here.

Ian Arch, Karen Jackson Design; Kathryn Banks, Pentland Ferries Ltd, Orkney; Brian Burnell; Brian A. Convery, Sales Development Manager, Isle of Man Steam Packet Company; John Crae; Paul Dashwood; Magnus Dixon, NorthLink Ferries; Keith Edwards, Manager, Gosport Ferry Ltd; Maj-Len Ehrnrooth, Transfennica, Helsinki; Michaela Farry, Marketing, Harwich International Port; Fred Fermor, John O'Groats Ferry; Stephen Ferres, Redboat; Alastair Gardiner; Hugh Gibson; Joy Gillan, Fastnet Line; Conor Gilligan, Passage East Car Ferry, Waterford; Rachel Gifford, Sales and Marketing Administrator, Condor Ferries Ltd; Lyndsey Green, Lundy Island; David Greer; Les Hamilton, Aberdeen; Jackie Hayman, Marketing Manager, Isles of Scilly Travel; Beverley Hayward, King Harry Steam Ferry Company Ltd; Emma Heard, King Harry Ferry Company; Elaine Jackson, Sales & Marketing Co-ordinator Passenger Irish Sea, DFDS Seaways; Mairi Johnston, West Coast Ferries, Campbeltown; Christopher Jones, Brittany Ferries; Andrew Kelly, Marketing and PR Manager, English Channel, DFDS Seaways, Dover; Lise Knudsen, Marketing Coordinator, DFDS Seaways, Copenhagen; David I. List, Manager, Tamar Bridge and Torpoint Ferry Joint Committee; Marion Lonsdale, Marketing Officer, Cumbria County Council; Ken Lussy, Undiscovered Scotland; Peter McCann; Duncan MacEachen, Isle of Kerrera Ferry; Louise McKibbin, The PR Agency, UK; Colin Manson, Resources Manager, Ferry Services, Shetland Islands Council, Sellaness; Michael Milne; Olivier Normand, Manche-iles-Express; Paul O'Brien, Fastnet Line; Tom Pell-Stevens, Red Funnel Ferries; David Punton, Press and Public Relations Officer, Nexus, Newcastle-upon-Tyne; Brian Rees of P&O Communications; David Ritchie; Sarah Roberts-Byrne, Company Supervisor, Isle of Sark Shipping Company Ltd; Paul and Sarah Smith; Kerry Southern, Dartmouth Higher Ferry; Darran Steel, Operations Manager, Transfennica UK Ltd; Nick Stevens, NLCH Associates Ltd; Tiffany Tate, Stena Line; Ivor Thomas; Michelle Ulyatt, Communications Executive, P&O Ferries; Captain B. Vaughn, WightLink; Mary Whirdy, Customer Support, Irish Ferries, Dublin; Jessica White, Marketing, Red Funnel Ferries; Sam Woodward and Lawrence Duffy.

This book is dedicated to the memory of Peter Coles, whose original concept it was. A yachtsman with a love of ships and the sea, Peter was one of the best and most knowledgeable editors I have ever worked with, and his sudden death in 2011 was an enormous personal loss to me. Wherever you sail now, Peter, I wish you blue skies and calm seas.

Freight loading and unloading takes place day and night. (© Portsmouth Port)

1: Penzance – Scilly Isles

Background

While the Isles of Scilly nowadays rely on seasonal tourism, including off-season bird-watchers, and the export of daffodils rather than fishing, transport across the 28-mile route to and from the Cornish coast is considered an essential lifeline that enables the islanders to carry on living there. Sail of course, was once universal and the Isles of Scilly Packet boat was taking passengers, cargo, communications and livestock to and from the mainland from as early as 1548. Sloops, cutters and smacks continued that dual role down the centuries until by 1825 it was announced that the *Cherub*, a new packet, would sail each Friday from Penzance for Scilly and would return to Penzance each Tuesday and that she was fitted with 'very superior accommodation for ladies and gentlemen …'.

The arrival of steam power and coal driven vessels did not immediately alter things as the early ships were both expensive to run and unreliable on anything other than short routes, which meant that it was often ferry services who pioneered their regular use rather than deep-sea traders. The roots of the ferry service to the Scillies, as presently understood, may be dated back to the June 1831, when first steamship to be christened *Sir Francis Drake*, built eight years earlier, began working to the Islands in June 1831 from Plymouth. In 1858 the eleven-year-old iron paddle steamer *Scotia* of 480-GT was chartered from her City of Dublin company owners to a Isles of Scilly consortium comprising two ship owners, James Phillips and Richard Edwards, two ship agents, Thomas Johns Buxton and Francis Banfield and one James Bluett, merchant, who together had formed the Scilly Isles Steam Navigation Company and began a regular mail and passenger service. She was only stop-gap until the arrival of a purpose-built 115-GT, 2-cylinder iron screw steam schooner which was being built by James Henderson at Renfrew, Scotland, the *Little Western*. This little vessel took over the route in 1859 making three 4-hour runs per week and she more-or-less had it to herself until 1871, when the West Cornwall Steamship Company arrived on the scene and commenced operating

The flagship of the Isles of Scilly fleet is the *Scillonian III*. (© Isles of Scilly Travel)

the ten-year-old, iron-built, 144-GT paddle steamer *Earl of Arran*, working from Penzance. The *Earl*'s tenure was brief for she came to grief on the Nornour Rock between St. Martins and the Eastern Rocks on 16 July 1872. Meanwhile the new company had purchased the *Little Western* but, on 6 October 1872, she was likewise wrecked on Southward Wells Reef, off the Scillies while attempting to aid a disabled brigantine.

After a series of chartered paddle steamers, the West Cornwall Steamship Company commissioned a replacement, the 152-GT *Lady of the Isles*, which started operating in 1875 and continued ferry working until 1905, but she also was equally unlucky when, on 1 September 1904, she struck the Heaver Rock and had to be beached. The *Deerhound*, of 483-GT, built by John Jones on the Mersey in 1901, was brought in to take her place while salvage work was done and a new boiler fitted, and this vessel was operated by the Royal Navy between 1905 and 1907 before being sold to Canada as a mail tender. With the termination of the West Cornwall SSC the route was operated by John Banfield for the next ten years. A bigger vessel, the 329-GT, 52 m steel screw steamer *Lyonnesse*, had arrived in 1889, being built by Harveys at Hayle, and likewise served long and well, and carried on the ferry service through to the First World War. In 1918 she was sold at Queenstown, and for a short period the government had to operate the route as an essential public service, requisitioning the 1903-built *Lapwing* from the Scottish company Clyde Cargo Steamers to do the job. *Lapwing* was a steel screw steamer of 194-GT.

In March 1920, the Isles of Scilly Steamship Company Limited was formed and *Lapwing* was replaced on 5 February 1920 by the purchase for £7,000 of the 380-GT steel screw steamer *Peninnis*, formerly the *Argon*, the Navy Examination Vessel at Berehaven, Ireland. She operated between 25 March and December 1920, when she was managed by E.N.V. Moyle but, by 31 December, she had been sold to William H. Ward, Woodford. The first custom-built ship for the new company,

The Chief Engineer of the *Scillonian III* with his charges. (© Isles of Scilly Travel)

built by Ailsa Shipbuilding at Troon at a cost of £24,500, was to have been the *Queen of the Isles*, but this 420-GT, 52 m long, vessel, able to carry 400 passengers was named *Scillonian* on her launch in November 1925. She plied the Penzance to Scilly route from 25 January 1926 for the next three decades, including work as a troopship in the Second World War. By the 1950s she was worn out and a replacement ship was ordered from John I. Thornycroft of Woolston, Southampton at a cost of £250,000. Of 921-GT and with an overall length of 63.55 m, she could carry 500 passengers and had a crew of 14.

She became the new *Scillonian* (and has become identified as *Scillonian II*, although she was never called anything else but *Scillonian* when in service). She was completed in 1956 and made her maiden voyage to the Isles of Scilly on 28 March that year; her larger size meant her operating from Albert Pier, Penzance. She was another reliable and much-loved vessel and continued service until replaced in her turn, in May 1977.

A second vessel, the 515-GT *Queen of the Isles*, built in 1964 at Bristol by Charles Hill & Sons, Albion Boatyard, was of 47.62 m length and could carry 300 passengers and 60 tons of cargo, and operated as a back-up ship at peak periods from 1965. But within a year she had proven inadequate for the waters off the Scillies and Land's End and was chartered out for work in kindlier climes before being sold in 1970.

Current Operator, Ships and Routes

The *Scillonian III* (IMO 7400259) is a passenger/cargo ferry which was especially constructed for the Isles of Scilly Steamship Company by Appledore Shipbuilders, Appledore, North Devon. After being christened by HRH Prince Charles, Duke of Cornwall, she entered service on 19 May 1977. She is of 1,346-GT and has an overall length of 67.7 m, a beam of 11.85 m and a draught of just 2.89 m, this latter allowing her to navigate the shallow waters of the Scillies. She is powered by two

The *Scillonian III* in her old livery. (© Isles of Scilly Steamship Company)

Mirrlees Blackstone ESL8 diesel engines which give her a maximum operational speed of 15.5 knots. She is also fitted with a *Flume* stabilizer which operates via slack water tanks to port and starboard joined by a transverse tunnel. In theory the water in the tanks is transported across the ship via the tunnel as she heels and rolls, and being directly out of phase with the motion, keeps her relatively steady. Following a £1,700,000 refit in 1998 the vessel had additional strengthening built into her and was fitted with a bow thruster to aid manoeuvrability, as well as three new generators. She is currently finishing her 35th season. Talk of a larger replacement being financed by Cornwall County Council with additional Government funding has become mired down in a bitter dispute involving the costings and the size of the new vessel among other matters. In July 2011, after the expenditure of some £4 million, the Government refused to back the scheme.

The *Scillonian III* and other ships make a peaceful backdrop to the glorious landscape of the Scilly Islands. (© Isles of Scilly Travel)

1: Penzance – Scilly Isles

The *Scillonian III* carries on as best she can. She is capable of accommodating 600 passengers and 6 cars. Aboard there is outside seating on A deck and bridge deck, and smoking is restricted to the open deck areas only. Views *en route* include Newlyn, Mousehole and the Wolf Rock Lighthouse. There is a bar with chair seating and tables, located on the middle deck forward, which serves various alcoholic and non-alcoholic beverages and hot drinks. There is a buffet area at the rear of the lower (C) deck, equipped with chairs and tables and which serves soft and hot drinks and snacks. There is also a baby-changing area and lounge seating. The lower saloon has quiet areas with some small couches, in which dogs are not allowed. A passenger shop has gifts, souvenirs, guide books and other sundries.

The onboard facilities include a person-only Dolphin Stairlift on the main stairway from the bridge deck to the upper deck, capable of conveying a single passenger and with a weight limit of 150 kg. Those who wish to use this lift have to be able to either transfer themselves or have their own helpers, as crew members are not allowed to lift passengers. The passenger gangway is unsuitable for motorized buggies, which have to be loaded as cargo. Wheelchairs are available but have to be pre-arranged. There are disabled access toilets aboard. There are certain luggage and freight restrictions which should be checked out with the company in advance as should the fares. The checked personal luggage allowance per passenger is limited to two items with a 25 kg maximum combined included in the price of the ticket. Single items are restricted to a maximum of 20 kg and any excess is additionally charged for and should be clearly marked. Day trip passengers have no luggage allowance; however, soft hand luggage is unrestricted. Various items are classed as freight and have to be booked and paid for in advance, these include boats of all types, camping gear, cycles, diving gear, motorized wheelchairs, windsurfing equipment, and trailers of less than 2 m for St. Agnes and St. Martins.

The *Scillonian III* currently operates a complex general schedule of crossings for an eight-month period each year, and some of these can be affected by extreme tidal conditions; as always it is essential to check with the company well in advance.

In 2012 this was as follows: between 26 March and 31 March and between 16 October and 3 November, there were sailings on Monday, Wednesday, Friday and Saturdays, the first leaving Penzance at 09.15 and the last returning from St. Mary's at 16.30.

Between 3 April and 26 May, between 11 June and 14 July and between 27 August and 13 October, there was a six-day service, excluding Sundays, which operated at the same first and last hours.

Between 28 May and 8 June and between 16 July and 25 August there was a five-day service, excluding Saturdays and Sundays, with the same first and last hours.

Between 2 and 9 June there was also a twice daily return sailing on Saturday, and between 16 July and 25 August there was single Saturday service departing Penzance at 10.30 and returning from St. Mary's at 15.00. In addition there were three 'Gig Weekend' sailings on 4, 5 and 7 May, and special Wednesday Sailings for *Race of Life* on 30 May. No Sunday service was scheduled.

The usual journey time is 2 hours 40 minutes. The *Scillonian III* has a comparatively shallow keel and there is sometimes rough water after leaving Land's End, but helicopters that provide an alternative can also be affected by weather conditions or even grounded by fog, and the ship is much cheaper.

At Penzance the ferry terminal has limited facilities; short-term pay and display parking is adjacent to the bus station but there are long-term secure garages available for other than day visitors.

The *Gry Maritha* (IMO 8008462) is a 590-GT class 1A NSC built in 1981 as a mini-pallet carrier. She was originally built by Moen Slip Og Mek Verksted, Kolvereid, Norway and was operated by Gjofor. She was

Offshore Ferry Services

The *Gry Maritha* freight ferry, here seen loading cargo, is part of the Isles of Scilly fleet and is based at Penzance, Cornwall. (© Isles of Scilly Travel)

named after the daughter of Captain Tor Sevaldsen, her first captain. Being built with a high freeboard, skeg and flared bows in order to cope with Norwegian sea conditions, she is particularly suited for the notorious large Atlantic combers in the seas off the Cornish coast in winter. She was purchased by ISSSCo in 1989 after it was recommended that *Scillonian III* continue in use, should be laid up during the worst winter weather, and that summer passenger and goods traffic be separated.

She is powered by two Caterpillar 34306B main diesel engines developing 350 bhp each at 1,800 rpm driving outward turning propellers through twin disc reversing gearboxes, making her manoeuvrability excellent in the small service terminals she operates from and obviates the need for tugs. This power unit gives her a working speed of 10.5 knots. She also has two Volvo auxiliary engines.

She has an overall length of 37.61 m, a beam of 9.81 m and a draught of 3.63 m full load and 2.9 m light and can carry 1,060 m^3 of cargo, including 25 tonnes of diesel gas oil for St. Mary's customers, along with a dedicated fuel discharge system, that can pump it ashore at 6,000 litres per hour; while petrol is carried in 1,250 litre tanks, which are loaded and discharged ashore. There is also a specially-adapted ballast tank that can convey 70 tonnes of fresh water to the islands. The *Gry Maritha* can also make available a further 30 tonnes of diesel oil tank capacity at short notice if required. She is fitted with 12.6 m × 4.7 m hatch covers and can accommodate a pair of 6 m ISO reefer containers. One can be maintained at a temperature of −25°C, for frozen food and the other at 1°C for chilled goods, important to the Scilly Island flower industry. Another 60 tonnes of deck cargo can be carried on the upper after deck. Three fork-lift trucks work inside the hold. The vessel has a starboard-mounted deck crane with a 14 m outreach, capable of lifting approximately 6 tonnes and has the advantage of a remote controlled side-shifter pallet hoist system to port, serving both the 'tween deck and lower cargo hold, which further reduces her dependence on shore-side cargo handling facilities.

There is certified space for 12 passengers, with overnight accommodation for 3; she has a crew of 4 and she can accommodate 5 cars and 1 truck in addition to general cargo. She operates an all-year freight and passenger service three times a week, sailing on Monday, Wednesday and Friday and returning to Penzance on Tuesday, Thursday and Saturday, taking just under 5 hours to make the round trip.

There is also the 32 m long *Ivor B*, (ex-*Guedel*) a former French coaster used as a freight ship and purchased in June 2010. She was named after Ivor Bone, contracts manager on the Five Islands new school project.

1: Penzance – Scilly Isles

The *Ivor B* freight ferry loading cargo. (© Isles of Scilly Travel)

For inter-island passenger and goods haulage the Isles of Scilly has the *Lyonesse Lady* here seen alongside embarking cargo. (© Isles of Scilly Travel)

Offshore Ferry Services

Another cargo vessel in the fleet is the *Lyonesse Lady*, originally built by Lochabar Marine, Fort William in 1991, which, in addition to freight, can carry 6 passengers. Finally there is the Rigid Inflatable Boat *Swift Lady*, purchased in 2004 and capable of 35 knots. She is used as an inter-island boat from St. Mary's to deliver and collect the mail at Bryher, Tresco, St. Agnes and St. Martins.

Contact Details
Port of Penzance, Penzance Harbour, Harbour Office, Wharf Road, Penzance, Cornwall, TR18 4AH
Tel: 01736 366113
Fax: 01736 366114
Isles of Scilly Steamship Company

Penzance Office
Steamship House, Quay Street, Penzance, Cornwall, TR18 4BZ

St. Mary's
PO Box 10, Hugh Town, St. Mary's, Isles of Scilly, TR2 0LJ
Tel: 0945 710 5555
Fax: 01736 334228
Email: sales@islesofscilly-travel.co.uk
Web: www.ios-travel.co.uk
Isles of Scilly Travel Centre, Quay Street, Penzance, Cornwall, TR18 4BZ
Tel: 0845 710 5555
Fax: 01736 334228

The smallest vessel of the Isles of Scilly fleet is the *Swift Lady*. (© Isles of Scilly Travel)

2: Plymouth – Roscoff – Santander

Background

No less than three attempts were made to operate a viable ferry route from Southampton to northern Spanish ports but the length of the route meant that none of them proved very popular or practical. It was not until 1978 that the French parent company of Brittany Ferries was able to negotiate special permission to sail ships through the dangerous waters between Ushant and the mainland and thus open a more westerly route between Plymouth and Santander. It was the consequent reduction in the time spent at sea to under 24 hours that made the whole thing feasible and commercial. The attraction of the hitherto small fishing port of Roscoff on the Breton coast for a similar opening up of a route to export for the French hinterland's largely agricultural produce had also led to lobbying of the French Government in 1968 and they agreed to fund a deep-water port and facilities.

Brittany Ferries was first founded in 1972 by Alexis Gourvennec with the prosaic task of conveying artichoke and cauliflower produce from the growing areas in Brittany to British markets via the deep-water port of Roscoff to Plymouth. This private venture also capitalized on the growing popularity of Brittany as a holiday destination. From this simple premise of shipping agricultural produce north and bringing tourists south across the western end of the English Channel, Brittany Ferries, which still has French farming co-operatives among its major shareholders, has grown into one of the largest and most progressive ferry and tour companies. The company has since extended operations to Cork in Ireland and Poole and Portsmouth in the UK, Cherbourg, St. Malo and Caen in France and to the Spanish Biscay ports of Bilbao and Santander. To cope with burgeoning demand Brittany now runs a modern fleet of superb vessels that in many ways vie with cruise ships for size and luxury and account for in excess of 50% of such traffic in this area of operations.

Brittany Ferries' *Armorique* at sea. (© Brittany Ferries)

Current Operators, Ships and Details
The current Brittany ferry flotilla operating from Plymouth comprises the *Armorique, Pont-Aven* and *Bretagne*.

Armorique (IMO 9364980) is a half-sister to the *Cotentin*, and is a combined passenger/freight ferry that was ordered from the Helsinki yard of STX Europe as a direct replacement for the *Pont L'Abbe* on the Plymouth to Roscoff crossing. Displacing 29,486 tons the *Armorique* has an overall length of 168.30 m, a beam of 26.80 m and a draught of 6.30 m, with a speed of 25 knots and a crew of 106. Costing £81 million, she can carry 1,500 passengers, 470 cars and up to 65 trucks, and has a double deck access via bow and stern doors and an internal ramp. She has high-quality accommodation for freight drivers. She made her maiden voyage on 10 February 2009.

The *Armorique* has 788 berths, with 248 cabins, including the external Commodore class, with twin beds, sofa-bed, *en-suite*, flat screen TV, DVD player, hair dryer, mini bar; Club4 Plus and Club4 standard and the Finistère Club cabins, along with 2- and 4-berth cabins with bunk style beds. Facilities include the Les Boutiques shopping mall, eating outlets at Le Restaurant, and the Lounge Café, while drinks are available at Le Bar in the main lounge. Entertainment includes an on-board cinema, the Games Planet and a slot arcade at Chance Planet as well as WiFi and dedicated play areas. There is the large Reserve Pullman lounge with reclining seating and a quiet area in the reading lounge. Disability toilets, children's area and baby-changing facilities are also provided.

She currently operates a twice-daily summer service between April and October on the Plymouth to Roscoff route with average journey times of 6 hours.

Pont-Aven (IMO 9268708) is a cruise/ferry vessel formerly known as the *Bretagne 2*. She is currently the company flagship and was constructed in the German yard of Meyer Werft, Papenburg, at a cost of £100 million, being completed in 2004 and making her maiden voyage that March. Of 41,748-GT she has an overall length of 184.6 m, a beam of 30.9 m and a 6.8 m draught. She is powered by four MAK 12V M 43 engines which provide 50,400 kW engine power, 43,200 kW propulsion power, and give her a service speed of 27 knots. She has a crew of 183. As befits such a ship she is lavishly equipped, with a passenger capacity of 2,400 and space to accommodate 650 cars.

The *Pont-Aven*'s facilities match this specification, with a pool and mezzanine, leisure area, a wrap-around promenade deck, a five-deck-tall atrium with panoramic viewing from the glass lifts. According to season the ship features live bands, a DJ, cabaret, pianists and a children's entertainment programme. There is a dance-floor and stage,

Comfortable and spacious bar area in the *Armorique*. (© Brittany Ferries)

2: Plymouth – Roscoff – Santander

The Brittany Ferries super-ferry *Pont Aven* at sea. (© Brittany Ferries)

Aboard the *Pont Aven* the pool is flanked by chairs and tables with inviting shopping area beyond. (© Brittany Ferries)

two cinemas with total surround-sound, Wi-Fi and internet access, the Casino video games room and slots, a relaxing lounge with forty-seven reclining seats for non-cabin passengers, and a special teenagers' room to chill out or play air hockey away from the oldies. Shopping includes a *bureau de change*.

Accommodation is 650 cabins including the eighteen Commodore-class outside cabins, suitable for up to three adults and a child; sixteen exterior De Luxe Cabins sleeping four adults, and fifty-six outside Club4 4-berth cabins, in addition to twelve exterior 2-berth cabins, and ninety-seven exterior 4-berth cabins, 158 inside 4-berth and 284 interior 2-berth cabins, also nine disabled 4-berth cabins with wheelchair access, all with full air-conditioning, reclining seats and cots if required. Catering is provided by Le Flora *à la carte* restaurant with choice of either set or buffet menus; with the two self-service outlets, La Belle Angele which features grill, world and traditional menus and Le Café

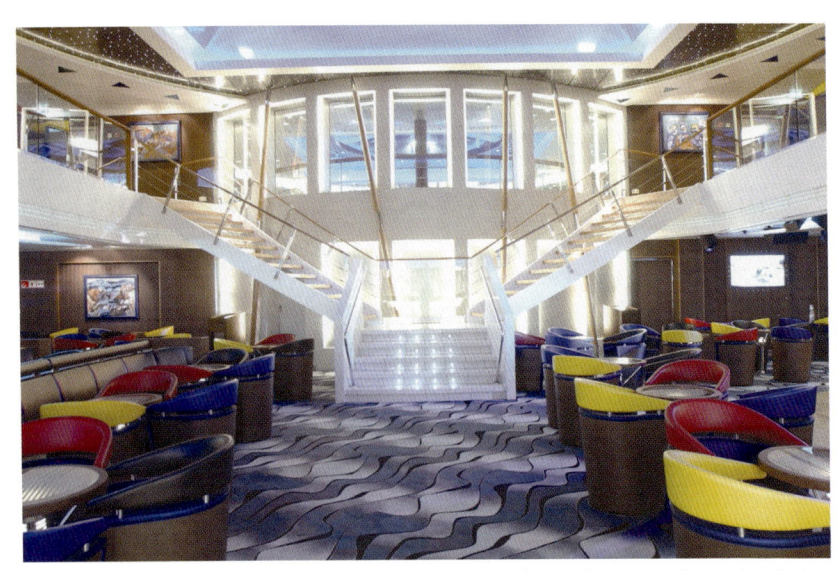

Contemporary styling and clean inviting spaces with ample space show the design concept of the Brittany Ferries *Pont Aven*. (© Brittany Ferries)

Spacious sun deck on the *Pont Aven*. (© Brittany Ferries)

du Festival, with a wide range of pastries and sandwiches; while for liquid refreshment there is two-tiered Le Grand Pavois main bar, Le Fastnet piano and cocktail bar and Les Finisteres pool bar. There is also a drivers' lounge and quiet space for truck drivers and passengers. There are also kennels for pet dog travellers.

The *Pont-Aven* currently operates over a variety of routes: between April and October 2012 she undertook the weekly Sunday sailing from Plymouth to Santander, returning every Wednesday, a voyage of 20.5 hours. She also operated the Portsmouth to Santander route between April and October, a 24 hour journey time, departing Santander each Monday and leaving Portsmouth each Tuesday. The Spanish port gives easy and relaxed access to southern France and northern Spain. The weekly Thursday service from Plymouth to Roscoff (returning on Sunday) takes 5.5 hours, for access to Brittany itself and western France. There is also currently a winter only service from Cork, Ireland to Roscoff, which takes 14 hours.

In the winter months this ship is relieved by the *Bretagne*, whose normal route is Portsmouth to St. Malo.

Plymouth can be reached by road from London via the M4, M5 and A38 in about 4 hours and the Ferry Port on Plymouth Sound is about

2: Plymouth – Roscoff – Santander

The Brittany Ferries super-ferry *Pont Aven* entering harbour. (© Brittany Ferries)

Offshore Ferry Services

20 minutes walk from the rail and bus stations and town centre. Between March and October there are up to two sailings per day to and from Roscoff. The terminal is well-equipped, having a cafeteria which opens for ferry arrivals and departures, payphone, a *bureau de change*, a baby-changing area, and there are showers for truck drivers at the freight office. There is daily pay car parking only at the terminal.

Roscoff is reached from Paris via the D69 and N58 via Morlaix and is situated conveniently for the Pink Granite Coast, Quimper, Bénodet and Concarneau and opens up a fast route to the Dordogne and Loire Valley or the Biscay coast. The ferry terminal is approximately 20 minutes walk from the rail station. The facilities include a limited opening cafeteria/bar/restaurant, ATM, a summer months only gift and newspaper shop, a baby-changing facility, toilets and disabled toilets and a tourist information desk in July and August only. There is a large open car park at own risk.

Santander, Cantabria, is not far from Bilbao, and the N634 is within easy reach with the N611 and N623, and the ferry port is signposted Puerto, Zona Maritima or Ferry. The rail and coach stations are a 15-minute walk away. At the terminal there is a ground floor cafeteria and gift shop, payphones, and a tourist information desk for arrivals and departures. There are toilets and disabled toilets. There are no car parks on site but paying car parks are nearby.

Contact Details

Plymouth Office
Brittany Ferries, Millbay, Plymouth, Devon, PL1 3EW
Tel: 0871 244 1401
Fax: 08709 011100
Email: enquiries@brittanyferries.com
Web: www.brittanyferries.co.uk/Plymouth

Roscoff Office
Brittany Ferries, Gare Maritime, Port de Bloscon, Roscoff, 29680
Tel: 0298 292813
Email: enquiries@brittanyferries.co.uk
Web: www.brittanyferries.co.uk

Santander Office
Brittany Ferries, Estacion Maritime, Santander, 39002
Tel: 942 360611
Email: enquiries@brittanyferries.com
Web: www.brittanyferries.co.uk

3: Weymouth – Channel Islands – St. Malo

Background

Weymouth has a proud history as a port, with records of shipping in the River Wey dating back to Roman times. The ferry terminal has an equally distinguished ancestry but in recent years has suffered a decline from its hey-day and is little used. There are currently plans to try and revitalize the harbour but in the current economic climate things are difficult, as problems with obtaining a much-needed by-pass road have illustrated.

The first sailing packet service was initiated in 1794 with regular sailings to the Channel Islands, a traffic that spurred much growth in the century that followed and in that respect at least Weymouth still delivers today. In 1857 the Weymouth and Channel Islands Steam Packet Services began operations, with the Great Western Railway (GWR) proving the spur, as with so many ferry routes, to drive the expansion forward at a far greater pace and set out Weymouth as a great boat train terminus. Established in 1880 was Cosens and Co. which although not and never a ferry concern, ran a fleet of excursions paddle steamers, that made occasional forays to the Channel Islands and even Cherbourg. Pride of their fleet became the *Monarch*, built in 1888. Meanwhile, with the extension of the line to the new terminal at the quay, tourists from London were able to make an almost seamless transit from the trains to the ships alongside. So popular did the service become that GWR began operating ferries of their own in 1889 with the three 672-GT sisters *Antelope*, *Gazelle* and *Lynx*, the former serving until the eve of the First World War before being sold and the other pair surviving to 1925. These three were joined by a fourth ship, the *Ibex*, in 1891, and she too lasted until 1925.

In 1897 two new vessels were constructed: the 1,193-GT *Reindeer* and the 1,186-GT *Roebuck*. They were built by the Naval Construction & Armaments Company at Barrow-in-Furness. Each had an overall length of 85.34 m, a 10.49 m beam and a draught of 5.08 m, and they were powered by two 3-cylinder engines for a speed of 18 knots. The *Roebuck* had a hair-raising career, being set afire and sunk in 1905; refloated, refurbished and placed back in service, in 1911 she grounded at St. Helier, survived that, was requisitioned by the Royal Navy in 1914

Bow view of the *Condor Express* (© Condorferries Ltd)

Offshore Ferry Services

to become a minesweeper as HMS *Roedean* and was sunk (again) the following year. *Reindeer*'s life was more prosaic and she survived until 1928. The 1,062-GT *Ibex* joined the fleet in 1897 and also remained until 1925.

After the First World War GWR built four new ships in 1925, the 1,885-GT pair *St. Helier* and *St. Julien* for passenger trade and the 776-GT second *Roebuck*, and *Sambur* for freight traffic. They all survived the Second World War, although the first pair only just. On 12 June 1940 they tried to enter St. Valery-en-Caux harbour, not realizing the German Army had already captured the port. Fired upon by artillery they beat a hasty retreat and got away with minor damage. The *St. Julien* was disposed of in 1946 while the other trio lasted until the 1960s.

In the aftermath of the Second World War the third *St. Patrick* was delivered in 1947. She was of 3,482-GT and right away began work on the Weymouth to Channel Islands crossing, where she remained until 1963, when she was superseded and moved over to the Southampton to St. Malo route. (She ended her days as the Greek *Thermopylae* from 1972 onward.) In 1948, under the post-war rail nationalization scheme, British Rail took over the fleet under the auspices of the British Transport Commission. Among the many vessels that sailed the route from Weymouth in these decades were the 3,543-GT *Normannia*, built for British Rail in 1952 and re-built ten years later as a stern-loading car ferry. She served briefly on the Weymouth, Channel Islands, Cherbourg route in 1974 and 1975.

The *Maid of Kent* was built in 1959 for service with BR/Sealink, and not finally disposed of until 1982.

In 1960 the nationalized British Rail started passenger ferries on the route with the *Caesarea*, built for the job by J. Samuel White at Cowes. She successfully operated from Weymouth for fifteen years when she was transferred to Dover. A contemporary was the much-loved *Sarnia*, another White-built ship completed a year later. She also ran for British

The *Condor Express* at speed. (© Condorferries Ltd)

Rail and then Sealink for sixteen trouble-free years before being sold in 1977.

In 1970 British Rail Ferries was re-branded as Sealink and in 1972 a Linkspan was built at Weymouth's No. 3 berth for Ro-Ro car and freight traffic. In 1974 a summer service to Cherbourg commenced and initially flourished. Another British Rail vessel commenced working from Weymouth during this period. The stern-door Ro-Ro *Caledonian Princess*, had been built by William Denny at Dumbarton in 1961 for the British Transport Commission and was used on the North Channel crossing between Stranraer and Larne. Of 3,360-GT she was 107.6 m overall length, had a beam of 17.4 m and a draught of 3.7 m. She was powered by two steam turbines which gave her a speed of 20.5 knots and she had a capacity for 1,400 passengers and 103 cars, after she underwent a modification in 1976 as part of the Sealink fleet which raised her tonnage to 4,042-GT. She was then used on the Weymouth to Channel Islands route, which she operated until 1981. She was subsequently sold, becoming the *Tuxedo Princess* floating nightclub on the Tyne and the Clyde and, as *Prince*, was scrapped in Turkey in 2008.

The *Earl Godwin* was the former *Svea Drott* built by Ab Öresundvarvet at Landskrona for Rederi AB Svea of Stockholm, Sweden in 1966. She was used by Sealink working from Weymouth to Cherbourg between 1975 and 1990 when she was sold. Sealink were also considering a Weymouth–Saint Malo service for which *Earl Godwin* was earmarked but this never came to fruition. The *Earl William* was another Scandinavian acquisition by Sealink, being the former Thoresen original *Viking II*, built in 1964 by Kaldnes Mekaniske Verksted A/S, Tönsberg. She was bought by Sealink British Rail in 1976 and renamed. She operated from Weymouth from 1981 to 1985 and later became a detention ship for foreign nationals trying to enter the UK by illegal means. The third Viking ship was the former *Viking IV*, built in 1973 and sold to Sealink in 1980, and she operated mainly from Portsmouth, but spent one brief period working from Weymouth in 1983.

In 1980 a new terminal was opened but in 1984 Sealink was sold to Sea Containers Ltd, and renamed Sealink British Ferries. Channel Island Ferries (CIF) began a competitive service around this time also and proved so successful that in 1987 Brittany Ferries took over the route from Sealink as British Channel Island Ferries.

Weybourg Ferries briefly utilized the *St. Julian* which worked from Weymouth to Cherbourg on a freight-only route in the 1980s. Another transit operator was Weymouth Maritime Services which operated as a passenger/car ferry service with just one vessel. Another contender was the Lo-Lo *Lowland Lancer*, the 6,390-GT former Royal Fleet Auxiliary and Falklands War veteran, *Sir Lancelot*, originally built in 1964 and purchased by Lowline (Rambler) Ltd in 1989 for commercial service, but she proved unsuitable. Likewise the proposed Starliner service did not, ultimately, work out. Even Townsend Thoresen at one time had contemplated using the port as one its terminals.

In March 1990 Sealink was taken over by Stena who shortly afterward closed down the Weymouth service. Their immediate replacement was Westward Ferries Limited in June 1990 but they were unable to generate sufficient traffic and quickly ceased trading.

Condor Ferries began services from Weymouth to the Channel Islands with the *Condor 12* in January 1987 then moved over to Poole in March. In 1991 the *Condor Wave Piercer* started operations but in February this service was moved to Poole. But the connection with Guernsey and St. Malo was again reinstated the following year. The *Condor Express* currently operates from both harbours, with a regular service from Weymouth to the Channel Islands with some terminating at St. Malo, and a summer service from Poole. She also experimented with a Cherbourg service in 2005 and 2008 in conjunction with Brittany Ferries.

Offshore Ferry Services

Condor Express against the backdrop of St. Malo. (© Condorferries Ltd)

3: Weymouth – Channel Islands – St. Malo

Current Operators, Ships and Details

Condor Ferries are now the only operators that work out of Weymouth indirectly to France, working a fast passenger and light freight ferry winter service to St. Malo interspersed by summer services via the Channel Islands both of which involve changing ferries in either Jersey or Guernsey *en route* in both directions. Consequently extra care should be made when booking to ensure the time involved in these changes is known and planned for (See also Section 8). Weymouth to Jersey takes around 3.5 hours with up to seven crossings per week while Weymouth to St. Malo takes about 5 hours 15 minutes while Guernsey to St. Malo is approximately 45 minutes to which waiting times must be added.

The usual vessel employed is the Bahamas-registered HSC *Condor Express* (IMO 9135896) a 86 m fast catamaran built by Incat, Hobart, Tasmania in 1996 at a cost of £27 million. She is of 5,007 tonnes, with an overall length of 86.62 m, a beam of 26 m and a draught of 3.5 m. She is powered by four Rushton 20RK270 engines with four Lips Lj145D waterjet propulsion units which give her a top speed of around 40 knots. She can carry 730 passengers and 185 cars, including pre-booked accompanied caravans.

The onboard facilities of the *Condor Express* include a café, a duty-free shop, the air-conditioned Club Lounge, children's playroom, baby-changing room and recliner seats all on her main deck; with a bar and kiosk on the upper deck.

Weymouth ferry terminal is reached via the A37 or A36 roads onto the A354 to the Quay. There is short- and long-term paid car parking available that requires pre-booking. There is a 1 hour check-in time for vehicles and 40 minutes for passengers. The rail station from Waterloo is 5 minutes walk away and the bus stop at Kings Statue is 10 minutes. Facilities for the disabled are very limited, although assistance with boarding may be arranged. There is a small café.

Contact Details

The Quay, Weymouth, Dorset, DT4 8DX
Tel: 01305 763003
Reservations: 0845 609 1024
Fax: 01305 760776; 01305 761551
Email: reservations@condorferries.uk
Web: www.condorferries.co.uk

4: Poole – Cherbourg

Background

One of the earliest forms of ferry service to operate in the area was the Bournemouth–Swanage Motor Road and Ferry Company, which was founded in July 1923. They commenced operations across the harbour mouth three years later with the appropriately named *Ferry Number 1*, a steam-driven vessel built by the Cowes, Isle of Wight company of J. Samuel White. She could carry 15 cars, a capacity soon expanded to 18, a sign of things to come. The coming of the Second World War saw the service closed down by the military but it was revived in 1946 and a second, smaller steam ferry, inevitably *No. 2*, with an eight car capacity, was added. Eventually both veterans were replaced by a diesel-electric vessel, *No. 3*, constructed by J. Bolson, a Poole shipbuilder. With a length of 47.85 m and a beam of 12.98 m she could carry 28 vehicles. It was not until 1994 that a new ferry arrived, the present *Bramble Bush Bay*.

Meanwhile by the late 1960s the principal cargo unloaded at Poole harbour itself was coal, and this did not sit totally happily with the expansion of the tourist trade and the yachting explosion. Despite its size, approximately 36 km^2, shipping was always restricted by the shallowness (48 cm average depth) of the harbour, which only had a single deep-water channel dredged through it at an average of 7.5 m depth and thus always lost out to Southampton along the coast.

The arrival of Truckline Ferries France S.A. to initiate a freight service from Poole to Cherbourg in 1972 brought a new facet to the harbour. Poole Harbour Commissioners embraced the concept and oversaw the construction of a new eight-acre Ro-Ro ferry berth and terminal on reclaimed land adjacent to New Quay. They were equipped with a modern Linkspan having a 7 m bridge width as well as side loading ramp. The first sailing was by the *Poole Antelope* on 29 June 1973. She was a 3,079-GT ferry built that year by Chantiers de Normandie, with an overall length of 75.63 m, a 14.7 m beam and a draught of 3.2 m. She had two Alpha 10V23Hu engines which gave her a speed of 11.5 knots, and she could carry 206 passengers and 50 cars in 193 lane meters. A second ship, the *Dauphine de Cherbourg*, built in 1974 of similar tonnage and beam but with an overall length of 74.9 m, arrived soon after, and expansion continued aided by a contract to import 25,000 Citroen cars and 2,000 tractors in 1974. Both ships were named after popular drinking venues, the Antelope Inn in Poole and the Hotel le Dauphin in Cherbourg but, neither of these vessels lasted long as they soon became too small for the traffic volume. The *Poole Antelope* was sold in 1976 and, after many changes of ownership and name, is currently the *Caledonia* working on the Odessa to Istanbul run, while the *Dauphine de Cherbourg* is now the Chinese survey support vessel *Bin Hai 504*.

The headlong growth of driver-accompanied freight traffic thus saw the replacement of the original pair of vessels by the two 6,507-GT sisters *Countances* and *Purbeck*, built in 1977 by the Societe Nouvelle des Ateliers et Chantiers due Havre, at Le Havre. They were 125.5 m overall, with a beam of 17.5 m and a 4.26 m draught and were powered by a pair of Krupp MaK 9M453AK diesel engines to give a speed of 18 knots. Each could carry 46 cars plus 33 lorries on two decks, in addition to the car deck, and they were later increased in length by 16 m to increase their truck capacity to 64. A second 10 m wide Linkspan was built to

4: Poole – Cherbourg

service these ships, which commenced operating in November 1978 and were so successful that the terminal was quadrupled in size by 1984.

Truckline itself was taken over by the French Brittany Ferries in 1985, although for a while they retained the old name on their livery, and on 30 March 1986 they expanded into the passenger traffic business, with the *Cornouailles* transferred to Truckline from service to Roscoff. This 6,018-GT ferry with bow visor and stern ramps had been built in 1977 by Trondheims Mekaniske Verkstedeer, at Trondheim, Norway being complete in May 1977. She was of 110 m overall, with a beam of 16.51 m and a draught of 5.18 m, with two Pielstick diesel engines and a speed of 17 knots. Her passenger capacity was 550 and car stowage 205. She also proved an instant success, so much so that a third Ro-Ro berth and more expansion was required and the *Corbiére* and then the *Tregastel* joined the booming fleet, replacing the *Cornouaille*s, which was sold to British Channel Island Ferries and renamed *Havelet*. Currently she still serves in Montenegro as the *Sveti Stefan*.

The 4,238-GT *Corbiére* was the lead ship of six identical ferries constructed by Jos. L. Meyer Werft at Papenburg, Germany, known collectively as the 'Papenburg Sisters'. Originally named *Apollo*, she had been built for the Viking Line for service between Sweden and Finland. She was 108.07 m overall, had a 17.2 beam a 4.6 m draught and was powered by two 12-cylinder Deutz S.B.V. diesel engines which gave her 18.5 knots. Her passenger capacity was 1,200 and her car stowage with bow and stern ramp loading was 260. Brittany Ferries had chartered her in 1984 from Nordisk Faergefart A.S. of Nassau, Bahamas, as the *Benodet* but by May 1989 when charted to Truckline she had already become the *Corbiére*. The 8,696-GT *Tregastel* was the former *Travemünde* built by Schiffbau Unterweser A.G. at Bremerhaven, Germany in 1971 and had an overall length of 118.01 m, a beam of 18.5 m and a draught of 5.01 m. She was powered by MAN engines which gave her a best

The *Normandie Express*, nearest, joins the Brittany fleet in the Channel. (© Brittany Ferries)

speed of 21 knots. She had served previously with Sally Line as the *Njegos* and could carry 1,500 passengers and 250 cars.

By 1991 some 781,000 passengers, and 219,000 cars passed through the terminal and freight tonnage rose to 2.35 million tonnes. Finally the *Barfleur* arrived in April 1992, which involved the erecting of an upper-deck Linkspan and dredging the main channel to accommodate her. She was the largest ship to enter the harbour up to that time, although she has since been eclipsed by the *Bretagne* and more recently the *Armorique*, and her arrival saw the *Corbiére* and *Tregastel* phased out: the former, after a dizzy array of owners and name changes, finally reverting to her original *Apollo* title and running a Labrador, Canada service between St. Barbe and Blanc Sablon; the latter passing through several hands and ending up as the *Barakat* working out of Jeddah, Saudia Arabia.

In 2001 the *Normandie Express* initiated yet another new phase with a 2-hour crossing. It seemed as if the port could only continue to grow and in July 2007 it was announced that the new freight-only ship *Contentin* would operate out of Poole to Cherbourg from November onward, as well as covering the Santander crossing at weekends. Of the older pair the *Purbeck* was sold in 2007 and is now the *Maria Rosario*, while *Countances* was sold in 2008 and renamed the *Rosa Eugenia*; both now work for Consolidated de Ferrys C.A. working out of St. Vincent in the West Indies. All seemed well for continued growth.

Then the blow struck. After seventeen years working the Cherbourg route Brittany Ferries made the shock announcement in December 2009 that they would be withdrawing the service due to declining passenger numbers and that it would close it down in the spring of 2004. About 80 per cent of the *Barfleur's* passengers were British but the towns had been twinned for thirty years and it was felt that as well as the loss of sixty local jobs, tourism at both ends of the crossing would be devastated. Brittany's spokesman said that the high-speed *Normandie Vitesse* had been less of a loss-maker since her introduction, and also that a new £75 million ferry would be introduced at the Portsmouth terminal and would operate across to Cherbourg three times a week in compensation. He also said that the freight service between Poole and Cherbourg would be remaining, and, indeed, be 'beefed up'. Thus the service closed in March 2010 and another operator was not forthcoming. However, in February 2011, in an apparent *volte-face*, Brittany announced the *Barfleur* would be brought back and the crossing reopened, at least on a trial basis from 27 February until 2 October, with a 450 passenger capacity and with the ship operating a daily daylight crossing from Poole and an overnight cruise back from Cherbourg, with extra passages on Friday and Saturday.

In 2011 *Barfleur* operated a daily summer service to and from Poole and Cherbourg, with additional schedules from Friday to Saturday. However, on 30 October 2011 this service ceased, and in March 2012 *Barfleur* was put under charter to LD Lines/DFDS to work their Dover to Calais service, from April.

Current Operators, Ships and Details

Normandie Express (IMO 9221358) is a High-Speed Craft (HSC) wave-piercing catamaran of the Evolution-10 type, originally built by Bob Clifford's Incat Company at Derwent Park, Hobart, Tasmania and launched in 1998. She is known as a 98 m WPC, (Hull Number 057) and was first named the *Incat Tasmania* and utilized by the Australian Trade Commission, under charter, as an afloat conference facility based at Darling Harbour, Sydney NSW in the 2000 Olympics during which she carried the Olympic Torch. Subsequently she was chartered out to Tranz Rail's Interisland Line, and between 2001 and 2003 operated a New Zealand service speeding between Picton, South Island and Wellington, North Island as *The Lynx*, but proved too large for the number of users and was laid up for a time back at Hobart. Back in

European waters, when P&O stated they were closing their Portsmouth to France service in 2004, Brittany Ferries saw their opportunity and determined to open their own direct service from Portsmouth to Ouistreham, Caen. This resulted in December 2004 in yet another chartering deal for the *Lynx*, with Condor Ferries, and she received her third name, *Normandie Express*, and was extensively refitted and repainted. She made her maiden Channel crossing in March 2005. On 15 January 2007 Brittany Ferries purchased her outright.

The *Normandie Express* has a tonnage of 6,581, a length of 97.22 m, a beam of 26.6 m, a draught of 2.7 m, and is powered by Paxman engines that give her a service speed of 42 knots and an alleged top speed of 46.5 knots. She originally had a passenger capacity of 850 passengers and 235 cars but now caters for only just 720 foot passengers and 185 cars. Initially registered under the flag of the Bahamas in Nassau, she has since been reflagged to Caen with an all-French crew. Her facilities are limited, comprising Le Café and two Le Bar watering holes; a shop, with a video game lounge, an open viewing sundeck, 850 reclining seats, a baby-changing room, a disabled toilet, a *bureau de change*, children's play area, slot machines and a tourist information desk. She has Commodore Lounge, reclining and standard seats. She operates daily leaving Poole at 07.15 and returning from Cherbourg at 11.15.

Currently *Normandie Express* runs two return passages per day between Portsmouth and Cherbourg between 18 March and 31 October, taking 180 minutes for the journey, but she also operates the Ouistreham route as a daily weekend service on the mornings of Friday to Saturday, and the *Normandie Vitesse* (*vide –Normandie Express*) currently provides the fastest crossing time to Cherbourg.

The *Normandie Express* photographed on 24 March 2011 outward bound. (© Brian Burnell)

Bow view of the HSC *Normandie Express* at speed. (© Brittany Ferries)

Aerial view of *Cotentin*. (© Brittany Ferries)

For operating freight-only services the *Cotentin* (IMO 9364978) was built by the Aker Finnyards, Helsinki, Finland in 2007 at a cost of €80 million. The 19,909-GT *Cotentin* is specialist freight-only ferry and can carry 120 trucks in 2,200 lane metres and convey them at 23 knots. She is of 167 m overall length, with a beam of 26.80 m and a 6.20 m draught and powered by two MAK diesel engines. She has a crew of 50. There are 216 berths with 116 freight cabins aboard providing every trucker with an air-conditioned, *en-suite* accommodation in which linen, towels and toiletries are provided. On-board facilities also include a self-service restaurant, a bar/lounge, boutique, games area, a crew fitness room and TV lounges.

Cotentin is the largest vessel to work out of Poole and operates a weekly 3 hour 45 minute service to and from Cherbourg, plus covering the Poole to Santander crossing during the week, providing a 'bypass' service at weekends to Santander, which enables truckers to avoid the French ban on weekend freight traffic

Poole ferry terminal is a 20 minute walk from Poole town centre and by car the B3068 access road is within easy journey time of the M27 and

Cotentin's smart restaurant area. (© Brittany Ferries)

M3 to London, as well as the A31 and A35 trunk roads to Dorchester and Exeter via the Lifting Bridge, and the A350 to Bristol and the M4 for the Midlands and North. There is a paying car park opposite the terminal itself. Caravans cannot be left there overnight but by arrangement and for a fee can be left in the car lanes (Tel: 01202 440220). The terminal itself has the many facilities, including a cafeteria open during summertime arrival and departure times only, a snack bar and small shop, likewise a *bureau de change*, a toilet block with showers near the check-in lanes, coin payphones and a baby-changing room. A shuttle bus operates between the terminal and the ship for foot passengers. There is an access ramp and disabled toilets in the terminal building and the check-in lane toilet block. There is no left luggage facility, however.

Cherbourg terminal is within 15 minutes walking time of the town centre and the train station is 40 minutes away. By vehicle the terminal is within easy access via the D901 the fast N13 motorway to Caen onto the main routes to Brittany itself, the Loire Valley and the south of France. The terminal has a short-stay only free car park, but with secure paid parking close by. There is a tourist information desk at arrival and departure times, (Tel: 33 233 935252). Amenities include a bar open during the day, and a *bureau de change*, free shower rooms, a newspaper and souvenir outlet, payphones and disabled facilities, including ramps and toilet facilities, with wheelchairs available from the desk.

Contact Details
Poole Office
New Harbour Road, Poole, Dorset, BH15 4AJ
Tel: 0871 244 1403
Reservations: 0871 244 0744
Fax: 0871 244 0912
Email: enquiries@brittanyferries.com
Web: www.brittany-ferries.co.uk

Cherbourg Office
Quai de Normandie, Cherbourg, 50100, France
Tel: 033 825 828 828
Reservations: 0233 884488
Fax: 0233 884440
Email: reservations@brittanyferries.com
Web: www.brittany-ferries.co.uk

5: Lymington – Yarmouth (IOW)

Background

On 5 April 1830 the first regular ferry service commenced from Lymington with the wooden paddle steamer *Glasgow* and in 1841 she was replaced by another paddle steamer, the *Solent*, which ran the route for twenty years. All these early vessels had, of necessity, very shallow draughts in order not to run aground in the shallow Lymington River. *Solent* was in turn replaced by the former Admiralty vessel, *Red Lion* which served until 1880, but meanwhile she was joined in 1866 by the 69-GT *Mayflower* on the crossing. *Mayflower* was a wooden hulled paddler, built by Marshalls at Newcastle for the Solent Steamship Company Ltd, and had a draught of 1.82 m. She gave sterling service for forty-six years not being retired until 1910.

With the arrival of the railways things took on a different complexion and in July 1884 the London and South Western Railway bought the Lymington service for the princely sum of £2,750, which included both *Mayflower* and the second *Solent*. Two steel paddle steamers replaced these two wooden ferries around the turn of the century, the *Lymington* of 1893 and the third *Solent* in 1902. Designed as a specific replacement for the *Mayflower*, the little 130-GT *Lymington* was built by Day, Summers & Co. of Northam with compound diagonal machinery. She served faithfully until 1927 when the *Freshwater* took over her work and lingered for a while towing barges before she was sold to become the *Glengarry* and then the training vessel *Lord Nelson*. The equally small *Solent* was also a 161-GT paddler with compound diagonal layout and was built for the L&SWR and featured a single raking funnel, mainmast forward of the wheelhouse and full-width saloons. She had limited capacity but was economical and remained in service until 1948, although she spent her latter days on the Portsmouth to Ryde crossing as befitted her age and fragility.

The paddle steamer *Freshwater* was a locally-built paddler steamer built in 1927 to replace the *Lymington* by J. Samuel White & Co., Cowes. She was of 264-GT which was larger than any of her predecessors on this route. She had a prominent wheelhouse before her single funnel but no bridge. She served until 1959 after which she served briefly under the names of *Sussex Queen* and *Swanage Queen* before being broken up.

The next *Lymington* was a very different beast, being a Ro-Ro vessel built in 1938 and serving through to the 1970s. Hitherto the old practice of using towboats laden with cars and cattle behind the passenger ferries had continued, with the *Solent* and *Freshwater* thus transporting heavy cargo to Yarmouth Pier, but on 1 May 1938 a very different approach was adopted with the arrival on the route of the purpose-built *Lymington*. Built by William Denny & Bros, Dumbarton, she was of 403-GT with an overall length of 45.1 m, and a beam of 8 m, and these dimensions were only possible because of her unique manoeuvering power. She was the first to use the Voith Schneider units containing five rotatable fins, which replaced propellers and rudders and enabled the ship to turn within her own length and which were still in use in 2003. She had two 4-stroke, 6-cylinder 653OB oil engines developing 200 bhp apiece which gave her a speed of 11 knots.

She commenced service in May 1938 and was capable of carrying 516 passengers and 17 cars, loaded and unloaded via ramps at either end, and made a 30 minute crossing time. Special slipways were constructed at Lymington Pier and adjacent to the castle at Yarmouth to accommodate her. She served throughout the Second World War and when sold in 1972 she continued to work for a further fifteen years on the Clyde as *Sound of Sanda*.

In 1948 and after railway nationalization, the 489-GT *Farringford* joined the former Southern Railways route. She was as revolutionary in her way as the *Lymington* had been and almost doubled car capacity with thirty-two being embarked on her open car deck with the bridge built above it. She was a hybrid diesel-electric paddle boat; each paddle could be controlled independently. She was another William Denny-built ship, with two 6-cylinder 420 bhp 4SCSA 6SKM Crossley oil engines connected to two English Electric, Stafford, electric motors to drive the paddlewheels. She was of 54.2 m overall length, with a beam of 15.08 m and a 1.98 m draught. She remained in service from February to 1974, becoming British Transport Commission property in 1953, and was finally retired and moved to the Humber under Sealink, being scrapped at Hull in 1984.

Another *Freshwater* arrived in 1959, she being a Ro-Ro Passenger Car Ferry constructed by Alisa Shipbuilding Company at Troon, for the British Transport Commission and she was transferred to Sealink in 1979. She was of 363-GT, and was just under 50 m overall, with a 13 m beam. Her engines were two Crossley 8-cylinder diesels which gave her 10.5 knots. She could carry 620 passengers and 26 cars. She worked until 1984 and later became the *Sound of Seil*, working for Western Ferries.

In 1973 the 3 C's were built by Robb Caledon Shipbuilders at Dundee for Sealink: the *Caedmon*, *Cenred* and *Cenwulf*. These were vehicle and passenger Ro-Ro ferries of the conventional type, each being of 761-GT, with an overall length of 58 m, a beam of 15.7 m and a 2.28 m draught. They could manage a good 10 knots in service. They each had a capacity of 512 passengers and 58 cars and the bridge and lounges were built over the vehicle deck with ramps at bow and stern. Later, hydraulically-powered mezzanine decks enabled them to carry extra cars. This trio served until 2009 when a new breed of ferries came into service.

Meanwhile changes kept occurring. The privatization of Sealink UK saw the purchase of the route by SeaContainers Ltd, Bermuda who introduced the name Wightlink to the route, and this was bought out

Wight Light showing her loading ramp. (© Paul & Sarah Smith)

by the management in 1995. Then, in 2005, Wightlink was acquired by the Macquarie European Infrastructure Fund, and two years later they ordered two new ferries for the Lymington–Yarmouth route with the option for a third. These vessels, *Wight Light*, *Wight Sky* and *Wight Sun* commenced operation on the Lymington–Yarmouth route in 2009 and replaced the 1970s built *Caedmon*, *Cenred* and *Cenwulf* on that crossing.

Current Operators, Ships and Details
Wightlink's Lymington to Yarmouth Car & Passenger Ferry is a 35 minute crossing operated by three new Ro-Ro ferries *Wight Light* (IMO 9446972), *Wight Sky* (IMO 9446984) and *Wight Sun* (IMO 9490416). These 2,546-GT passenger and freight ferries have an overall length of 62.4 m, a beam of 16.1 m and a 2.3 m draught. They are powered by four Volvo D16MHs 6-cylinder engines driving two Voith Schneider 21 R5/135 units. They have a capacity for 360 passengers carried on two decks, a vehicle deck holding 65 cars and with 110 m of freight area, and have a crew of 10. They were built by Brodogradiliste Kraljevica, Croatia and were delivered in 2008/9. They have lounges with bar, café, gift shop, video & gaming machines, lifts, baby-changing rooms and toilet facilities. They also have observation decks and they are designed for disabled access.

At the terminals there is a 30 minute check-in time for cars and 15 minutes for passengers. Currently there are approximately twenty-five crossings per day made in both directions on the summer schedule between 4 April and 30 October but all are subject to alteration and should be checked prior to a journey. The terminals have only limited facilities but there are both short and long term pay and display car parks. For those with special needs there are lifts from car decks to passenger lounges, disabled toilets, and wheelchairs available onboard, as well as in the terminal. Lymington Ferry Port is approached from the A31/M27 via the A337. At Yarmouth the Wightlink office is at Quay

Loading vehicles onto *Wight Light*. (© Paul & Sarah Smith)

5: Lymington – Yarmouth (IOW)

Street; at the terminal itself there is a ticket office, toilets, payphones and a pay and display car park.

Contact Details
Freight
Wightlink, Undershore Road, Lymington, Hants, SO41 5SB
Tel: 0871 376100
Fax: 023928 55218
Email: enquiries@wightlinkfreight.co.uk
Web: www.wightlink.co.uk/coach-and-freight

Wight Sun amongst small boats in Lymington harbour. (© Paul & Sarah Smith)

Bridge of *Wight Light*. (© Paul & Sarah Smith)

6: Southampton – Cowes

Background

The regular sailing service linking the Isle of Wight to the mainland can be traced back to 1420, but at Cowes, already established on either bank of the Medina River as a natural anchorage, its long-established popularity as a maritime centre was reinforced by the first regatta to be held in 1812 and which brought public interest to that area. In 1820 the 71-GT paddle steam *Prince of Coburg*, originally built on the River Trent at Gainsborough, Lincolnshire in 1817, began a service between Cowes and Southampton. She was 23.3 m long with a beam of 4.38 m. and her engines were built by Aaron Maney of Staffordshire. The Isle of Wight Royal Mail Steam Packet Company was set up to operate steamers between Cowes, Isle of Wight and Southampton in 1820. In 1826 a competing service was introduced by the Isle of Wight Steam Packet Company and among their paddle steamers was the 87-GT *Gem* of 1840; George Ward owned the Isle of Wight Royal Mail Steam Packet Company and built a 17 m long quay to dock his fleet and in 1841 his son later extended it with a 30.48 m pier which had cellars to hold coal for the growing numbers of paddlers, which included the *Earl of Malmsey*, *George IV* and *Medina*.

Passenger trade to the Isle of Wight increased when, on 16 June 1862, the first railway on the Isle of Wight, the Cowes and Newport line, opened. This led to an increase in traffic and resulted in a new pontoon, constructed in 1873, which extended the pier again to a length of 36.576 m. The 87-GT *Gem* was built locally by J. White in 1883, for the IWSPC, and survived for more than forty years on the route; it was followed by the 103-GT *Ruby*, built by Day, Summers & Co, Northam for the South Western & Isle of Wight Steam Navigation Company in 1841 as the *Pride of the Waters*. The 1844-built, 64-GT *Pearl*; the 1848-built, 93-GT *Queen*; the 1857-built, 69-GT *Emerald* and 1860-built, 82-GT *Sapphire*, all followed from the same builder down the years.

In 1860 another company, the Southampton Isle of Wight and Portsmouth Improved Steamboat Company started operating on the same

Aft view of the *Red Jet 4* powering along. (© Red Funnel Ferries)

6: Southampton – Cowes

Aerial view of the *Red Falcon* showing car and truck decks. (© Red Funnel Ferries)

route with the 126-GT *Lord of the Isles* and the 124-GT *Lady of the Lake*, both built by Thames Shipbuilders and featuring Promenade decks for passengers, but the company failed and went bankrupt the following year. IWSP and IWRMSP merged in 1861 to form the Southampton, Isle of Wight & South of England Royal Mail Steam Packet Company. This company also absorbed the third Isle of Wight company in 1865 and also bought Bournemouth and South Coast Steam Packets Ltd in 1908. One of the ships taken over at the time was the 203-GT paddle steamer *Lord Elgin*, built by Richardson, Duck & Co of Stockton in 1876 and which survived on various duties until 1955. The unwieldy title eventually became simplified to Red Funnel Ferries when they adopted the red with a black top style in 1935, and the company has operated as such ever since. The colours of the design of the house flag design were those of the names of some of their original fleet, *Emerald*, *Pearl*, *Ruby* and *Sapphire*.

Meanwhile the longevity of some of the Cowes paddle steamers was incredible, The *Princess Helena* for example, a 246-GT vessel of 53.4 m with a beam of 6.14 m, and powered by a 90 bhp compound diagonal, was built and first entered service in July 1883. After various re-boilering and modifications this old lady survived two world wars, and was not retired from the fleet until 1952. Others were less fortunate: the *Princess of Wales*, a 32-GT paddler built by Barclay, Curle at Glasgow in June 1888 and capable of carrying 600 passengers was still on her trials at Skelmorlie on 16th of that month when she was cut in half by the liner *Balmoral Castle* and sunk. Another Day, Summers & Co.-built craft which was designed specifically to introduce a fast (35 minutes) summer service was the motor cruiser *Island Enterprise*, a 9-tonne vessel which could carry eleven passengers between Cowes and Southampton at 20 knots and was fitted with toilets, hand luggage stowage and a luxury cabin for all-weather commuting. She served between 1933 and 1938 before being withdrawn. She had been a concept ahead of her time.

In 1959 Red Funnel began to operate passenger/car ferries and introduced the Castle class ships, *Carisbrooke Castle*, 672-GT, in 1959; *Osborne Castle*, 736-GT, in 1962; *Cowes Castle*, 786-GT, in 1965 and *Norris Castle*, 734-GT, in 1968, all built by J.I. Thornycroft at Woolston. The latter pair were converted to Ro-Ro ships with extra capacity added in the form of mezzanine decks for another 30 cars, and all served until the mid-1990s. The arrival of high speed hydrofoils revived the fast passenger service concept in the early 1970s and saw the introduction of the Shearwater series, two being built by Seaflight S.p.A. at Trapani, Sicily: the 26-ton *Shearwater* and *Shearwater II* capable of carrying 54 passengers at

32 knots; and a second pair built by Rodriguez, Messina, somewhat larger at 35.1 tons but with similar speed and capable of carrying 67 passengers, these being the *Shearwater III* and *Shearwater IV*. These two made the passage in 23 minutes on an all-year service and were far more successful. They were not withdrawn until 1992. A fifth and sixth such vessels, *Shearwater V* and *Shearwater VI*, joined them in 1982 and served until 1998. There were also two hovercraft obtained from Hovermarine Ltd in 1981, *HM2 GH2019* and *HM2 GH2024*, but they were not successful and were quickly disposed of.

Finally the first catamaran was acquired from the local builder FMB Marine, this was the *RedJet 1* of 168-GT and capable of conveying 138 passengers on the crossing reliably in 22 minutes, at speeds of up to 35.5 knots, and she remained in service until 2009 before being sold.

Current Operators, Ships and Details

The current Red Funnel fleet comprises the *Red Falcon* (IMO 9064047) and *Red Osprey* (IMO 9064059), Ro-Ro double-ended vehicle ferries, all built by Ferguson Shipbuilders, Port Glasgow, in 1994. Designed with a central bridge high up on the block superstructure for all-round vision, they are of 3,953-GT, with a length of 93.22 m and a beam of 17.5 m. They have two FHD240 Wåtsilå diesel engines and two Volth Schneider propellers which give them maximum manoeuvrability. Their passenger capacity is 895 and, after being lengthened at the Remontawa Shipyard, Gdansk, Poland in 2004, can carry 220 cars. *Red Eagle* (IMO 9117337) is similar, built by Ferguson in 1996 with the same dimensions and power-plant but she is of 4,075-GT and has a larger passenger accommodation deck, which entailed raising her bridge and funnel to increase crew space which, after similar lengthening, makes her the largest ferry to serve the Isle of Wight.

The *Red Jet 3* (IMO 901323) hi-speed catamaran was built locally by FMB Marines, Cowes, in 1998 and is of 213-GT, and is 32.90 m long with a beam of 8.32 m. She has two 1,500 kW 12V 396TE74L MTU diesel engines and two MJP waterjets which give her a speed of 38 knots. She is fitted with trim-tabs and, following a refit in 2007, has leather seats and LCS screens, along with more luggage capacity for her 190 seated passengers. Her larger companion, *Red Jet 4* (IMO 906937), arrived in 2003, having been constructed in Hobart, Tasmania by North West Bay Ships Pty. She is of 342-GT, and is 39.88 m long with a 10.82 m beam. She has two more powerful 1,740 kW 12 V 4000 M70 MTU diesels and can carry 275 seated passengers at speeds of up to 42 knots, making her the fastest commercial vessel working the Solent.

The *Red Jet 5* (IMO8954415) was built in 1999 by Pequot River Shipworks, New London, and Connecticut, USA and joined the Red Funnel

Stern view of the *Red Eagle*. (© Red Funnel Ferries)

6: Southampton – Cowes

The *Red Jet 3* at speed. (© Red Funnel Ferries)

fleet in 2009. She is a Solent class Catamaran, designed by FBM Marine Ltd, Cowes, Isle of Wight, and is built of aluminium alloy. She has a service speed of 35 knots at 85 per cent maximum continuous rating; a maximum speed of 38 knots and a range of 510 nautical miles. She has a crew of 3, while her passenger capacity is 187 seated. She has an overall length of 32.9 m, a beam of 8.32 m and a draught (loaded) of 1.25 m, with a 1.80 m freeboard. Her tonnage is 209-GT.

She is fitted with the following navigational equipment – a Sperry Bridge Master E 250 series radar with high RPM scanners; a Plath SR 180 Mk.1 Gyro compass; C. Plath Venus compass; a Furuno FE-700 echo-sounder; a Walker 4040 Log; a Furuno FM-8500 VHF DSC; 1 × ICOM IC-M127 VHF; a IESM Rescuer 9.2–9.5 GHz SART; a Simrad GN33 GPS; a GPS/Wi-Fi receiver; a Transas Navi Sailor 3000 electronic chart plotter; a Furuno FA 150 AIS Transponder; a Airchime WT 15604 Whistle and a Guest searchlight. She is powered by two MTU/DDC 4000 Series 4-stroke direct injection liquid cooled turbocharged intercooled diesels developing 3,476 kW at 2,000 rpm. She has DDC-supplied engine management and monitoring with propulsion provided by two KAMEWA SII waterjet drives; and has Kamewa Independent Combinator Control steering.

Her equipment also includes RFD Ferryman self-inflating life rafts; Kon Tiki 98 SOLAS approved lifejackets; a Jason's Cradle MOB; two Ikarus MOB Markers; SOLAS approved Lifebuoys; twelve red parachute flares and two Pains Wessex Linethrower 250.

Her facilities include leather seats with cup holders and seat pockets; double sided central luggage rack; full air conditioning; tinted (electrically heated on bridge) windows; a Navaho MediaCat 3 with bridge video stream; and the ReFuel Express hot and cold drinks service.

The three Raptor class Ro-Ro ferries run a 55-minute passenger and vehicle service at 15 knots between East Cowes and Southampton up to eighteen times daily, which can take 800 passengers and approximately 200 cars. Aboard the *Red Falcon, Red Osprey* and *Red Eagle* there are the following facilities: the ReFuel café restaurant, which has hot meals, sandwiches, salads, pastries and confectionary, smoothies, juice, wines, spirits and hot drinks; The Steam Coffee Company; and Bar1861, which stocks bottled and draught beers, wine and spirits. For children there is Ferry Fun with kids' meals, pre-arranged visits to the bridge and entertainment during selected weekends. The WiFi Zone is available via the Hotspot, there are also 240v power points for charging laptops or mobile phones on B deck. There is onboard TV and an out-

Overhead bow view of the *Red Jet 4*. (© Red Funnel Ferries)

side deck. There are toilet facilities, passenger lifts for wheelchair users and baby-changing facilities

The two remaining Red Jet Hi-Speed waterjets ferries, *Red Jet 3* and *Red Jet 4*, run a 25 minute passenger-only service between West Cowes and Southampton at 35 knots. There is an 'at-seat' refreshment service with drinks and light snacks but all passengers have to remain seated for safety reasons. It should be noted that there are no toilets aboard. These boats are wheelchair-friendly, but bicycles are *not* permitted. Booking is not required.

The Southampton Terminal 1 is at Royal Pier, Dock Gate 7, Town Quay Road and Terminal 2 is located at Town Quay and has the bus City Link service, taxi rank, ATM, disabled assistance, heated waiting area, luggage trolleys, Parcel Point, the Steam Coffee Company, ticket office, toilets, vending machines, visitor information point and wheelchairs. Parking is available at the Triangle car park.

The West Cowes terminal is at Fountain Yard and the East Cowes terminal is at Trinity Wharf and both have similar facilities including drop-off/pick-up only parking only, payphones, toilets, heated waiting area, luggage trolleys, ticket office, vending machines and Parcel Point.

Contact Details
Office
Red Funnel Ferries, 12 Bugle Street, Southampton, SO14 2JY
Tel: 0844 844 9988
Fax: 0844 844 2698
Email: post@redfunnel.co.uk
Web: www.redfunnel.co.uk

Freight
Red Funnel Freight Centre, Riverway, Newport, Isle of Wight, PO30 5UX
Tel: 0844 844 2666
Fax: 0844 844 2667
Email: freight@redfunnel.co.uk
Web: www.redfunnel.co.uk/freight

7: Portsmouth – St. Malo – Ouistreham (Caen) – Le Havre – Cherbourg

Background

Sitting strategically on the tip of the Contentin peninsula in Normandy, Cherbourg has for centuries been the major French Navy base for Atlantic operations and a major port for mercantile trade.

The first regular ferry route was operated by Thoresen Car Ferries from 1976 when they decided to start moving their ferry services to Cherbourg away from the under-performing Southampton Port Authority to the more efficiently run Portsmouth. Starting on 17 June and running through to 12 September, their distinctively orange-hulled *Viking I* commenced a summer service that was ultimately to run until 1986. This vessel was a 3,671-GT ship built in Norway in 1964 by Kaldness M/V A/S at Tonsberg, and designed to the Otto Thoresen concept that customer comfort and care took priority, in stark contrast to British Rail's austere and shabby treatment of its passengers afloat and ashore. In honour of the move the *Viking I* was re-christened as the *Viking Victory*.

In 1968 the Townsend Ferry Company took over the shares of Thoresen and in 1969 became the European Ferries Group, with the ferry companies known as Townsend Thoresen. As a result, a new class of 'Super-Vikings' was ordered. In the interim, as passenger numbers increased, the 6,387-GT *Viking Valiant* also began operating more and more from Portsmouth, commencing with a weekend crossing in 1977. This enlarged ferry, one of a trio, was built in 1975 by Aalborg Vaerft A/S at Aalborg, Denmark; she could convey 1,200 passengers and 275 cars at 18 knots and proved most popular. By the 1980s Thoresen was operating morning crossings from Portsmouth to Cherbourg and by 1984 Southampton had been abandoned totally. The *Valiant*'s sister ships, *Viking Viscount* and *Viking Voyager*, moved to Portsmouth from the failing Felixstowe route and a period of upgrading of the fleet ('Jumboization') took place. In 1985 P&O sold all its cross-Channel interests to Townsend Thoresen.

The modernized *Viking Valiant* resumed work in July 1986 on the route Portsmouth to Le Havre. In December 1986 another take-over occurred and Townsend Thoresen were merged into the P&O Group of companies and *Viking Viscount* was renamed *Pride of Winchester* and *Viking Voyage* became *Pride of Cherbourg*, and both continued sailings until 1994. They operated two 5-hour sailings by day in each direction and a single 8-hour overnight passage. In 1993 the *Pride of Bilbao* was also used. Ultimately the so-termed 'Super Vikings' arrived. Named *Pride of Cherbourg* and *Pride of Hampshire*, they served until 2002 when they were replaced by yet another *Pride of Cherbourg*. She was the 37,799-GT Ro-Pax ferry, originally built in 1995 as the *Isle of Innisfree* for Irish Ferries by Van der Giessen-de Noord at Rotterdam. She had served on various routes until 2002, when P&O Portsmouth took her under charter and had her refitted with extra cabins and other updates.

Various ferry companies have tried to operate a viable and profitable service to Cherbourg in recent years but have been defeated by the downturns in the economy and resultant heavy fall-off in traffic. Stena

The *Bretagne* makes a fine picture steaming past the lighthouse as she leaves for yet another crossing. (© Brittany Ferries)

The mighty and state-of-the-art ferry *Mont St. Michel* dwarfs her fellow fleet companion as she passes her at speed. (© Brittany Ferries)

Line ran two crossings a day from Southampton until 1996; P&O Irish Sea sailed three times a week to Rosslare and to Dublin at weekends, but the former was sold and the latter closed down in 2004. Hoverspeed Great Britain began a Portsmouth–Cherbourg service using a wave-piercing catamaran but this was abandoned after just a single season.

Between 1998 to 2004 the P&O FastCat service operated a 3-hour service with the *Superstar Express* on charter from Star Cruises, and then in 2000 with the *Portsmouth Express* catamaran, the former *Catalonia*. She later became the *Express* then finally *Cherbourg Express*. In 2002 the two conventional ships were replaced by the new *Pride of Cherbourg* on her own and running two daily crossings, morning and evening. All services were terminated in 2005.

Finally HD Ferries attempted the more modest Cherbourg to Channel Islands service in 2007 but lack of custom brought this quickly to an end. Even Brittany Ferries stuttered, temporarily withdrawing their Poole service in 2010.

Le Havre was originally served by Thoresen Car Ferries between 1954 until 1968 when they made three daily sailings: morning, afternoon and overnight. All three vessels used both this and the Cherbourg route.

In 1967 another company, Normandy Ferries, began operating the same route, twice daily only with no overnight service. Eventually this company was taken over by P&O and became P&O Normandy Ferries and was in turn sold to Townsend Thoresen which operated this route between 1968 to 1987.

The *Pride of Le Havre* and *Pride of Portsmouth* arrived from German shipbuilders in 1994. They reduced the crossing time to just over 5 hours. They worked until 2005 when P&O (European) Ferries shut the route down and the two ships were sold to Italy as the *SNAV Lazio* and *SNAV Sardegna*.

LD Lines (Louis Dreyfus Amateurs) ran a passenger and freight service for several seasons from September 2005 with the *Norman*

An overhead view of the *Normandie* showing her helo-pad forward. (© Brittany Ferries)

Voyager, along with the freighter *Cote d'Albatre*. For a season the HSC *Norman Arrow* took over the route but she too was withdrawn and replaced by the *Norman Spirit*.

Ouistreham at the mouth of the river Orne, is another former fishing port fairly recently made-over into a ferry port, and was perhaps most famous in recent decades as *Sword* Beach, one of the British assault landing beaches during the Normandy invasion of 1944. Linked to Caen by a canal and lock system, it was chosen by Brittany Ferries as one of their terminals when their ferry services to Plymouth began to expand. The service was initiated on 6 June 1986, an appropriately auspicious date, no doubt well-chosen to cement Anglo–French trade and relations for the new crossing. However it was not until 2004 that a direct service to Portsmouth was initiated by P&O Ferries. They chartered an Incat 91 catamaran from Mols Linien and changed her operating name from *Max Mols* to *Caen Express*. It was hardly worth the effort for by September the route had been shut down again and the *Max Mols* reverted to her owner once more.

St. Malo in Brittany has a long seafaring history, and not always of the peaceful trading type that typifies it today, for it once was a notorious nest of corsairs and pirates that raided up and down the Channel until the Royal Navy smoked them out in 1758. The development of the modern ferry port has revitalized the old town and now there are crossings to Poole and Weymouth as well as Portsmouth.

Current Operators, Ships and Details
Brittany Ferries
This company runs a summer service from Portsmouth to St. Malo.

Bretagne (IMO 8707329) is one of the smallest and oldest of the Brittany ships – she was built by Chantiers de l'Atlantique at a cost of £55 million and was completed in 1989. She has a GT of 24,534, an overall length of 151.20 m, a beam of 26 m, a draught of 6.20 m, and is powered by Wärtsilä diesel which gives her a top speed of 21 knots. She has a capacity of 2,056 passengers and 580 vehicles (with 39 trucks) and is served by a crew of 130. Her facilities include Les Aubers, which is an *à la carte* restaurant; La Baule, a self-service eatery; and the La Gerbe de Locronan Wi-Fi café. There are two bars, the Gwenn Ha Du and The Yacht Club piano bar and a coffee shop. Onboard shopping can be conducted at La Boutique, Le Kiosque, La Vitrine and there is also a photo shop. For entertainment the ship has a Games Planet zone, cinemas, and a children's playroom. Her 1,146-berth accommodation includes 376 cabins of Commodore class and also fifty of Club4 standard, fully air-conditioned, with 2- and 4-berth cabins, plus 454 reclining seats.

Bretagne currently operates between Portsmouth and St. Malo with a 9-hour daily crossing up to November, when Saturdays are excluded.

The English Channel commercial vehicle ferry *Commodore Clipper* of Condor Ferries outbound from Portsmouth Ferry Port on 16 February 2011. (© Brian Burnell)

Offshore Ferry Services

Brittany Ferries' liner-like *Bretagne*. (© Brittany Ferries)

Bretagne's popular Le Café offers a modern concept and choice of menu.(© Brittany Ferries)

Brittany Ferries also runs a service from Portsmouth to Ouistreham. *Mont St Michel* (IMO 9238337) is a 35,592-GT ferry built by the Dutch shipyard of Van der Giessen-de Noord and completed in 2002. She made her maiden voyage on 20 December 2002 and previously had been referred to as the *Deauville*, the *Honfleur* and the *Normandie 2* before the adoption of her present name. In the latter case this was understandable because she is, internally at least, a near-sister to the current *Normandie*. The vessel is 173 m overall, with a beam of 28.5 m and a draught of 6.21 m. She is powered by Krupp MAK engines giving her a top speed of about 22 knots.

The *Mont St Michel* can carry 2,123 passengers, and has a car carrying capability of 830 in 2 km of vehicle space, with a crew of 135. The passenger accommodation has 224 cabins, which includes Commodore-class (three adults and one child); 4-berth internal and external cabins, 2-berth internal cabins, wheelchair access cabins, all with full air-conditioning, plus ample provision of 460 fully-reclining seats and cots. Other facilities include baby-changing rooms and disabled toilets. The food outlets are the Les Romantiques, an *à la carte* restaurant; the self-service La Galerie as well as the Café du Festival de Thé coffee shop and the Blue Note bar. Shopping outlets are La Boutique, Le Kiosque, La Vitrine and a photo shop. For entertainment aboard there is a DJ and

7: Portsmouth – St. Malo – Ouistreham (Caen) – Le Havre – Cherbourg

A family cabin aboard the Brittany Ferries' *Bretagne*. (© Brittany Ferries)

One of the seating areas and lounges aboard the Brittany Ferries *Mont St. Michel*. (© Brittany Ferries)

children's entertainment programme; two cinemas; the Games Planet for video gaming entertainments and slot machines; Wi-Fi and internet access, a sundeck and a *bureau de change*.

At the present time the *Mont St Michel* is utilized on the Portsmouth Ouistreham, Caen crossing, with four 6-hour sailings daily.

Normandie (IMO 9006253) is a 27,541-GT passenger/car ferry completed in May 1992 by the Kvaerner Masa-Yards at Turku, Finland. She is 161.40 m overall length with a beam of 26 m and a maximum draught of 6 m. Powered by four 4,440 kW engines she has a best speed of 20.5 knots. She can carry 600 cars and 84 trucks, and her passenger capacity is 2,123, accommodated in 775 berths with 220 cabins, which include Commodore-class cabins and a range of 2- and 4-berth cabins with air conditioning. There are also special disability cabins as well as 416 reclining seats and cots.

Facilities include the Deauville Restaurant offering *à la carte* service; the Riva Bella, a self-service restaurant; Le Pays d'Auge Salone de Thé; Le Derby bar; as well as a freight drivers' lounge, a *bureau de change* and a cinema. There is shopping at La Boutique, Le Kiosque, La Vitrine and there is a photo shop. Entertainment includes a seasonal children's entertainer and children's programme of events, two cinemas, games

Offshore Ferry Services

Brittany Ferries *Mont St. Michel*, one of the newest and largest ships of the fleet, resembles a cruise liner in her array of afloat facilities. (© Brittany Ferries)

7: Portsmouth – St. Malo – Ouistreham (Caen) – Le Havre – Cherbourg

The cavernous maw of the truck deck with night loading in progress onto the Brittany Ferries Mont St. Michel. *(© Brittany Ferries)*

room and slot machines, DJ, WiFi and internet access, a sun deck, and a children's playroom. There is also a baby-changing facility and disabled access toilets.

Since she was first commissioned in 1992 the *Normandie* has diligently plied the busy Portsmouth Ouistreham, Caen route with an average time of 6 hours per daytime crossing.

Contact Details
Brittany Ferries, Wharf Road Portsmouth, Hants, PO2 8RU
Tel: 0871 244 1402; 0871 244 0744
Fax: 08709 011100
Email: enquiries@ldferries.com
Web: www.brittanyferries.com

LD Lines

This company has, for many years, run a daily 5 hour 30 minute route between Portsmouth to Le Havre, sailing from the latter port at 17.00 each day and with the return ferry from Portsmouth at 23.00. This service was until recently provided by the *Norman Spirit*. However, on 28 November 2011 it was announced that she was being chartered by DFDS Seaways and transferring over to the Dover to Boulogne crossing, where she would temporarily replace the high-speed catamaran *Norman Arrow*. After a short period, on 17 February 2012, she was revamped and 're-launched' by actress Kelly Brook to serve on the Dover to Calais route.

Contact Details
LD Lines, Continental Ferry Port, Wharf Road, Portsmouth, PO2 8QW
Tel: 0870 428 4335
Freight: 0870 428 4336
Fax: 01235 845608
Email: ferry@ldlines.com
Web: www.ldlines.com; www.transmancheferries.com

Condor Ferries

Condor Ferries also run a daily seasonal route from Portsmouth to Cherbourg using a purpose-built ship catering principally for caravan traffic heading across the Channel. The *Commodore Clipper* (IMO 9201750) is a 13,456-GT Ro-Pax ferry with an overall length of 129.14 m, a beam of 23.4 and a 5.8 m draught, and her two MaK 9M32 11,746 bhp diesel engines give her a speed of 18.25 knots. For manoeuvring in small Channel Island harbours at Guernsey and Jersey, she is equipped with two controllable pitch propellers port and starboard and two fixed-pitch bow thrusters. She has a crew of 38 and a passenger seating capacity of 500. She can also convey 100 cars and 92 trucks/trailers. She was built by Van der Giessen-de Noord, Krimpen aan den Ijssel, Rotterdam in 1999 as a replacement for the freighter *Island Commodore* and is designed for year-round, all-weather service. The crossing takes between 6 and 8 hours depending on the route.

Her amenities include 160 berths, with a choice from forty 2-, 3- or 4-berth cabins, including two for wheelchair access, and Superior Cabins. Passenger accommodation includes Club-class and reclining

LD Lines' *Norman Spirit*. (© Portsmouth Port)

seating, a self-service restaurant, a lounge, a panoramic bar, a VIP lounge, the Condor Traveller Bar and duty-free shop.

Portsmouth is easily reached from London via the M3 and M27. Embarkation is at least 1 hour before sailing. The Portsmouth International Ferry Port is at Wharf Road, and is fully signposted, and for rail passengers from Waterloo there are shuttle buses to save a 30-minute walk. Car parking, including ground floor disabled car parking, is inside the port, where there are 516 places with a pay on exit scheme. Facilities include the Amigo shop and newsagent, Costa Coffee outlets, ATM, payphones, a licensed bar, the World Marché café, photo booths, public fax machine, left luggage, a baby-changing room, and a viewing deck, while there is a 24-hour truck drivers' rest room, with a vending service and nearby shower rooms.

Cherbourg ferry terminal is at the Quai de Normandie, and is accessed by car via the E46, then the N13, N132 and D901. There is a free short-stay car park, with disabled places near the ferry port, and also a paid and secure long-term car park further from the terminal. The train station is 45 minutes walk away, however, and currently there is no bus service. There are both car and passenger check-in desks, and other facilities include a bar, a newsagent which also vends snacks and gifts, payphones, a *bureau de change*, baby-changing area, toilets, ATMs, and there is also disabled access and assistance.

Le Havre's LD Terminal is at the Bassin de la Citadelle and the town itself is the closest port to Paris, at 200 km distant. The ferry port is accessed via the A13, the A131 and the Normandy Bridge, and is signed to the terminal. There is both short- and paid long-term parking and also some disabled driver spaces. The rail and bus stations are a short distance away at the Terminal de Grande Bretagne, which connects with the SNCF station at Cours de la Republique. There are shuttle buses. There is a 45-minute embarkation limit prior to sailing. Facilities include a cafeteria, toilets, seating area, satellite TV, baby-changing area, disabled facilities and a tourist information kiosk.

Ouistreham terminal is at the Avenue du Grand Large near the Caen Canal entrance and is car accessed via the A13 and signed to the Car Ferry. There are both short- and long-term car parks and some disabled driver spaces nearby. The Bus Verts runs a shuttle service from Caen to

The transport ferry *Condor Clipper*. (© Condorferries Ltd)

the ferry port but not in the evenings, and the nearest rail station is also at Caen, some 18 km distant, with TGV trains to Paris. Facilities at the port include a cafeteria/bar open between 06.30 and 23.00, a *bureau de change*, toilets, card payphones, tourist information office, disabled facilities, including wheel chair assistance and shuttle bus. Latest check-in is 45 minutes prior departure

St. Malo is accessed via the N137 with a rail connection to Rennes, and the terminal is signed. The terminal is located at the Gare Maritime du Naye and is signed. It is also served by local shuttle buses from a stop 3 minutes walk away near the pool. The main SNCF station for Paris is at the Square Jean Coquelin which is best reached by taxi. There are both short- and long-term paid car parks. Services at the terminal include a cafeteria open during arrival and departure times, a newsagent and gift shop, a left luggage office, showers, toilets, disabled access and facilities, a baby-changing room and a tourist information desk.

Contact Details
Continental Ferry Port, George Byng Way, Portsmouth, Hampshire, PO2 6SP
Tel: 0870 243 5140
Fax: 01305 760776
Email: enquiries@condorferries.co.uk
Web: www.condorferries.com

Manche-iles-Express
This is a French company which operates the HSCs *Marie-Marins*, *Tocqueville* and *Victor Hugo* on a summer service (April to September) between the French ports of Granville, Barneville-Carteret and Diélette, and the Channel Islands of Alderney, Guernsey, Sark and Jersey.

Contact Details
Rue des Iles, Granville, France or Albert Quay, St. Helier, Jersey
Tel: Granville (+33) 825 133 050
Tel: Jersey 01534 880756/880314
Tel: Guernsey 01481 701316
Tel: Carteret (+33) 0233 011011
Email: info@manche-iles-express.com
Web: www.manche-iles-express.com

8: Portsmouth – Bilbao

Background

In 1993 the P&O European Ferries company initiated what was to be their longest direct route, from Portsmouth to the Basque port of Bilbao (more precisely to Zierbena, which houses the Port of Bilbao facilities, near Santurtzi, some 14 km down the Nervión river) with the chartered *Pride of Bilbao* operating a twice weekly service. She was originally built by Wärtsilä, Turku, Finland for Rederi AB Slite, Sweden as a Viking Line ship. She was 37,799-GT with an overall length of 177.10 m, a beam of 28.4 m and a 6.51 m draught. She could carry 2,500 passengers and 580 cars on 1,115 lane meters of vehicle deck, and had a speed of 22 knots. She was taken over by the Irish Continental Group in 1993 who leased her to P&O for seventeen years.

Despite her size, there was some doubt expressed about the practicality of the proposed route by those who knew the reputation of the Bay of Biscay for rough weather, when even in pre-war days British battleships had their bridges swamped by the huge seas. Nonetheless the enterprise went ahead as it saved tourists a long car journey south from the French ports to the sun. Despite such dire predictions, and several instances of huge delays for just such reasons, the route continued to operate until January 2010, with a passage being made on average every three days. However despite many innovations the route proved to be a loss-maker for the operator and was therefore shut down. The last crossing was made in September of that year, when the *Pride of Bilbao* was returned to her owners who intended to sell her on after a refit, to the St. Peter Line.

Brittany Ferries, however, still considered the route a feasible operation, and took it over in 2011 and began operations with the *Cap Finistère*.

Current Operator and Ships

Cap Finistère (IMO 9198927) is currently the newest vessel to join the Brittany fleet. This ferry was originally built for the Greek Attica Group by Howaldtswerke-Deutsche Weft AG, Kiel, Germany and was launched in 2001 as the *Superfast V*, and as such she operated in the Adriatic between Patras and Ancona. In March 2010 the vessel was purchased by Brittany Ferries at a price of €81.5 million specifically for use on the new routes from the UK to Spain. She was re-named *Cap Finistère* and delivered to Brittany. She underwent a purpose-designed refit at Dunkerque and was repainted in her new livery, before commencing operations in March 2011.

The *Cap Finistère* is of 32,728-GT, has an overall length of 203.90 m, a beam of 25 m and a draught of 6.40 m, with a normal service speed of 22 knots. Her facilities are extensive, and venues for meals are Le Café du Pont Brassiere with *à la carte* menu and fine wines; Le Petit Marché and Blue Marine café and salad bar; along with the Planets bar and the Belle View bar. Shopping can be indulged at 5th Avenue/L'Atelier, which sell spirits, tobaccos, toys, confectionery, perfumes and cosmetics, fashion wear, leather goods decoration, souvenirs, magazine and book outlets. The ship has a cinema and a heated outdoor swimming pool, a children's play area, Chance Planet for games and slots,

Offshore Ferry Services

Brittany Ferries 32,728 GRT Ro-Ro ferry MV *Cap Finistère* outward bound from Portsmouth to Bilbao. (© Brian Burnell)

A cosy and comfortable corner of the main bar area on the *Cap Finistère*. (© Brittany Ferries)

sun deck with covered verandas, lounges, and kennel accommodation for man's best friend. There is a well-equipped sick bay and disabled access and toilets.

Accommodation for 1,600 passengers has 790 berths and includes 2-berth outside cabins and 4-berth exterior and interior cabins, all with air-conditioning. There is also a capacity for 712 cars.

Cap Finistère currently sails twice-weekly on the Portsmouth to Bilbao route, a 24 hours service interspersed with a weekly service from Portsmouth to Santander. Sunday sailings from Portsmouth also service Roscoff for crewing purposes, which takes 33 hours. As with all the company's routes they operate a pets travel scheme.

Contact Details
Bilbao Office
Terminal de Brittany Ferries, Puerto de Bilbao, Muelle A3, Zierbena 48508, Spain
Tel: 0871 244 0744; 0871 244 1400
Email: customer.feedback@brittanyferries.com
Web: www.brittanyferries.com

9: St. Malo – Channel Islands

Background

During the nineteenth century the long period of stability and peace that followed the Napoleonic Wars saw the blossoming of sea communications between the Channel Islands and France, which the arrival of steamships enhanced. The French shipping company Bateaux de la Cote D'Emeraude (BCE) was originally founded in 1904 to transport passengers and general cargo along northern Brittany's so-termed 'Emerald Coast', and for over four decades operated a conventional ferry service to the Channel Islands, interrupted only by the German occupation between 1940 and 1945. With the building of a new road from Dinard to St. Malo in 1969, the existing car ferry was rendered obsolete and a new route to Jersey was selected the following year. By 1976 Emeraude started operating the *Westamarin W86*, a fast catamaran built by Norwegian Shipyards, with routes between Jersey, Sark and Guernsey.

Although initially there was little or no competition, in May 1964 clouds appeared on the hitherto rosy horizon with the arrival of Condor Ferries and their high-speed vessels, which soon eclipsed the traditional methods of sea transport. In 1964 Peter Dorey and Jack Norman had founded Condor Ferries as an alternative to the conventional ferries operating from the Channel Islands to French ports. They started their route by purchasing the *Condor-1*, a Rodriquez PT50 hydrofoil built in Messina, Italy. She was Jersey-based and ran to Guernsey, Sark and St. Malo; with her high speed she soon proved popular and in the first year of the summer-only operation carried 10,000 passengers. Within two years this number had increased six-fold.

Suddenly shorn of their old easy monopoly, Emeraude's financial problems began to rapidly accrue. A new company, the Le Havre-based Sogestran Group, took over and in 1976 their Vedettes Blancs company purchased the second of the Westermoen W86 hydrofoils, the Norwegian *Karmsund*, and renamed her as *Belle de Dinard* and later *Trident I*. Subsequently they operated several of these vessels during the summer season from various ports but mainly on St. Malo – St. Helier, the *Trident I* being sold in 1987 and being replaced by the Italian company Alilauro-owned *Celestina*, which became *Trident IV* in 1988. Meanwhile 1977 had seen the service re-flagged as Emeraude Ferries, using a traditional car ferry, the *Solidor I* to operate a daily service to and from Jersey. This vessel was the former 1965-built *Langeland* which had been built for the Kiel to Bagenkop, Denmark route and had a length of 68 m, a beam of 12 m and a 3 m draught, with a speed of 11.2 knots. She had a capacity of 500 passengers and 50 cars.

Condor expanded rapidly, adding to their hydrofoil fleet with *Condor 2*, chartered in 1969–70; *Condor 3*, which arrived in 1970; *Condor 4* in 1974 and *Condor 5* in 1976. The next vessel was the Westmarin gas-turbine powered catamaran *Condor 6* with a 250-passenger capacity, but which proved rather prone to mechanical failures. *Condor 7* was another Rodriquez hydrofoil which was purchased in 1985 and she served for nine years. Two more additions followed, this time high-speed catamarans. In 1988 the 300-passenger *Condor 8* arrived, built in Singapore by Fairey Marinteknik Shipbuilders, of 387-GT and designed to operate with a 19-strong crew, arrived transported by the *Kestrel* bulk carrier ship and started work on 17 May. In 1990 another quantum leap was

9: St. Malo – Channel Islands

The *Condor Vitesse*. (© Condorferries Ltd)

made with the British-built 450-passenger capacity *Condor 9* delivered by Aluminium Shipbuilders, Fareham.

With the specific role of providing a similar high-speed car ferry to Jersey from St. Malo and determined on fighting fire with fire, Emeraude emulated their new competitor in a last-ditch effort to regain their earlier dominance. Initially they brought into operation the catamaran *Solidor 3* and then between 2000 and 2005 they operated the custom-tailored 2,369-GT *Solidor 5*, another JumboCat 60 catamaran owned by S.N.A.V. She had been built by Fjellstrand A.S. (Finlande), and had an overall length of 60 m, a 16.43 m beam and a draught of 2.2 m. She was powered by a pair of Caterpillar 3618 engines of 7,200 kW each, driving a Kamewa 112 SII water-jet system, which gave her 36 knots. Her capacities were 450 passengers and 52 cars and she was fitted with a Light Craft Design motion-dampening system (MDS) to compensate for the rough seas experienced in her designated area. In 2005 the company became Emeraude Jersey Ferries and continued using the *Solidor 5* until an even larger vessel was obtained. The *Solidor 5* was returned to S.N.A.V. and commenced working from Naples as the HSC *Don Franceso*.

The Emeraude Company's high-speed hydrofoil fleet were all formally renamed as Trident's in 1983, and a Westamarin W95 type high-speed hydrofoil was bought. She was again built by Westermoen Hydrofoil, Mandal, Norway, one of the unique Herald Heinriksen designs with asymmetrical hulls. She was of 228-GT, had an overall length of 29 m, a beam of 8 m and a 3.1 m draught. She was powered by two 1,800 bhp engines and could carry 200 passengers. Named the *Venture 84* (IMO 8205694), she was completed in 1982 and began operating in April 1983, remaining on the route until 1996 when she was sold to Fergün Denizcilik and started operations from northern Cyprus as the *Fergün Express II* and later *Trident II*. Later Emeraude additions included the *Trident 5* (ex-Flaggruten, Norwegian *Vingtor*), *Trident 6* (ex-Spanish Allisur *Alisur Amarillo*), *Trident 7* (ex-Danish *DSØ Tumleren*), the ex-Service Maritime Carteret–Jersey *Pegasus*, which retained her name intact, and the *Emeraude Express*, (ex-Hong Kong *Oregrund*), which could carry 306 passengers at 36 knots.

After six years the *Solidor II* replaced the older car ferry, and *Solidor I* was to end her days several decades later, as the Naples-based *Redentore Primo*. Her replacement was another former *Langeland* originally built for Langeland-Kiel Linien in 1977 by Scheepswerf Ferus Smith BN, Netherlands. She was of 1,599-GT, with a length of 70 m a beam of 16.25 m and 3.8 m draught. Powered by Krupp MAK engines she had a speed of 15 knots with a 650 passenger capacity and space for 90 cars and freight accommodation. She remained in service until 2001 with various companies, including Rainbow and Fast Ferry. A new high-speed vessel was ordered from Kvaerner Fjellstrand in 1996, being launched that June and named *Solidor III*, and she was joined by a second vessel in 1999, the *Solidor IV*.

Meanwhile Vedettes Blanches et Vertes, as it had become, had been fully taken into the Emeraude fold. In 1988 the ferry part of the larger operation was re-named as Emeraude Lines. In 1991 the Saint Quay Portrieux to the Channel Islands route commenced but was not a success. The leasing of the high-speed car ferry *Emeraude* from Marinteknik Verkstads, Sweden, in 1994 replaced the *Solidor II* and she also started working to Guernsey.

The 3,012-GT HSC *Emeraude France* was originally built in 1990 as the *Seacat Tasmania* for Tasmanian Ferry Services by Incat, Tasmania. She had an overall length of 74 m a beam of 26 m and a 3.09 m draught and was powered by four Ruston 16R K270 engines that gave her an operational speed of 36 knots. She could carry 450 passengers and 88 cars. Between 1993 she was operated by a variety of companies, Hoverspeed, Ferry Linas and S.N.A.V. under the names *SeaCat Calais*, *Atlantic II*, *Croazia Jet* and *SeaCat France* before Emeraude Jersey Ferries took her over in 2005 and operated her for two years. However, despite their best efforts they could not compete for various reasons and repeated technical faults saw her withdrawal and the re-installation of *Solidor II* once more in 1995. With losses of €15 million since the arrival of Condor on the scene, in 2006 the company was dissolved. The *Emeraude France* was re-allocated and in 2007 she was briefly operated by the Isle of Man Steam Packet Company, and then, under the ownership of Maritime Charter Sales Limited, in 2007 she was laid up at Tilbury. With the demise of Emeraude Line's brief challenger, another operator appeared upon the scene in response to the desire of Jersey and Guernsey States and the Brittany Regional Council for a second operator to offer competition. After nine months pondering the scene, HD Ferries, a subsidiary of the Two M Group of ferry operators, had the notion that they could provide an affordable and reliable daily high-speed 'missing transport link' with a fast catamaran service, for passenger and freight traffic wishing to use the route between the Channel Islands and Paris via St. Malo.

The *HD1* (IMO 9160114) was a high-speed, aluminium catamaran of the Incat 80 m K50 design, originally the *Afai 08* and one of a pair built at Panyu, Guangzhou, China in July 1998 by AFAI Ships Ltd, Hong Kong, in conjunction with Incat, Tasmania, Australia. She was 2,357-GT and was 80.1 m overall with a moulded beam of 19 m and a 2.16 m draught. She could carry 450 passengers in Tier 1, built over a hull that was sub-divided into eight watertight compartments, with lounges, a cafeteria, a bar, a duty-free shop and wheelhouse set upon anti-vibration mountings. Tier 2 contained the three-lane car deck, with a height of 3.1 m, in which 89 cars could be driven on to starboard rear ramps and stacked round the whole deck to be driven off the port hand side of the same ramp. Her four Ruston 16 RK 270 marine diesel engines developed 22,000 kW, and fed four Kamewa 80 SII water jets which gave her a registered speed in 1997 of 47.5 knots.

In 1998 she was chartered to Bay Ferries as the *Incat K3* and worked the route between Miami and Nassau, Bahamas until 2003, then moved to the Caribbean to operate between Guadaloupe and Martinique and then moved to the Mediterranean where she worked for Transmediterranea on the Palma, Mallorca, Ibiza and Alicante triangle in 2006. The following year Incat Chartering leased her to HD Ferries who renamed her *HD1*. With the co-operation of the UK and French Maritime Coastguard Agencies a new stern loading ramp was prepared and installed at Portsmouth, strong enough to take 10 trucks as well as 100 cars, along with 400 passengers, and a passenger shuttle bus service laid on at each terminus. The new service was inaugurated on 15 March 2007 when she commenced operations from St. Helier, Jersey to St. Malo, a crossing time of 1 hour being promised, and later via St. Peter Port, Guernsey on a triangular route. At one time six crossings per day were made and the company announced plans to extend the service to Alderney and Cherbourg, but the former concept was overtaken by events, although a twice weekly service was commenced to the latter port but this quickly withered through lack of sufficient custom.

A collision between the *HD1* and Condor's *Commodore Goodwill* at Jersey in May 2007 did not help matters as it led to the cancellation of services and the resignation of her captain. Unfortunately a similar incident happened at St. Helier in July and caused considerable damage to *HD1*. By September 2008 high fuel prices and the general economic slump made the service less well-used than originally envisaged and the summer service was halted early. In February 2009 HD Ferries went further and announced it was not resuming services in 2009 at all, citing lack of support for its problems.

After being laid up at Newhaven for a period, in November 2011 the *HD1* was sold to a Republic of Korea ferry operator at Pusan and was renamed *Moonflower*, joining her sister (now *Sunflower*) and working to Kaohsiung, Taiwan.

Another brief contender was the *Britannia*, operated by the French state-controlled Sealink SNAT subsidiary, Channiland. She was the former *Ternoy*, ex-*Fjorddrott*, another Westermoen Hydrofoil, built in June 1976. She commenced operations from St. Malo and Granville to Jersey and Guernsey, but in 1977 she was sold locally. Another Channiland fast ferry, the *Saint-Malo*, refitted at a cost of £2 million, was run onto the La Frouquie rock off Jersey at high speed on 17 April 1995 with 300 passengers and crew of 9, of whom 55 were injured

In 2007 yet another operator, the French Compagnie Corsair, another offshoot of Emeraude but operating from the Gare Maritime De La Bourse, Saint Malo, had been approached and had announced it planned to operate a passenger-only service to and from St. Malo and the Albert Pier, St. Helier.

The *Jacques Cartier* (IMO 9447689) was built in 2007 by Strategic Marine at Henderson, Australia. She was 37 m long, had a 7 m beam and 2.3 m draught, could carry 200 passengers, had a crew of 5 and was capable of a speed of 29 knots. She had a snack bar, duty-free shopping, air-conditioned lounges, stabilizers, observation decks, seating behind panoramic windows and sundecks. Loaded aboard the heavylift ship *Annemieke*, she was delivered to St. Malo on 27 July 2007 and commenced operating on 4 August. She had a schedule of one rotational voyage each day.

Having seen off every attempt at competition, Condor Ferries thrived and continued to introduce improved vessels to enhance the crossing as the years went by. The Bahamas-registered *Condor Vitesse*, formerly the *Incat 044*, was built at Hobart in 1997 and in March 1998 Condor briefly chartered her for use on the Guernsey to St. Malo crossing, with 500 passengers and 90 cars, as an intermittent summer service. The catamaran *Condor 10* was completed by Incat, Hobart, in 1993, and was of 3,240 tonnes, with a length of 74.15 m, a beam of 26 m and a 2.62 m draught. She had four Ruston 16RK270 M engines and four Lips LJ145D waterjets which gave her a speed of 35 knots. Her passenger capacity was 576, she had a crew of 24 and could carry 90 vehicles. After working out of Weymouth she was switched to the St. Malo route in March 2002 following earlier technical faults, replacing *Condor 9*. In June 2010 the *Condor 10* was retired after seventeen years service and replaced by the *Condor Rapide*, which could carry 700 passengers and three times as many cars. In September 2010, however, it was announced that the *Condor 10* was being temporarily brought back into service after the *Condor Vitesse* had two of her four engines damaged.

Current Operators, Ships and Details

The current Condor arrangement sees the *Condor Rapide* (IMO 9161560) working the Guernsey/Jersey to Saint Malo crossing, while the *Condor Vitesse* (IMO 9151008) (alternately and seemingly randomly known as *Normandie Vitesse*, or merely, *Vitesse*) seasonally operates out of Poole via the Channel Islands to St. Malo. Condor Ferries Freight operates a Ro-Ro service from Portsmouth that includes the Channel Islands and, at some weekends, onward to St. Malo with the *Commodore Goodwill*.

Condor Rapide is a wave-piercing catamaran which was built in 1997 by Incat, Hobart, Tasmania, as *Incat 045*. She is of 5,005-GT with a length of 86.62 m, a beam of 26 m and a 3.6 m draught. She has four Rushton 20RK270 diesel engines developing 28,320 kW, and four Lips waterjets which give her a speed of 48 knots.

Initially she was chartered out to Transport Tasmania under the name *Tascat* as a intermediate relief ferry provider across the Bass Strait, between Devonport and Melbourne. After being taken out of service, she was commissioned into the Royal Australian Navy between May 1999 and May 2001 under the name HMAS *Jervis Bay* (AKR 45) and based at Darwin for work with the INTERFET Task Group, carrying up to 500 troops and light equipment rapidly into action during the crisis in East Timor. In 2002 she was returned to Incat to resume her civilian career. After then she was chartered out to TRIS at Genoa, Italy as *Winner*, and later with SpeedFerries as *HSC SpeedOne* and in 2009 as *Sea Leopard*. On 26 March 2010 she was purchased by Condor and given the old name from the earlier catamaran operated by the company.

She can carry 741 passengers in spacious air-conditioned lounges with a guaranteed seat for each one, and has a crew of 30. There is a cafeteria, a duty-free shop, an upper deck bar and shop and children's TV room, and she can accommodate 175 cars. Club class includes a private seating area with tables, complimentary newspapers, beverages. Reclining seats are *not* available however.

Condor Vitesse is of 5,007 tonnes, with a length of 86.62 m, a beam of 26 m and 3.5 m draught. She is powered by four Ruston 20 RK270 engines with four Lips LJ145D waterjets, which give her a speed of 39 knots. She can currently carry 741 passengers in lounges that are fully air-conditioned and with guaranteed seats and recliner options; she has a crew of 30 and a maximum capacity for 175 cars. Her onboard amenities include a café on her main deck and a bar on her upper deck; a duty-free shop (where applicable), a Club-class lounge, a children's playroom and reclining seats all on the main deck.

The 11,116-GT, Bahamas registered *Commodore Goodwill* (IMO 9117985) is an all-weather, purpose-built, dry cargo ship built in 1996 by Schelde Koninklijke at Vlissingen in the Netherlands for NYDA Shipping Ltd and is operated by Condor Ferries Freight. She has a length of 126.3 m, a beam of 21.4 m and 6.01 m draught. She has MaK engines which provide a working speed of 18.3 knots. She has 1,250 lane meters of car space for 100 cars, and facilities aboard include twelve *en-suite* cabins, Club class, reclining seats, a Brasserie, a lounge bar, duty-free shop and a special children's area.

The Jersey Ferry Port at St. Helier on St. Aubrin's Bay at the southern end of the island is opened daily from 06.00 to 22.30 each day. The road approach is via the Route De La Liberation roundabout and La Route De La Port Elizabeth. The ports amenities include paid short- and long-stay car parking nearby, cafeteria, a bar, duty-free shopping, *bureau de change*, ATM, payphones, toilets, disabled toilets, baby-changing area, and lost property/left luggage. Travel times to Guernsey are around 1 hour and to St. Malo 70 minutes. The Guernsey ferry terminal is at St. Peter Port and is open between 09.00 to 17.00 all year round. Travel times to Jersey are about 1 hour and to St. Malo 1 hour 45 minutes.

Condor Ferries currently operate a variable timed daily summer timetable with first sailings from Guernsey, Jersey and St. Malo which should be carefully checked well prior departure and are subject to weather and other conditions.

The St. Malo Ferry Port is one of the largest in France, with a million passengers each year, and, as one would expect, has many facilities. There are two ferry terminal buildings, a café, toilets and disabled toilets, and there are shower facilities during opening hours. There is no *bureau de change* or ATM at the terminal but as the town is just 5 minutes walk away this is strange but not too inconvenient.

Contact Details
Condor Head Office
New Jetty Offices, White Rock, St. Peter Port, Guernsey, GY1 2LL
Tel: Guernsey 01481 728521
UK: 01202 207216
Jersey: 01534 872240
St. Malo: 0825 165 463
Fax: 01202 685184
Freight: 01481 728521
Email: customer.service@condorferries.co.uk or
Reservations: reservations@condorferries.co.uk
Freight: len.lepage@condorferries.co.uk
Web: www.condorferries.com

10: Isle of Wight – Wootton Creek and Ryde

Background
Records exist which reveal that in medieval times sailing boats plied between Barnsley Creek east of present-day Ryde over to Portsmouth, but when the creek became silted up the traffic transferred to Ryde itself. Certainly the Lord of the Manor in Ashey and Buckland was responsible for boats crossing from Portsmouth to La Richte or La Rye ('little stream') late, Ride, which may mean Monkton Brook. The local craft so used was known as a Ryde or Portsmouth Wherry or Hoy, described as a light rowboat for use in transporting goods and passengers. The Old Portsmouth Wherry was both described and illustrated in Robert Charles Leslie's book *Old Seas Wings, Ways and Words, In the Day of Oak & Hemp*, published by Chapman & Hall, London, in 1890. How they were employed in practice was graphically described by another writer. In Brannon's *Picture of The Isle of Wight*, George Brannon described how a time of '... favorable (sic) weather, at the moment of high tide. The practice then was, to cram the passengers promiscuously into a common luggage-cart, till it was drawn out upon the almost level sands sufficiently far for a large Wherry to float alongside, into which they were then transferred, and conveyed to the sailing-packet, perhaps lying off at some considerable distance.'

By the 1600s boatmen plying their living at Ryde's East Key or Quay, which had a small jetty, were required to take turns in making a daily return crossing to Portsmouth as frequently as every 2 hours, or suffer penalty. In 1703 one Henry Player purchased the Manor of Ashey and Ryde, as it had become in 1578, from Sir John Dillington, and built wharves and Brewhouse Quay. By 1788 he had also built the Passage Hoy inn there, which was later renamed The Bugle, and became a place where the skippers and crews of the ferry boats congregated.

As Portsmouth grew into Britain's premier naval base so did Ryde flourish by proximity as a recreational area, and by 1796 traffic was sufficient for the very first twice-daily regular sailing packet from The Bugle to the Quebec Tavern, Portsmouth, while in 1814 a proper embarkation pier was completed and ten years later much enlarged. With the coming of steam this service was taken over by the 76-GT passenger steamer *Britannia*, a vessel constructed far from the sea in Gainsborough, Lincolnshire in 1817, but she proved unsuitable for the task and was soon withdrawn and the *Prince Coburg* arrived in 1820. Nonetheless the Portsmouth & Ryde United Steam Packet Company persevered, and on 5 April 1825 commenced operating a succession of paddle steamers on the passage, *Union* (1825), *Arrow* (1825), *Lord Yarborough* (1826) and *Earl Spencer* (1833). By May 1842 up to ten daily sailings were being made from Ryde to Portsmouth's newly-opened Victoria Pier and four years later the even grander Albert Pier allowed paddle steamers easy embarkation and disembarkation alongside.

The first direct railway link to London arrived in 1847, along with one of the first fully-integrated tourist services, with the London Brighton & South Coast Railway transferring holidaymakers from Portsmouth Station to Victoria Pier by omnibus. The paddle steamer *Prince Albert* of 1847 reflected this new trend. In 1849 a brief period of intense, and destructive, competition was signalled with the arrival on the scene of The Portsea, Portsmouth, Gosport and Isle of Wight New Steam Packet Company who commenced rival operations with a flourish with a trio of vessels, the *Prince of Wales, Princess Royal* and *Her Majesty*. The competition was too hot and in 1851 the two companies decided to merge. However, in defiance, the grandly-named Port of Portsmouth and Ryde United Steam Packet Company Ltd commenced its own service on New Year's Day 1852.

The Victorian boom continued and at Ryde the new Clarence Pier opened on 1st July 1861, and as many as seven steamers were soon using it for the Portsmouth crossing. Typical of the era and built in 1873 by William Whites & Sons at Cowes, for the PPRUSP, the *Ryde* was a 75-GT vessel with a 39 bhp two-cylinder engine, a length of 30.27 m, a beam of 4.9 m and a draught of 2.16 m, but she was soon sold to William Johnston at Liverpool.

A new boom period commenced on 31 March 1880 with the purchase of the company by the London & South West and the London, Brighton and South Coast Railways, and their passengers made possible thirteen daily sailings on the crossing, plus five on Sundays. The 336-GT paddle steamer *Duchess of Fife* was built by Clydebank Engineering & Shipbuilding, Glasgow for the SW&BRCSPS in 1899. She was another veteran who served until 1929 after war service in the First World War. There seemed no end to expansion and by 1912 there were some twenty-six crossings being made by similar steamers on the route, including the *Duchess of Kent, Duchess of Richmond* and *Duchess of Norfolk*. The arrival of the automobile had been catered for with the construction of a slipway at George Street in Ryde, and just before the First World War brought a drastic reduction in the service, some 742 cars had been transported across along with 845,000 passengers.

Many ferries were pressed into war service and lost, and the post-war amalgamation of the rail services saw the establishment in 1923 of the Southern Railway monopoly of the ferries under Government aegis and saw passenger numbers rise to 1.3 million along with 1,163 vehicles.

The rise of the car continued and in April 1925 work commenced on the construction of a new road for cattle and traffic expected at the new Southern Railway Company's landing slipway, south of the old coastguard building and north of Hayles yacht yard at Fishbourne, while work was underway dredging the entrance to Wootton Creek. This made the establishment of a regular service to and from Portsmouth non-dependent upon the tides. It was expected the journey would take about 35 minutes.

By 1927 the first exclusive, custom-built ferry to cater for it was the *Fishbourne*, built by William Denny & Bros in Dumbarton. Double-ended in design she was 40 m by 7.62 m, 2.438 m deep and powered by a pair of two diesel engines that provided a service speed of just 8 knots. She could carry 18 cars in just under an hour from Portsmouth to the new Fishbourne slipway, loading and unloading from her ramps, and with their owners and passengers carried below the car deck. She had commenced operations in July 1927 and was soon joined by the similar *Wootton*, their names reflecting their operating area. New passenger ferries were also built to cater for the increased traffic, including the *Shanklin, Merstone*, and *Portsdown*, followed in the 1930s by *Southsea, Whippingham, Sandown* and a new *Ryde*, the last Ryde to Portsmouth paddle steamer built before the Second World War intervened.

In the aftermath of the war, nationalization took place 1st September 1948 with the setting up of British Rail, which in 1971 would re-brand its ferry business as Sealink. Two new motor vessel ferries were built, the 837-GT *Brading* and *Southsea*, built by William Denny Bros. of Dumbarton. Each is of 60 m overall length with a beam of 13 m. They could carry over 1,000 passengers in two classes at a speed of 14.5 knots and were the first Isle of Wight ships to carry radar. In 1951 the duo were joined by the similar *Shanklin* to cope with up to 60,000 passengers per day at peak periods. More car ferries were built for Fishbourne, which saw a similar increase in numbers with, in the mid-1960s,

Offshore Ferry Services

St Faith alongside the *Wight Ryder I* and *FastCat Ryde* catamarans.

54,919 cars being conveyed to Wootton Creek, rising to 59,982 a year later and to 273,566 cars and 24,000 trucks by the end of the decade. In 1969 the 750-GT *Cuthred*, built in Lowestoft by Richards shipbuilders, was added to the fleet, and she had the capacity for 48 cars and 400 passengers. Even larger was the 1973 addition, the 761-GT *Caedmon*, which had an overall length of 61 m, a 15 m beam and could carry 52 cars and 756 passengers at 11 knots. To meet demand these ships were operated round-the-clock and were all upgraded in 1977–78 by the addition of mezzanine decks, increasing their capacity from 48 and 52 to 72 and 76 cars respectively.

As well as bulk travel, experiments had been made with high-speed passenger services with, in 1968, the introduction of Hovermarine HM2 side-walled hovercraft. In the 1980s a catamaran, the *Highland Seabird* was also briefly chartered from Western Ferries for the Ryde service. Also, in the summer of 1983 the side-walled hovercraft *Ryde Rapid* introduced daily crossings from between Ryde Pier to Clarence Pier in Southsea.

The new Linkspan terminal opened at Portsmouth which entailed modification to the existing car ferries, and in August 1982 the same modification at Fishbourne Linkspan began with the widening and deepening of the main channel at Wootton Creek. This paved the way for the introduction of the 2,036-GT *St. Catherine* the following July, followed by the 2,983-GT *St. Helen* in November. They had overall lengths of 77 m, a beam of 17 m, and carried 142 cars plus 1,000 passengers at 12.5 knots for a 35 minute passage time. A third vessel, the 2,968-GT *St. Cecilia* joined them in March 1987. Meanwhile the age of privatization appeared with Sealink being sold off by the government to Sea Containers in July 1984 and the next year being rebranded as Sealink British Ferries.

The high-speed concept was again re-introduced in March 1986 with acquisition of the Tasmanian-built *Our Lady Patricia* and *Our Lady Pamela*. They had an operational speed of 29.5 knots, taking just 15 minutes to convey their 470 passengers. They operated a 20-minute frequency summer service.

In July 1990 the 3,009-GT, £7.5 million price-tagged *St. Faith* arrived on station, giving the route a quartet of 'super-ferries'. 1991, however, saw the sale of Sealink British Ferries to the Swedish Stena company, which renamed the service as Wightlink and this, in turn, was sold by Sea Containers to a management team headed up by Michael Aiken with finance from CinVen. In 1999 the two catamarans were re-branded as FastCat and two further vessels, built in Singapore in 1996, were added. Used on the Ryde service, these were the *FastCat Ryde* and *FastCat Shanklin*. There were equipped with stabilizers and water jet propulsion and had a 34 knot top speed. Passenger amenities included TVs and a café bar for the service. For the first time on HSS the passengers were not confined to their seats during the passage. However, by the beginning of the new millennium, passenger numbers again surged and another big ferry was introduced. This was the 5,300-GT, Polish-built, £11.5 million *St. Clare*. She is of double-ended design and her dimensions are an overall length of 86 m and a beam of 18 m, with the capacity to haul 180 cars and 770 passengers at 13.5 knots.

In 2005 Wightlink was acquired by the Macquarie European Infrastructure Fund, and the following year Wightlink announced plans for new catamarans for the Portsmouth – Ryde service and enlargements to the Portsmouth – Fishbourne car ferries. The *Wight Ryder I* and *II*, built in the Philippines, started working on the Portsmouth to Ryde crossing on 29 September 2009.

Current Operators, Ships and Details

Wightlinks Portsmouth to Fishbourne service is operated by four vessels and the 2011 spring to autumn schedule had 30 minute sailings in both directions for which a 30 minute check-in time is recommended.

The 2,968-GT *St. Cecilia* (IMO 8518546) and the 3009-GT *St. Faith* (IMO 8907228) were originally built for Sealink in 1987 and 1989 respectively by Cochrane Shipbuilders, Selby. They have three 6-cylinder Harland & Wolff-MAN engines with three Voith Schneider propellers and a speed of 12.5 knots. Their dimensions are a length of 77.05 m, a beam of 17.22 m and a 2.48 m draught, and they can carry 771 passengers and 142 cars with a crew of 10–12. Both passenger decks have lounges with a café/bar on the lower one, are accessible via lifts, and there is also some open sun deck seating. *St. Cecilia* has undergone a refurbishment recently with a new retail outlet installed and seating areas modernized.

The 5,359-GT *St. Clare* (IMO 9236949), the fleet flagship and the largest Wightlink vessel, is double-ended and was built by Stocznia Remotowa, at Gdansk, Poland in 2001. Her dimensions are a length of 86 m, beam of 18 m and draught of 2.6 m. She is powered by four Wärtsilä 3,300 kW engines driving four Voith Schneider propellers and a speed of 13 knots. She can convey 186 cars and 878 passengers and has a crew of 10–12. The *St. Clare* has a central bridge and three passenger decks all served by lifts, with many lounges and a shop on the main deck. Her facilities include a full Costa Coffee outlet on her upper lounge which as well as the full Costa range will have newspapers and magazines available, while adjacent is an art gallery featuring local artists whose work is for sale. There is a dedicated dog area for man's best friend to also make a comfortable crossing.

The 2,983-GT *St. Helen* (IMO 8120569) was originally built for Sealink at the Henry Robb Caledon Yard at Leith. Her overall length is 77.05 m, with a 17.22 m beam and a draught of 2.48 m. She has three MAN H&W 1,876 kW engines driving three Voith Schneider propellers and has a speed of 12.5 knots. Capacity is 771 passengers and 142 cars and she has a crew of 10–12. She has two decks with lounges, with the lower one having a café/bar. There is a lift from the car deck to the main lounge.

Since September 2009 on the direct Portsmouth to Ryde service, Wightlink have operated two passenger-only HSC 2000 Cat A, 520-GT catamarans, the *Wight Ryder I* (IMO 9512537) and *Wight Ryder II* (IMO 9512549), which take about 22 minutes to cross the Solent, connecting the two rail stations. Both were built in the Isle of Wight-originated, Aboitz Transport System Corporation-owned, FBMA yard at Balamban, Cebu, in the Philippines. They are of 41 m overall length, with a 12 m beam and 1.6 m draught. They have Caterpillar water-cooled engines with an improved fuel management system to reduce costs and make them more environmentally friendly in use. With an operating speed of 20.1 knots they can carry 260 passengers and 20 bicycles and have a crew of 4–5. Both have comfortable lounges and some open sun-deck seating. Currently the 2 April to 22 December timetable has around thirty crossings Monday to Friday with slightly fewer on Saturday and Sunday, but weather can affect timings and checks should be made ahead of journeys.

Contact Details
Wightlink Isle of Wight Ferries Ltd, Gunwharf Road, Portsmouth, Hants, PO1 2LA
Tel: 0871 376 1000
Coach/Freight: 023 9285 5260
Fax: 02392 855257
Email: enquiries@wightlink.co.uk
Web: www.wightlink.co.uk

11: Newhaven – Dieppe

Background

A regular service of sailing vessels between Sussex and the French coast had been in place as early as 1790, with the British packet *Princess Royal* leaving Shoreham each Tuesday for Dieppe, returning each Saturday. Similar concerns to those that worry ferry customers today were evident, with the service promising two 'elegant' cabins, with eight beds apiece, but that accompanying horses and carriages had to arrive the day prior to sailing.

In 1792 packets were also plying between Brighton and Dieppe. The long period of the Napoleonic Wars interrupted and disrupted the service but after 1815 and the restoration of normal trading it was resumed. By 1824 the first steam vessel, the *Rapid*, had made the crossing, and in June of the following year the General Steam Navigation Company (GSN) introduced the paddle steamer *Eclipse* for a twice-weekly passage sailing instead from Newhaven, for the first time calling at Brighton Chain Pier *en route* to Dieppe. Crossings were made on Tuesday and Saturday with her return passages being made on Monday and Thursday ('weather permitting' of course).

With the establishment of reliable rail links on both side of the Channel, traffic promised to expand. In 1847 the Brighton and Continental Steam Packet Company was established and commenced operations with a twice weekly crossing from Brighton to Dieppe and also worked a route from Shoreham to Le Havre with the MS *Manai*. They later added two more steamers, *Fame* and *Magnet*, for a four-times-a-week ferry from Shoreham to Dieppe. Both the English termini eventually became too expensive for commercial operations and the ferries moved back to Newhaven, where the London Brighton and South Coast Railway Company (LB&SCR) had opened a railway terminus also in 1847. In the first year of operations 5,000 passengers made the Newhaven to Dieppe passage, a journey time then of 6 hours.

Both French and British railway-based ferry companies continued to develop the route from both ends with the introduction of screw ships, Newhaven harbour was expanded and the channel dredged to take larger ships, which in 1863 led the LB&SCR and the French Chemins de Fer de l'Ouest company to invigorate a new Newhaven to Dieppe venture.

In 1885 the LB&SCR ordered two new 471-GT cargo ships from J. Elder & Co., these being the *Italy* and the *Lyons*. On completion in 1887 both were given French crews and became *Italie* and *Lyon*, and they served until 1910 and 1911 respectively.

The single-funnelled *Seaford* was built in 1892 by William Denny & Bros for the LB&SCR specifically for the crossing. She was of 997-GT, had a length of 80.06 m, a beam of 10.38 m and a draught of 4.26 m. She was powered by Denny Bros 4-cylinder, triple-expansion engines developing 292 bhp which gave her a 20 knot speed. The *Seaford* worked the route for only a short period for, on 20 August 1895, while *en route* to Newhaven in thick fog, was in collision some 20 miles offshore with another ferry, the *Lyons*, and sank. Another disaster involved the 531-GT *Victoria*, built in 1878, which was wrecked at Dieppe with the loss of nineteen lives.

In total, some forty ferries were built for the company between 1863 and 1923, when the company merged into the Southern Railway, among them three *Brightons*, three *Dieppes*, three named *Rouen* and four named *Paris*. The final addition was the 1,903-GT *Versailles* which survived until 1945.

The two world wars in the twentieth century caused further disruption (including one ghastly British landing fiasco at Dieppe in 1942) and the route followed the normal post-war story of nationalization followed by privatization, the boom of the car ferries and the bust of the Channel Tunnel and the container revolution. By the early 1990s ferry traffic had peaked with a million plus making the crossing, but the austerity years hit hard and this was sharply reduced so that by 2010 only a third of that number were using the route, and current government cut-backs threaten even that declining figure. Long before then, the then current operator, P&O Stena, took the decision to concentrate services at Dover and their last sailing from Newhaven was on 31 January 1998 with the *Stena Cambria*.

Hoverspeed entered the scene in April 1999 with the *SuperSeaCat 1* for a high-speed passenger-only service. They utilized the Fincantieri-Cant Nav. Italiani S.p.A., La Spezia-built vessel which was built in 1997 and had an overall length of 100 m and could carry 782 passengers at a speed of 38 knots. She gave a summer season service between April and October in 2000 and again between 2002 and 2004 before operational costs caused a cessation of operations, when she was sold to Italy and became the *Almudaina Does*.

By the early twenty-first century the service almost ceased entirely and Newhaven as a ferry port was very run down and threatened with extinction. Little was achieved at the British end, but fortunately the French proved more enterprising and the Conseil Général de la Seine-Maritime, Dieppe stepped in. They formed Transmanche Ferries which took over both the ferry operation terminals and invested in ships to reintroduce an all-year ferry service once more. Initially they chartered two stern-loading vessels in order to initiate the service while two brand-new Ro-Pax ships, the *Côte d'Albâtre* and the *Seven Sisters* were being built in Vigo, Spain, by De Hijos De J. Barreras De Vigo.

The first chartered ship was the rear-door loading Corsica Ferries *Sarinia Vera* (formerly *Corsica Vera*, ex-*Marine Atlantica*) which had been built in 1975. She served the route between 2001 and 2006 making two return crossings weekdays and one at weekends. The second chartered ship was the *Dieppe*, originally built in 1981 by Fartygesentreprendader AB at Uddevalla TT-Line as *Saga Star*, and then re-named *Girolata* with CMN. She commenced working from Dieppe in 2002 and on arrival of the *Seven Sisters* was disposed of and became the *Baltiva*.

Of the two new ships, both are 18,900-GT ships, with 142.71 m overall length, a beam of 24.2 m and a draught of 5.89 m. They are powered by two Wärtsilä 8L46C diesels giving 16,800 kW with a speed of 22 knots and are fitted with stabilizers. They can carry 600 passengers, have 196 berths and have 1,270 lane meters for car capacity. The *Côte d'Albâtre* was completed in 2005 and the *Seven Sisters* in 2006. Both ships were subsequently entrusted to the French LD Lines, but they later moved the *Côte d'Albâtre* across to the Portsmouth to Le Havre crossing.

Current Operators, Ships and Details

Transmanche Ferries currently operate thirteen 4-hour crossings per week on the route to a varying seasonal timetable, which should be consulted in advance.

Newhaven has excellent road and rail links to London via the A26 and being the closest port to the capital is still favoured by many over the more well-known Dover terminal. However foot passengers need to check in at the car terminal at the Town Station. There is the Haven café in the port terminal building and a freight drivers lounge open 2 hours before departures, shower facilities, disabled access and toilets, and assistance with boarding.

11: Newhaven – Dieppe

Côte d'Albâtre worked the Newhaven to Dieppe route alongside her Transmanche sister ship *Seven Sisters*. (© LD Lines)

Dieppe is 121 km from Paris via the N27, but there is very limited free parking along the seafront and a small car park with a 96-hour time limit opposite the terminal itself. Dieppe also suffers from the reduced service but has a wider range of amenities on offer.

The facilities aboard the French-crewed *Seven Sisters* (IMO 9320130) include a choice from fifty cabins, with both 4-berth interior and exterior, and one reduced-mobility cabin plus small Commodore cabins on Deck 6. Also on Deck 6 is: the Agatha Christie Saloon; The Lane's cafeteria with a self-service section; the Brighton Pier truck-drivers' lounge; The Devil's Dyke Salon; a gift shop with books, cameras, perfumes etc; a TV lounge showing both British and French channels; a video gaming arcade; a children's play area and an information counter. Deck 7 has the Beachy Head bar offering all alcoholic beverages, soft drinks and coffee, and the Rudyard Kipling, Hilaire Belloc, Sir Arthur Conan Doyle and Angus Wilson seating saloons. Toilets and disabled toilets are on both Decks 6 and 7, while the Royal Pavilion salon and open promenade deck are on Deck 8.

Contact Details

Newhaven Office
Newhaven Ferry Port, Railway Approach, Newhaven, East Sussex, BN9 0DF
Tel: 01273 612864; 0800 917 1201
Fax: 01273 612875
Email: transmancheferries.com
Web: www.transmancheferries.co.uk

Dieppe
7 Quai Gaston Lalitte, 76200 Dieppe, France
Tel: 33 232 145200
Fax: 33 232 145206
Web: www.transmancheferries.com

12: Dover – Boulogne – Calais – Dunkirk

Background

The 21 miles of salt water between Dover and Calais make it the shortest route between England and the Continent and a natural faucet for trade down the ages, such that the much-used epithet 'Gateway to Europe' is not misplaced. Today millions of passengers and tens of thousands of cars, lorries, coaches and other transport pass through these ports and across the English Channel each year. With such a long-established position of eminence, these ports have a long and detailed history, and we can but touch upon some highlights here.

From the beginnings a regular route between the UK and Calais was plied by sailing vessels, most of them small, shallow-draught cutters and their like, with capacity of about 30 or 40 passengers. Of course with little or no facilities at either end of the route, such services were dependent on the tides for embarkation and landings, and if high tide was missed, you could be transhipped (at considerable cost) or even piggy-backed, ashore with no small discomfort. For long periods the constant interruption of wars between the two growing empires interfered and halted this sail packet trade, culminating in the French revolution and the long period of conflict with Great Britain that followed, which lasted until 1815. In the aftermath of the Napoleonic wars restoration of normal ferry service between the two nations was again commenced, with up to twenty such craft plying their trade, including even the likes of the notorious Tom Souville, the Calais-born and Dover-educated corsair who now turned legitimate businessman and began carrying mails between Calais and Dover. Initially serious consideration was given for regulation whereby the ships of each nation would carry only their own citizens, but this agreement did not last long in the face of commercialism, and the usual free-for-all soon prevailed once more. Then, as now, the majority of the travellers were British.

With the coming of steam the crossing times were reduced and more reliable schedules could be adhered to. The British *Rob Roy*, a wooden-hulled steam paddle ship built on the Clyde, of 24.70 m overall length with a beam of 4.75 m, could make the daily crossing in 2 hours 45 minutes in good conditions. She made her first such passage from Dover to Calais on 15 June 1821, heralding the dawn of a new era. The French postal authorities acquired *Rob Roy* for their own use and re-named her *Henri IV* and she remained active until 1830. The Royal Mail scorned such innovations and continued using the three sail packets, such as the *Lord Duncan* and *Prince Leopold*, on the Calais route, but she easily outpaced them and quickly forced a re-think. The result was the arrival of two British steam packets at Dover, the *Dasher* in October 1821 and the *Arrow* the following January. Private operators followed the same trend, gradually eclipsing the sailing ships. The 149-GT wood-hulled paddle steamer *Arrow* became the Admiralty *Ariel* in February 1837, and among her noted passengers under Lieutenant and Commander Robert Mudge, RN, was HRH Prince Albert in 1840 *en route* to his marriage to Queen Victoria. By 1837, the Royal Mail service was carried by no less than six postal steam vessels.

As the railways spread their tentacles across England, more and more potential travellers arrived at Dover for passage to the Continent and the rail companies themselves were not long in taking advantage of the situation they had brought about. At Dover a new hotel was opened in

12: Dover – Boulogne – Calais – Dunkirk

P&O's new Superferry *Spirit of Britain* sails past the White Cliffs of Dover in 2011. (© P&O)

1840 to cope with this new breed of continental traveller, with embarkation from adjacent stone steps or alternatively from the Admiralty Pier which was in place by the following decade. The first iron-built ship, the *Dover*, also appeared there in 1840. Built by Cammell Laird at Birkenhead she was taken over by the Admiralty, although they made little use of her. At Dover difficulties with landing persisted and regular timetables could still not be adhered to, in stark contrast to the railways that fed the ferries. All of which led to the South Eastern Railway developing the Folkestone to Boulogne route as an alternative crossing point between London and Paris.

One ingenious vessel, years ahead of her time, was the *Express*, a catamaran steamer built in 1878 and purchased by the London, Chatham, Dover Railway. She had an overall length of 111 m and a 30 m beam. She made a 90-minute crossing and served for a decade before being withdrawn as uncompetitive. By 1882 the twin-funnelled paddle steamer *Invicta* appeared on the route, a great step forward. She was steel-built and had electrical fittings throughout. She was built by Thames Iron Works and was the last to be built in the capital. She was of 1,197-GT and was fitted with a fore-and-aft stem and had a rudder at both ends. The 600 bhp Maudsley, Son & Field engines gave her a maximum speed of 22 knots and she once made a record passage of 65 minutes, but her operating speed was normally a more modest 18.5 knots. After a few years service she was chartered to the Northern Railway of France in 1896, but was withdrawn and broken up three years later. Similar ships that came after her included the 1,065-GT *Calais-Douvres*, built in 1889 by Fairfield at Govan, and the *Calais* and the *Dover* of 1896.

Similarly, the first propeller and turbine driven ferry, the *Queen*, arrived in June 1903 and marked the demise of the paddle steamer, being followed by a new *Invicta* in 1905, *Empress* and *Victoria* in 1907 and 1,674-GT *Riviera* in 1911. The latter was a two-funnelled, two-masted, triple screw ship built by William Denny & Bros at Dumbarton for the South Eastern and Chatham Railway. She had an overall length of 98.5 m, a beam of 12.45 m, a 5.03 m draught and was unique in that as well as 105 first-class and 45 second-class passengers, she was designed to carry cars. She made her maiden voyage on the Dover to Calais crossing on 8 June 1911. After seeing war service as a seaplane carrier, she was re-converted and continued in service from 1920 to 1925 when she was sold to Burns & Laird and became *Laird's Isle*.

The Admiralty constructed the huge outer harbour and basins that we know today between 1895 and 1909 as accommodation for the Channel Fleet, but, by the time it was ready, it was deemed largely unnecessary, for the enemy was now Germany across the North Sea while the *entente cordiale* of 1904 had made France, across the Channel, a friend if not an ally. The harbour therefore inadvertently became an unexpected bonus to the ferry operators who could use large parts of it, even though it had been constructed at Government expense!

In 1928 a former Army officer, Captain Stuart Townsend, who had founded Townsend Brothers in 1916, chartered an old collier, the *Artificer*, which could be loaded with 15 cars and 12 passengers, to make the Dover to Calais crossing in 2 hours 30 minutes, while their drivers and passengers proceeded by mail boat and rejoined their vehicles on the other side. As an extension of this service, which undercut Southern Railways' own route by a margin, he then bought and converted a surplus Royal Navy Hunt class minesweeper, the 710-ton HMS *Ford*, to cater for the new market of people who wanted to take their car with them to the continent. She had been built in 1918 by Dunlop Bremner, at Port Glasgow, and was 70 m overall length, with a beam of 8.5 m and a 2.4 m draught, and was coal fired and good for 16 knots. He renamed her *Forde* and had her converted to carry 165 passengers within three saloons, one for ladies only, and three private state rooms. She could carry up to 26 cars and was converted with a folding stern door for

12: Dover – Boulogne – Calais – Dunkirk

Another view of *Spirit of Britain*. (© P&O)

loading and unloading, but this proved impracticable. The cars were therefore loaded aboard her by crane. She served right through to October 1949 on the Dover to Calais route, with intervening war service and a post-war refit. In her first year of operations she carried 6,000 cars annually, and this figure had reached 31,000 in 1939 before the Second World War intervened.

The Southern Railway responded with the purpose-built 985-GT *Autocarrier*, which made her maiden voyage from the Admiralty Pier on 30 March 1931. She was built by D. & W. Henderson on the Clyde and had an overall length of 67.13 m, a beam of 10.2 m and a draught of 4.29 m. She was powered by two sets of 4-cylinder triple-expansion engines from her builders which gave her a trials speed of 16 knots. Originally designed as a cargo vessel, she was changed while under construction and had the capacity for 307 passengers and 26 cars, operating on the Dover to Calais route throughout the summer and switching to the Folkestone to Boulogne crossing during the winter months. During the war she served at Dunkirk, surviving to resume service from Dover in 1946 and not finally being withdrawn until 1954.

In May 1929 the British Southern Railway and the French Societe Nationale de Chemins de Fer Francais (SNCF) together started a new Pullman Car service, the Train Ferry. The trains from London and Paris left simultaneously at 11.00, ran straight to the docks at Dover and Calais, where specially built ferries with a cargo deck with rail lines built onto them, received them in adjustable docks. Thus the Night Ferry was born, with the same coaches being used for the entire passage. There was also the glamorous *Golden Arrow* service which used different trains at each side of the Channel, in conjunction with the French *Flèche d'Or*, which had already been running the Compagnie Internationale des *Wagon Lits* service for three years, with the passengers transferring from the new *Invicta* and the second *Canterbury*. The latter was specially built for the Golden Arrow luxury service and carried only first-class passengers initially. She was a 2,910-GT steel twin screw steamer, built and engined by Denny of Dumbarton for S.R. in 1929. She had a length of 100.43 m, a beam of 14.35 m and a 5.1 m draught. She also served during the war, being at both Dunkirk in 1940 and Normandy in 1944. Post-war she served as the Golden Arrow ship until September 1964.

Meanwhile the French contribution to the route was the *Côte d'Azur* in 1931 and the *Côte d'Argent* in 1933. Of 111 m overall length, they were

The brand-new P&O Superferry *Spirit of France* in the building dock at Rauma, Finland, February 2011. (© P&O)

powered by 1,400 bhp engines that reduced the regular crossing time to 75 minutes. They could carry 1,450 passengers. Both these ships were lost during the war, in 1940 and 1944 respectively.

Post-1945, the unstoppable rise in car ownership continued and led to the inevitable innovation of the drive-on car terminal, and this was initiated on the Dover to Calais route in 1953, using movable loading bridges which made the tides irrelevant to the loading/unloading routine. The Townsend company thrived, and repeated their earlier experience by purchasing another former Royal Navy vessel, the River class frigate *Halladale* in April 1949 for £15,000. She had been built in 1943 by A. & J. Inglis, Pointhouse, Glasgow, and was 91.0 m overall length, 11.19 m beam and a 3.30 m draught, with a speed of 20 knots. After conversion by Cork Dockyard she could carry 388 passengers and 40 cars. A special car ramp was built for her at Calais which lowered onto her after deck enabling drive-on/drive-off operations. She served until November 1961 before being sold and becoming the Finnish *Norden*.

The SNCF's 3,467-GT *Compiegne* which was built by Chantiers Reunis Loire-Normandie at Rouen in 1958 was another landmark ship. With an overall length of 115.03 m and a beam of 8.35 m, she could carry 1,000 passengers and 164 cars at 20 knots and featured such innovations as being of all-welded construction, and had variable-pitch propellers and bow thrusters controlled from the rear bridge to help her align with the link-span. She made her maiden crossing on 22 July and serviced most of the Channel ports down the years, making her final Dover to Calais run in February 1981 before being laid up and sold to become the *Ionian Glory*.

In 1962 the first purpose-built ship for the Townsend company was the 2,607-GT, twin-funnelled, *Free Enterprise*, built by N.V. Werf 'Gusto' at Schiedam, Rotterdam. She was of 96.5 m length overall with a beam of 15.8 m and a 4.3 m draught. Powered by two 12-cylinder MAN diesels she had a speed of 17 knots and could carry 850 passengers, with 120 cars and 6 lorries on two decks. She commenced work on the route on 22 April and featured open-plan and 'luxurious' conditions whose lounges, saloons, bars, restaurant, snack bar, shop, *bureau de change* and ladies' rest room all spoke of a totally different concept to the former railway boats. She proved to be such a hit with the public that similar ships followed: the 4,011-GT *Free Enterprise II* in 1965 and the 4,657-GT *Free Enterprise III* in 1966.

By 1968 the Townsend Brother Ferries company and the Thoresen Car Ferry Company had amalgamated as Townsend Thoresen and serviced the Dover to Calais route for almost two more decades until acquired by P&O in the 1980s.

Perhaps the most famous vessel of the Townsend Thoresen fleet, for all the wrong reasons, was the *The Herald of Free Enterprise*, one of three Ro-Ro Spirit class sisters built especially for the Dover – Calais crossing by Schichau Unterweser AG, at Bremerhaven in 1980–81, the others being the *Pride of Free Enterprise* and the *Spirit of Free Enterprise*. They were 131.91 m overall length, 23.19 m beam and had a draught of 5.72 m. Powered by three Sulzer 12ZV 40/48 engines they had a speed of 22 knots and a passenger capacity of 1,400 with vehicle decks for 350 cars over three decks and were fitted with watertight bow and stern doors. On 6 March 1987, while off her normal route, she capsized off Zeebrugge with the loss of 193 passengers and crew, a subsequent Court of Enquiry citing negligence and bad working practices as well as design flaws for her loss. By October the now disgraced Townsend Thoresen name had been obliterated and the company became P&O European Ferries and her sisters were renamed.

On 25 July 1959 the first hover vehicle, the Saunders Roe *SRN1*, an invention of Sir Christopher Cockerell, traversed the waters of the English Channel exactly fifty years since the French aviator Blériot first flew across, and powered up the beach inside Dover Harbour offering what was thought a simpler and swifter (if ear-shattering) method of travel. These revolutionary vehicles rapidly increased in size and power so that they soon were carrying many hundreds of passengers and also cars and other light vehicles. Concrete pads were constructed at Dover and Calais and competing companies, the private Hoverspeed and the rail-based British Rail and SNCF, all began running regular services, the first such being the British Rail Seaspeed SRN4 *Princess Margaret* on 1 August to Boulogne, but with a Dover to Calais service the following year by her sister, *Princess Anne*. These vehicles were modified to cope with extra passengers, increasing their capacities to 424 passengers and 54 cars from 1978 onward, and began working from the new Dover Hoverport, making the crossing in an average time of 35 minutes. The French SNCF *Jean Bertin*, a Sedam N500 version, operated briefly but was beset with mechanical problems. The third contender was Hoverlloyd, operating since 1966, which merged with Seaspeed at Dover in October 1981 to form Hoverspeed. They operated two SRN6 vehicles, the *Swift* and the *Sure*. The hovercraft, besides the unwholesome din they made, had two, what were to ultimately prove fatal, flaws. No matter their size they were unable to cope with bad weather, for which the Channel is notorious, and secondly they used a lot of fuel, which, with successive oil crises down the decades, eventually made them uneconomical to run. By the end of 1983 they had all gone.

From 1996 until 2011 one of three major ferry companies operating on the Dover to Calais route was SeaFrance, totally owned by the SNCF French railways. They operated up to eleven daily 75-minute sailings across the English Channel in each direction, with hourly turn-around periods, and was by then the only French company operating on this route. They sailed the two Calais-registered 'Superferries' *SeaFrance Berlioz* (IMO 9305843) and *SeaFrance Rodin* (IMO 9232527) each with eleven decks. Although generally considered sister ships they were built at different times, in different shipyards in different countries, and vary in some details.

The 33,796-GT *SeaFrance Rodin* was built by Aker Finnyards, Rauma, Finland in 2001 and the 33,800-GT *SeaFrance Berlioz* was built in France by Chantiers de l'Atlantique/ALSTOM in 2005. Sea France in Calais had a total of 1,850 employees while a further 200 were employed ashore in Dover. Heavy losses began to be incurred from 2005 onward and four years later the latest of several proposed restructuring plans was implemented, with both Brittany Ferries and LD Lines expressing interest in taking over the company. However, on 16 November 2011, the Commercial Court of France ordered the winding up of the company and, despite last-ditch attempts by the French unions involved, final liquidation was announced on 9 January 2012.

On 11 June 2012 a new ferry company was established named 'MyFerryLink' with former Sea France employees and two former Sea France vessels leased from Eurotunnel, the *Berlioz* and the *Rodin*. Both commenced operations between Dover and Calais on 20 August 2012.

Dover – Calais

P&O Ferries currently operates a fleet of five multi-purpose passenger ferries and two freight-only vessels.

The *Pride of Dover* and *Pride of Calais* were originally ordered by Townsend Thoresen as purpose-built vessels for the Dover to Calais route. Following the purchase of Townsend Thoresen during construction, they were delivered to P&O European Ferries in 1987 and began operating soon after. They were built by Schichau Unterweser in Bremen-Vegesack, Germany.

Following the closure of the Dover to Zeebrugge route in 2002, *European Pathway* and *European Highway* returned to their builders and were converted to full passenger mode, eventually re-entering service as the *Pride of Canterbury* and the *Pride of Kent*. The fourth vessel, *European*

The P&O ferry *Pride of Calais* leaves her home port. (© P&O)

The P&O ferry *Pride of Canterbury* leaving Dover. (© P&O)

Seaway, was transferred to the Dover – Calais route in early 2005 where she still operates as a freight-only replacement to *Pride of Provence*. P&O also introduced the Spirit class ferries in the 1980s as representing a great leap forward in design for the route, with features like 'free-flow' passenger accommodation and twin-level vehicle decks, these vessels being the *Pride of Dover*, *Pride of Calais* and *Pride of Burgundy*. Two other ships, *Pride of Aquitaine* and the *Pride of Provence*, were withdrawn from service in a review of P&O Ferries operations announced in September 2004.

On 17 December 2007 the Dover fleet was joined by the MS *European Endeavour*, the ex-Norfolk Line *Midnight Merchant*, to run along with the *European Seaway* on the freight side of the business. It was announced on 8 August 2008 that P&O Ferries had placed a €360 million order with STX Europe for two 49,000-GT new ships to replace the *Pride of Dover* and *Pride of Calais*. They were to be the first ships in the world to comply with the new SOLAS 'Safe Return to Port' requirements.

P&O's *Spirit of Britain* made her maiden voyage in service on 21 January 2011. Originally to have been named *Olympic Spirit* and *Olympic Pride* to commemorate the 2012 London Olympic Games, their names were changed to prevent any infringement of copyright. The duo, of the Spirit 2 class, cost a staggering £300 million pounds and

Offshore Ferry Services

The new P&O Superferry, *Spirit of Britain* on arrival at Dover in 2011. (© P&O)

replace the *Pride of Dover*, *Pride of Calais* and *Pride of Burgundy* but it is hoped that by doubling capacity per crossing for the same fuel outlay, profitability will be achieved.

Current Operators, Ships and Details

Four ferry companies operate from Dover to Calais and Dunkirk, these being DFDS Seaways (Dover to Dunkirk), P&O Ferries (Dover to Calais), LD Lines (Dover to Calais) and MyFerryLink (Dover to Calais).

P&O Ferries currently have two brand-new ships, making five sailings over the route every 24 hours, these being the 'Superferries' *Spirit of Britain* (IMO 9524231) and *Spirit of France* (IMO 9533816) which arrived in 2011. These huge ships were built by STX Europe at the Rauma yards in Finland and are of 49,000 tonnes with overall length of 210 m, a beam of 31.4 m and a draught of 6.5 m. Their size is the maximum that can be safely operated from the two ports. They are powered by four MAN 7L 48/60 diesel engines developing 30,400 kW and driving two controllable pitch propellers for a speed of 22 knots. They are also equipped with three bow thrusters. They have a capacity of 1,750 passengers and 1,079 cars and 180 lorries on 2,700 lane meters, spread over an unprecedented three vehicle decks.

On the Upper Deck 9 the amenities include floor-to-ceiling stained glass picture windows in the select Club Lounge, with its own private

The Spirit Club, one of the many facilities aboard the new P&O *Spirit of Britain*. (© P&O)

shelter deck; there are adjacent toilets and a disabled toilet, while opposite the Blue Stair Zone is a small smoking deck. Next door is the Brasserie restaurant with waiter service with more toilets; and then near the Yellow Stair Zone is the Routemasters' Lounge for commercial freight drivers, which has private showers, a restaurant, relaxation area and outside deck area. At the Red Stair Zone are disabled facilities and baby-changing area and finally the self-service food court with more toilets. On Lower Deck 8, there are conventional and disabled toilets, an outside deck area and the aft lounge with the Terrace Bar; with the main bar forward; towards the Yellow Stair Zone are more mixed toilets, the video arcade and Vegas Slots for teenagers; and further along the shop near the reception desk and *bureau de change*; there is also the coffee bar featuring Costa Coffee; more mixed toilets, and finally the Horizon Family Lounge and a baby-changing and children's area.

In December 2009 DFDS A/S acquired Norfolkline from A. P. Moeller-Maersk for €346 million and re-branded it as DFDS Seaways. The line has the Dover to Dunkirk route to itself and claims it offers less congestion and shorter (approx 50 km) driving times to the Netherlands, Belgium and Germany. There are a maximum of twelve 2-hour crossings per day, according to season, using the 35,923-GT Dover-registered sisters *Dunkerque Seaways* (IMO 9293076), *Dover Seaways* (IMO 9318345) and *Delft Seaways* (IMO 9293088). These vessels were built for Norfolkline by Samsung Heavy Industries at Geoje, South Korea in 2005 and 2006 respectively, as the *Maersk Dunkerque*, *Maersk Dover* and *Maersk*

The *Dunkerque Seaways* a Ro-Pax vessel built in 2005 operates on the Dunkerque to Dover route for DFDS. (© DFDS Seaways)

Another of the DFDS trio of Ro-Pax vessels built in 2005 is the *Dover Seaways* which plies the Dover to Dunkerque route. (© DFDS Seaways)

Delft. All three were renamed in 2010. Of 186.65 m overall length, they have a beam of 28.4 m and a 6.75m draught. Their engines are MAN B&W 8L48/60B Diesel, developing 38,400 kW for a speed of 25 knots. The capacities are 780 passengers, on two decks, along with a 70-strong crew, 200 cars and 120 trucks carried on 1,800 lane meters of vehicle decking and are designed for separate Ro-Ro decks for cars and lorries.

The facilities aboard include three restaurants the forward one fitted with large panoramic windows for unrivalled ahead views and the passenger decks are served by seven lifts.

For meals onboard there is the self-service restaurant on Deck 6 with both a breakfast and a lunch menu; the Café Bistro on Deck 7, the upper deck, next to the first-class lounge, with waiter service and both snack and main meal menus. The lounge bar is on Deck 6 and serves tea coffee and pastries, snacks, confectionery, soft drinks, alcohol and has widescreen TV. On this deck there is also ample seating and good covered deck spaces, showers and a squall shelter. Also available is a dedicated children's play area; a games arcade and a *bureau de change*. There is a bar and also a retail shop for clothes, souvenirs and gifts. Shopping includes beers, wines, and spirits, cosmetics and fragrances, jewellery, watches and sunglasses. For commercial freight drivers there is Road Kings, which is a dedicated lounge situated at the bows, which includes a restaurant, complimentary tea and coffee and exclusive shower facilities.

Following the disappearance of SeaFrance, DFDS announced that, in conjunction with LD, a new Dover–Calais route with two vessels would be implemented to help fill the gap. The first ferry to ply this route was our old friend, the *Norman Spirit*, now re-flagged as a French vessel, and she commenced operations on 17 February 2012. A second ferry, *Barfleur*, joined her on this route from April 2012 and many former SeaFrance employees have been taken on.

The *Barfleur* (IMO 9007130) was originally built in the Kvaerner Masa Yards at Turku in Finland and, having been lengthened by 9 m on the slipway, was finally completed in 1992 as part of the Brittany Ferries subsidiary Truckline Ferries fleet. Taken into the main fleet in 1999 and repainted, she is a combined passenger/vehicle ferry, originally built with a capacity for 1,212 passengers and 590 cars or 112 trucks, but now reduced to 450 passengers, 590 cars and 75 trucks on a tonnage of 20,133, overall length of 157.7 m, beam of 23.3 m and a 5.8 m draught. She has a crew of 185. She is powered by four Wartsilla-Vasa 8R32 diesel engines which give her a top speed of 19.5 knots. Her onboard facilities include the Turquoise self-service restaurant and Les Alizés bar, but the Arc en ciel café has been closed. For entertainment she has

12: Dover – Boulogne – Calais – Dunkirk

The DFDS vessel *Delft Seaways* built in 2005 is a Ro-Pax ship working the routes from Dover to Dunkerque. (© DFDS Seaways)

Offshore Ferry Services

The *Barfleur* at speed showing her fine, uncluttered lines and open upper deck areas. (© Brittany Ferries)

Good food, attentive service and fine wine, some of the attributes that are found aboard the Brittany Ferries *Barfleur*. (© Brittany Ferries)

the Chance Planet games area and Games Planet video games room, WiFi and internet, children's playroom, baby-changing room, disabled toilets, a baggage room, lifts, a *bureau de change* and shopping outlets at la Boutique and le Kiosque. There are a total of seventy-two 4-berth cabins, and 295 recliner seats, cots and a sundeck.

The *Norman Prince*, which joined her on this route in the wake of the SeaFrance closures, now makes five daily crossings. *Norman Prince* was built in 1991 by Boelwerf Themse, Belgium for Regie voor Maritiem Transport (RMT) as the *Prins Filip* and later served with P&O, Stena, P&O Ferries and Transeuropa Ferries under a dizzying variety of names including *Stena Royal*, *Aquitaine*, *Pride of Aquitaine* and *Ostend Spirit*, before re-adopting her current identity in 2011. She is currently owned by Louis Dreyfus Ferries and operated by LD Lines. She is of 28,838-GT, has a 163.6 m overall length, with a beam of 27.7 m and a 6.35 m draught. Powered by four Sulzer 8ZA S40 engines she has a speed of 21 knots and is fully stabilized. Since her modification in 1999 her carrying capacity is 1,850 passengers, with 434 berths, 600 cars and 100 trucks. Her many on-board amenities include shops, restaurants, bars, comfortable seating and cabins, luxurious sleeper seating, outside decks, children's play area, internet access and games arcade.

The DFDS terminal at Dunkirk is reached by car from the A16, exiting at sortie 53 onto the N316. Calais main terminal is signposted Port Rapide/Car Ferry from the A16 and D600 or from Dunkirk via A16 sortie 24, signed to Loon Plage/Car Ferry or via the RN1. There is a 90 minutes minimum check-in time. The rail station is in Calais centre and is linked by a bus service to the port. Beside the P&O booking desk there is a *bureau de change* (not Sundays, not 24 hour), car hire, a fast-food outlet and restaurants (neither 24 hour).

Dover Ferry Port is accessed via the M2 from London, then the A2, or the M20 and A20 and both Eastern & Western Docks ferry terminals are signed. Rail from London Victoria or Charing Cross stations to Dover Priory. All P&O and DFDS Terminals are at Eastern Docks and are open between 06.00 and 19.30, with a minimum of 60 minute check-in times recommended. Facilities at the Passenger Services Building WEST include a Travelex *bureau de change*, bank and ATMs; massage chairs; information desk, toilets and baby-changing facilities, the Café Ritazza, Burger King, and the Boardwalk shopping for snacks, drinks, confectionery, newspapers, books and sundries. There are toilets, disabled toilets, showers and baby-changing facilities. There is also a harbour viewing platform. The Passenger Services Building EAST has the same amenities and also G-Scape Games Zone and the Barnacles Bar.

In 2011 plans were put forward to privatize the port of Dover with the setting up of the Port of Dover Community Trust (PDCT) and at the time of writing this is under Government consideration.

Contact Details

Dover P&O Ferries Office
P&O Ferries, Channel House, Channel View Road, Dover, Kent, CT17 9TJ
Tel: 08716 642121
Freight: 01304 866866
Fax (freight): 01304 866888
Email: customer.services@poferries.com
Web: www.poferries.com

DFDS Office
DFDS Seaways, Dover Eastern Docks, Dover, Kent, CT16 1JA
Tel: 0871 574 7235
Freight: 01304 218416
Fax (freight): 01304 218420
Email: diver.pax@dfds.com
Web: www.dfdsseaways.com.uk
DFDS have a 45-minutes check-in time prior departure plus UK Border Control check times.

Calais P&O Office
P&O Ferries Ltd, Terminal Car Ferry, Bp 421, 6226 Calais Cedex France
Tel: 0321 177029
Tel: 0825 120 156
Fax: 00321 003200
Email: info@poferries.com
Web: www.poferries.fr

Dunkirk DFDS Office
Terminal Roulier du Port Ouest, Dunkerque, France
Tel: +33 3282895 50
Fax: +33 328 2895 44
Email: doverpax@norfolkline.com
Web: www.norfolkline.com

MyFerryLink Office
MyFerryLink UK Terminal, Ashford Road, Folkestone, Kent, CT18 8XX
Tel: 0844 2482 100
Email: clientservice@myferrylink.com
Web: www.seafrance.com/uk

13: Ramsgate – Ostend

Background

Ramsgate Royal Harbour has an ancient lineage, the first excavations commenced in 1749 and were not completed until a century later.

Ferry operators working from Ramsgate briefly included Ole Lauritzen, of Ribe, Denmark. This company inaugurated a Ramsgate to Dunkirk service on 15 May 1980 with the 4,471-GT Ro-Pax ferry *Nuits Saint George*, the former *Fred Scamaroni* which had been originally built in 1965 by Forges & Ateliers et Chantiers de Mediterranee at La Seyne, France. However, the route proved uneconomical and was quickly terminated in September when the company was declared bankrupt after *Nuits Saint George* ran aground at Ramsgate. She was later laid up Vlissingen, the Netherlands before being sold to Egypt as the *Lord Sinai*.

Sally Viking Line was established in 1981 and as Sally Line UK. Later the Holyman Sally Line operated from 1993 for five years on the Ramsgate to Ostend crossing. Initially they used the Ro-Ro *Sally Euroroute*, which they had chartered in 1993. She was built in 1985 by Santierul Naval Galatz SA, Romania, for the Balder Company in the Black Sea as the *Balder Sten*, and subsequently served with Navrom as the *Bazias 3*. She was 9,088-GT, 121.48 m overall, with a beam of 21 m and a draught of 5.3 m. She was powered by a pair of Krupp 9M453AK 9-cylinder diesels and had a speed of 15.5 knots. She could carry 12 passengers, a crew of 18 and had 1,272 lane metres for 94 trucks.

She served until 1996, before being sold and replaced by the *Eurotraveller*, the former *Sally Sky*, ex-*Viking2*, ex-*Gedser*, which had originally been built in 1976 by Schichau Unterweser AG for Gedser-Travemunde Ruten. The *Eurotraveller* only served for just over a year on the Ramsgate to Ostend route before Sally Line folded, when she was leased to Transeuropa Ferries as *Larkspur*.

The French Schiaffino Line operated the route from 1989 with the 6,041-GT *Schiaffino*, which was the former Ro-Ro *Mashala* built in 1977 by Krögerwerft GmbH, Rendsburg, Germany, and which had served variously as both the *Halla* and the *Tikal*. She could carry 12 passengers and had 350 lane meters for vehicles via a rear-loading ramp. This company was taken over by Sally Line in 1990 and she was renamed as the *Sally Eurobridge* and finally ended her days as the *Riverdance* with Seatruck.

The Belgian state-operated Holyman, Regie voor Maritiem Transport (RMT) Company, which had operated crossings on the Ostend to Dover route since 1846, established Oostende Lines in 1993 in direct competition to the opening of the Channel Tunnel, in the hope that a big ships and jetfoil combination might prove to be a viable competitor. The 28,828-GT *Prins Filip* delivered in 1992 was one end of that equation; two Boeing Jetfoils for a fast passenger traffic service was the other. By February 1997 the experiment had failed.

Prins Filip was a steel twin-screw Ro-Pax ship and is described later. She made her maiden voyage on 12 May 1992 from Ostend to Dover but at the end of 1993 a deal was done with Sally Line and on 27 January 1994 she commenced working between Ramsgate and Ostend. Despite their best efforts the Tunnel won the battle and she made her last crossing on 28 February 1997 before being laid up at Dunkirk. After many changes of name and ownership she briefly returned to the route as the *Ostend Spirit* in 2010–2011.

Offshore Ferry Services

The Slovenian Transeuropa Shipping Lines (TSL) first commenced a Ro-Ro freight service from Ramsgate to Ostend in November 1998, but when it expanded into passenger services it established a subsidiary, Transeuropa Ferries N.V., based at Ostend, as its cross-Channel arm. Among their vessels which worked for part of their time on this route were the *Laburnum* between 1993 and 2003, she being the former *Free Enterprise V*, built in 1970 for Townsend Thoresen; and the *Primrose*, between 1998 and 2010, the former *Princesse Marie Christine*, and later being sold to Italy.

Until recently a long-time veteran was the *Eurovoyager*. As recorded she was 6,019-GT freight and passenger ferry, formerly the Belgian Maritiem Transport Belgie ship *Prins Albert*, built by Belliard Hoboken, Belgium. She has a length of 118.4 m, a beam of 23.32 m and a 5.05 m draught and was powered by two Pielstick 18PC2V400 engines which provided a 21 knot top speed. She had capacity for 1,400 passengers, with eighty beds, and 250 cars on 700 lane meters. Her route was initially Ostend to Dover until 1994 when she transferred over to Ramsgate to Ostend. She was renamed in 1998 and briefly chartered by Sally Line before coming under the Transeuropa Ferries flag. She served for many years on this crossing but since 2010 has been withdrawn and now plies between Algeciras, Tangier, and Gibraltar.

Larkspur was originally built in 1976 in Germany by Schichau-Unterweser, at Bremerhaven, for the Gedser-Travemünde Ruten as the *Gedser*. After a decade she was sold to Thorsviks Rederi A/S then to Johnson Line Ab before finally joining Sally Line in 1999 after successively bearing the names *Viking 2*, *Sally Sky* and *Eurotraveller*. She is owned by Forsythia Maritime Company and operated between Ramsgate and Ostend by Transeuropa. She is of 5,314-GT, has an overall length of 123.02 m, a beam of 20.5 and a 5.81 m draught. Powered by two SWD 9TM410 engines she has a best speed of 18.5 knots. Her capacity is 800 passengers, with forty-eight beds, and she can carry 325 cars on her 870 lane metres of vehicle deck.

The 7,951-GT *Oleander* is a Ro-Ro ferry built in 1980 for Townsend Thoresen in Germany by Schichau Unterweser AG, Bremerhaven as the *Pride of Free Enterprise*, to work between Dover and Calais. After a period with P&O Ferries and Stena to 2001 as the *Pride of Bruge* and then the *P&OSL Picardy* respectively, she was bought by Transeuropa in 2001. She commenced freight-only operations between Ramsgate and Ostend in July 2002 and later began to carry passengers also. She has now left the route and works the Algeciras, Spain to Tangier crossing. There was also the *Begonia* between 2002 and 2005 before she was sold to Baltic Scandinavian Lines.

The 8,097-GT *Gardenia* (IMO 7711139) is a former Townsend Thoresen freight ferry built by Schichau Unterweser AG, Bremerhaven, Germany, in 1977 as the *European Enterprise*. She has an overall length of 117.85 m, beam of 20.27 m and a draught of 5.82 m. She has two Stork Werkspoor 9TM410 engines giving her a best speed of 18.4 knots. She later became the P&O vessel *European Endeavour* before being laid up by Abbey National Leasing and then chartered in July 2002 by Transeuropa and refurbished for the Ostend–Ramsgate crossing. She started operations in January 2003 and is still currently in service. She can carry 107 passengers and has 1,140 lane meters of vehicle loading space.

Using such older vessels to those on rival routes, the high ratio of crew-to-passenger provided a good quality of service and competitive prices that ensured the service flourished.

In February 2010 it was announced the LD Lines and Transeuropa Ferries had made a commercial agreement to launch a freight and passenger service between Ramsgate and Ostend, to start in March. The deal involved the re-naming of the LD Line ferry *Norman Spirit* as the *Ostend Spirit* and that the ship would operate two 4-hour crossings a day and supplement the existing Transeuropa fleet. The companies also

The *Oleander* in TransEuropa Ferries livery approaching Ostend.

planned to co-operate fully, and the *Ostend Spirit* was to continue to operate under the British flag and be branded in LD Line and Transeuropa Ferries colours and with LD Line tourist fares for cars and passengers, cars and caravans, motor homes and motorcycles.

Built in 1991 as the *Prins Filip*, the *Ostend Spirit* (IMO 8908466) is a Ro-Pax ferry built for the Belgian company Regie voor Maritiem Transport, she was used on their Dover–Ostend route from 1992 and then worked from Ramsgate until 1997 when following an accident at Ramsgate, she was taken out of service. In 1998 Stena Line rescued her from obscurity and renamed her as *Stena Royal*, refurbished her for P&O Stena then again re-branded her as the *Aquitaine*, the *PO Aquitaine* and then the *Pride of Aquitaine* in quick succession. Another accident followed, this time at Calais, before she was again withdrawn until 2006 when, as *Norman Spirit*, she re-commenced operations for LD on the Portsmouth to Le Havre route before being chartered for a period in 2010. She is a 28,838-GT vessel with an overall length of 163.4 m, a beam of 27.6 m and a 6.2 m draught. She is powered by four Sulzer 8ZAL40S diesel engines driving two shafts and has a best speed of 21 knots. Her capacity is 1,850 passengers and 700 cars.

However the experiment was short-lived and in March 2011 Transeuropa Ferries and LD Lines decided to end their joint operation arrangement on the Ramsgate – Ostende route. LD's tourist pricing strategy had resulted in a steep increase in passenger fares during 2010, but no significant improvement in carryings. Some industry commentators pointed to this as the reason for the poor results of the service. Transeuropa terminated their charter of LD's *Ostend Spirit*. She departed to Gdansk, Poland for repainting in LD livery once more and reverted back to her previous name of *Norman Spirit*. Currently Transeuropa Ferries resumed operating just *Larkspur* and *Gardenia* whilst their other two remaining fleet units are still away on charter.

Current Operators, Ships and Details
Ramsgate Ferry Port is the only terminal in the south of the UK with a direct ferry service to Belgium. Facilities include car parking, with dedicated passenger parking and a drinks vending machine. There are up to four crossings per day with current sailings at 07.00, 12.00, 13.30, 18.30 and 22.30.

Currently Transeuropa operate two of their four ferries on the Ramsgate to Ostend crossing, providing the only direct ferry link between the two ports. They note that they only carry passengers travelling in vehicles. The travel time is around 3.5 hours. At the time of writing there are temporary changes which mean that wheelchair users cannot be accommodated. Checks should be made well in advance while this situation remains, as there are twenty-five stairs to the customer facilities.

The *Gardenia* currently has no separate area for freight drivers and passengers and lacks a children's play area. On board there is English, Belgian and Italian cuisine available from the *à la carte* restaurant, or light snacks in the family area. Cabins can be booked if required.

The *Larkspur* (IMO 7500451) has similar amenities, including the 114-seat self-service restaurant Buffet Europa, and the Ostend Spirit self-service outlet, the Crows Nest Bar with 22 seats, which serves cakes and coffee in addition to wines, spirits and beer. There are 364 seats and there are tables in the Marco Polo Lounge on Deck 6, with children's playroom, information desk and Purser's office, as well as large promenade decks when the weather is clement.

Contact Details
Ramsgate
Transeuropa Ferries UK, Ferry Terminal, Port of Ramsgate, Ramsgate, Kent, CT11 9FT
Tel: 01843 853833; 01843 595522
Freight: 0844 5760060
Fax: 01843 594663
Email: infouk@transeuropaferries.com
Web: www.transeuropaferries.com

Ostend
Transeuropa Ferries N.V., Slijksesteenweg 2, B-8400 Oostende, Belgium
Tel: 0032 059 340 260
Fax: 0032 059 340 261
Email: info@transeuropaferries.com
Web: www.transeuropaferries.com

14: Pembroke – Rosslare

Background

Ferries operated from Pembroke to Haverfordwest as early as the twelfth century and the harbour occupies the closest position to the Irish coast of any. In medieval times vessels regularly ran to and from Ireland, but it was the foundation of the Royal Navy dockyard in 1814 that saw the beginning of its present importance. Smaller ferries used the Passage even after the opening in 1827 of the Hard. The Irish packets used the custom-built facility at Hobbs Point from 1832 until around 1848 when the service was moved elsewhere. Not until 1979 did the terminal return to the Dockyard which Government enforced economies had forced the Admiralty to close in 1925.

The British & Irish Steam Packet Company (the B+I) had operated ferries between Great Britain and Ireland since 1836, but it was not until 22 May 1979 that their *Connacht* inaugurated a new B+I service from Pembroke to Cork. She had been launched the previous year and had been built by Verolme Cork Dockyards, Cork, for Morrison Ship Trading. She was of 9,796-GT, 122 m overall length, 18.83 m in the beam and had a draught of 4.83 m. Four MAK 4T 8-cylinder engines gave her a speed of 20 knots and she could accommodate 306 passengers, with 306 berths, and could carry 332 cars.

Unfortunately B+I's courage was not backed by performance, and lack of customers saw this first experiment terminate prematurely as passengers preferred the easier land access and extra facilities offered at Swansea. By 1989 she had been sold on. Other vessels were chartered for the route, including the *Viking III*, and *Stena Nordica*.

In 1981 as losses escalated, the service was 'rationalized' and the *Leinster* was moved to cover both the Rosslare and Cork services to Pembroke and re-named to become the fourth *Innisfallen*. She was another Verolme-built ship, of 4,849-GT, with a length of 118 m and a beam of 18 m and built in 1969. But by 1986 the company had decided to switch the failing Rosslare to Pembroke route to Fishguard. They reinforced the *Innisfallen* with the *St. Brendan* (ex-*Stena Normandica*) and marketed them in Ireland under the banner Southern Seaways. Meanwhile, in another switch to try and stave off the inevitable, the company's long-established Dublin to Liverpool service was shut down, enabling the *Connaught* to try again on the Pembroke to Rosslare route, commencing sailings on 12 January. It was to no avail and she was sold to Brittany Ferries at the end of the summer to became their *Duchess Anne*. Further chartered ships were tried on the Rosslare route, including *St. Patrick II*, *The Viking*, *Earl Harold*, *Norrona* and *Munster*, the former *Cruise Muhibah*.

In 1990 the company was privatized, with Irish Continental taking control on 1 January 1992. Having been taken over by Irish Ferries, B+I had already taken the *Stena Nautica* under charter from her then current owners, Stena, and re-named her as *Isle of Innisfree*. She was of 20,000-GT and had the capacity for 1,840 passengers and 410 cars. She commenced working the Rosslare to Pembroke Dock passage and also the Dún Laoghaire to Holyhead route but she only operated until 1995 when she was re-chartered to Lion Ferry, becoming the *Lion King*.

In 1973 the companies Irish Shipping, Fearnley & Eger and the Swedish Lion Ferry A/B came together and founded the Irish Continental Line (ICL), working from Rosslare to Le Havre. Lion dropped out in 1977 and when Irish Shipping was liquidated in 1984, ICL became privatized. In 1992 they absorbed the British and Irish Steampacket Company Limited (B+I) to become Irish Ferries, and instigated a period of investment in both ships and shore facilities.

A second *Isle of Innisreef* was custom-built in 1995 for Irish Ferries for the Holyhead to Dublin crossing but in 1997 she was replaced by the *Isle of Inishmore* and transferred to the Rosslare to Pembroke Dock route. In 2001 she was taken out of service and the next year charted to P&O to become their *Pride of Cherbourg*.

The Rosslare to Pembroke route is currently worked by the large, modern Ro-Ro *Isle of Inishmore*. In March 2011 a meeting between the Secretary of State for Wales and the Milford Haven Port Authority confirmed a new ten-year agreement with Irish Ferries to safeguard the route which currently carries 300,000 passengers and 80,000 freight units annually.

Current Operators, Ships and Details

Irish Ferries is the sole operator with the *Isle of Inishmore* (IMO 9142605) which sails from Rosslare at 02.45 and 14.45 each day and returns at 06.45 and 18.45. She takes 3 hours 45 minutes to make the crossing.

Built in February 1997 in Holland by Van der Giessen-de Noord, Rotterdam, at a cost of IR£60 million, the Cyprus-registered vessel is of 34,031-GT, and has an overall length of 182.5 m, a beam of 237.8 m and a 5.8 m draught. She has four Sulzer 8ZA40S diesel engines which gives her a speed of 21.5 knots. She can carry 2,200 passengers and 856 cars and 122 trucks on 2,060 lane meters of vehicle decks, and has a crew of approximately 90. She commenced operations in March 1997 on the Dublin to Holyhead crossing before switching to Rosslare in March 2001 when she relieved the *Isle of Innisfree* for charter work.

Her many onboard facilities include 186 berths in overnight *en-suite* cabins from 5-star to 2-star class. On Deck 7 there is the reception desk and *bureau de change*, the Café Lafayette for light refreshments, a relaxing lounge known as the Kilronan Motorist's Club and a gaming area with the latest machines. Deck 8 hosts Boylan's Brasserie and the Freight Drivers' Club which has a restaurant and lounge especially reserved for truckers. Deck 8 has a good shopping area, The Travel Galleria; meals from Druid's Delights; the Cyber Zone and the children's play area, while on Deck 11 there is the Dún Aengus Club-class lounge. WiFi is available and there is internet access at the Surf Box on Deck 7. There is also outer deck seating on both Decks 11 and 9, with a dedicated smoking area.

Pembroke Dock in south-west Wales is close to the A40 for the M4 direct link to London and is part of the Milford Haven Port Authority, the third largest in the UK. Amenities are comprehensive and include the passenger terminal lounge with TV, toilets, disabled access and toilets, and help on request for boarding, as well as refreshment vending machines, but very limited car parking.

Passengers are required to check in 30 minutes prior departure, more if tickets are to be collected.

Rosslare is in the south-east of the Republic of Ireland within easy reach of Cork. It has several Linkspans, including at Berth 1, a two-tier section built in 1998 which serves the *Isle of Innisfree* and other vessels. Facilities are comprehensive and include a restaurant and waiting area, the Waterfront Bar and a check-in area, while at the Europort there is a car park, car rental offices, payphones, toilets including disabled toilets, shops, a *bureau de change*, a children's play area and baby-changing facilities.

Contact Details

Port Office, Pembroke Dock. Pembrokeshire, SA72 6TW
Tel: 08705 329543

Irish Ferries, The Ferryport, Pembroke Dock, Pembrokeshire, SA72 6TW
Tel: 0870 329543
Fax: 01646 621125
Email: info@irishferries.com
Web: www.irishferries.com

Irish Ferries, Rosslare Harbour, Co. Wexford, Eire
Tel: 053 913 3158
Fax: 053 913 3544
Email: info@irishferries.com
Web: www.irishferries.com

15: Harwich – Esbjerg – Hook

Background

The early history of this route concerns ferries of the two linked nations. We will briefly examine each in turn.

In The Netherlands the ferry company Stoomvaart Maatschappij 'Zeeland' (SMZ) was originally founded in 1875 and, commenced operations with two ships, the 1,816-GT sisters *Stad Middelburg* and *Stad Vlissingen*, built by Jones, Quigguin of Liverpool as the *Midland* and *Great Northern* respectively, and after serving as blockade-runners during the American Civil War, were bought in London by SMZ for £18,000 apiece and rebuilt in Amsterdam. They were joined by the 1,604-GT *Sneafell* purchased for £15,000 from the Isle of Man Steam Packet Company and renamed *Stad Breda*.

Down the decades the SMZ ships plied from Vlissingen (Flushing) to the English ports of Sheerness, Queenborough and Port Victoria (all on the River Medway), and Dover, London, Tilbury and Folkestone. In 1886/87 the existing fleet was enhanced by a trio of new ships built by the Fairfield Shipbuilding & Engineering Company, at Glasgow, these being the 1,648-GT *Engeland*, the 1,653-GT *Duitschland* and the 1,660-GT *Nederland*. They carried their 240 passengers between Vlissingen and Queenborough

It was not until 1926 that the company settled on Harwich as its main British terminal for day sailing traffic, a move brought on by decreasing traffic and the devaluation of the Belgian currency at the time, when a deal was struck with the British Government. Even then a full and final transfer had to wait until the aftermath of the Second World War, before Harwich became fully utilized by SMZ. Likewise Vlissingen remained the main Dutch terminal until the same era when operations were re-centred on the Hook of Holland (Hoek van Holland).

With the partial move to Harwich, SMZ began working from the same base as its British competitor, the London & North Eastern Railway, with its direct route from the capital's Liverpool Street Station, although their ships worked to the Hook of Holland. Already in direct

The Commodore Lounge aboard the *Dana Sirena*. (© DFDS Seaways)

15: Harwich – Esbjerg – Hook

The *Dana Sirena* is part of the DFDS fleet and operates between Harwich and Esbjerg.
(© DFDS Seaways)

competition for decades, the arrival of turbine-driven ships in LNER's fleet in 1903 with better speeds and increased crossings had led to increased rivalry as SMZ's paddle steamers were increasingly unable to compete. The Dutch company responded in 1908/1909 with a trio of its own such ships, the Fairfield-built 3,051-GT *Prinses Juliana*, the 3,053-GT *Oranje Nassau* and 3,052-GT *Mecklenberg*. All were of 110.64 m overall length with a beam of 13.5 m and a 7.24 m draught, with two 3-cylinder Fairfield steam engines for 22 knots and could carry 24 first-class passengers and 110 second-class passengers, but only *Oranje Nassau* briefly served on the Vlissingen to Harwich crossing in 1927. The other two became casualties in the First World War and were replaced by two new Dutch-built namesakes in 1920 and 1922.

In 1939, on the eve of the second conflict, two 4,353-GT diesel-driven Ro-Ro ships arrived, these being the *Koningin Emma* and the *Prinses Beatrix*, which were built by Kininklijke Mij, De Schelde, at Vlissingen. They were 115.82 m overall length, had a 14.38 m beam and a 4.40 m draught and were powered by two TEW 10-cylinder Schelde-Sulzer diesels for a speed of 23 knots. They had a capacity of 1,800 passengers and 35 cars. Both of these new ferries briefly served between Vlissingen and Harwich, and both escaped the German invasion but were requisitioned by the Royal Navy who modified them as Landing Ships. The first *Prinses Juliana* was not so fortunate and was sunk by German Stuka dive-bombers off Ijmuiden in 1940.

Post-war, because Vlissingen had suffered enormous damage, SMZ transferred to the Hook as already related, and re-commenced operations in 1948 with the two renovated sisters, both of which survived for another twenty years.

During the immediate post-war period SMZ worked increasingly closely with the nationalized British Railways, and later, Sealink. A new 6.228-GT Ro-Ro ferry was built at N.V. Scheepswerf & Machinefabriek De Merwede at Hardinxveld in 1960, she being the second *Koningin*

Wilhelmina. She had two TEW 12-cylinder MAN diesel engines, a speed of 21 knots and could carry 1,600 passengers and 60 cars. She served for eighteen years before being sold in 1979.

The 6,682-GT Ro-Ro *Koningin Juliana*, which arrived in 1968, was built by Cammell Laird at Birkenhead. Of 131.02 m overall length, with a 20.48 m beam and a 5.00 m draught, she was powered by four TEW 9-cylinder MAN diesel engines which gave a speed of 20 knots. Her car capacity was much increased, to 220, and she could carry 1,200 passengers. Delayed by a fire during construction, she commenced working the Hook to Harwich crossing later the same year and continued in service until 1985 when she was sold and became the Italian-owned *Moby Prince*. She was followed in 1978 by the second *Prinses Beatrix*, a 9,353-GT Ro-Ro constructed in the yard of Scheepswerf Verolme at Heusden. Of 132.16 m overall, a beam of 22.56 m and a 5.17 m draught, she was powered by four TEW 8-cylinder Stork-Werkspoor engines and had a 21-knot top speed. Her capacity was 1,500 passengers and 320 cars. She served until 1985 before being sold to Brittany Ferries and becoming their *Duc de Normandie*.

In the same year Sealink and SMZ finally merged. The arrangement was for each company to contribute two new ships to the route and this profile was maintained for several years. However, in 1984 Sealink was 'privatized' by the UK Government and sold off to Sea Containers. 'Rationalization' duly followed in its train and the four ships were reduced to just two new vessels, one from each company, namely the British *St. Nicholas*, the first so-termed 'Superferry' in 1983, and the Dutch *Koningin Beatrix*, with a 2,100 passenger capacity, in 1987. This vessel was built by Van der Giessen-de Noord, Krimpen aan den Ijssel and was of 31,189-GT, with an overall length of 161.78 m, a 27.6 m beam and a draught of 6.2 m. Her engines were four 8-cylinder MAN diesels for 21 knots and her passenger capacity up to 2,100, with space for 500 cars. She served on the Hook to Harwich crossing from 1986 to 1998 before being switched to other routes.

The Dutch Government bowed to the inevitable in 1988, selling its share in SMZ and this enabled Stena Line to take over a year later. In 1989 they also purchased Sealink from Sea Containers and the whole Harwich to the Hook route was consolidated under the flag of Stena Line Holland BV.

The British side of the joint venture has its origins in the expansion of the railway, when it first reached Harwich in 1854 with the tracks running through the town to the waterfront. This was to prove the saviour of the port because the mail packets had moved to Dover in 1836. In 1862 the GER obtained permission to run steamships and began chartering in 1863 for a route to be run from their newly built Continental Pier, with sailings to Rotterdam and Antwerp. It was in 1883 that the Great Eastern Railway (GER) decided to establish its main English ferry terminal at Harwich Parkeston Quay, on reclaimed land of the former Ray Island on the south bank of the River Stour, which they named in honour of their then chairman Charles H. Parkes. They also re-routed the railway line to pass through the new port. However, it was not until 1893 that the first direct service between Parkeston and the Hook commenced and the British end of the route became first established.

The 1,196-GT twin-screw steamer *Cambridge* was the first vessel on the crossing, making her maiden voyage on 12 February 1887, and her ports of call were Harwich, Rotterdam, Amsterdam and the Hook; she served until 1912 before being sold to the Anglo-Ottoman Steamship Company. She had already been superseded by the specially-built 1,635-GT twin-screw ship *Chelmsford*, which in May 1893 began a night service, thus establishing a route from London to Berlin via Amsterdam with a 24-hour journey time, no mean feat. She was eventually sold to the Great Western Railway in June 1910 and became their *Bretonne*.

Traffic rapidly grew and the line flourished, with a succession of vessels including the trio of twin-screw steamers built especially for the route by Earle Shipbuilding & Engineering, at Hull in 1894: the 1,745-GT *Berlin, Amsterdam* and the 1,753-GT *Vienna*. The *Berlin* was wrecked in February 1907 at the entrance to the Nieuwe Waterweg, with the loss of 128 lives as well as important government dispatches; the others survived until 1928 and 1930. In 1897 a replacement was built by Earle, the 1,830-GT *Dresden*. She achieved notoriety in 1913 when the inventor Rudolf Diesel disappeared from his cabin and his body was later found drowned, leading to an early conspiracy theory. The 1,380-GT *Brussels* joined the fleet in 1902 and three more ships, the 2,570-GT *Copenhagen*, *Munich* and *St. Petersburg* arrived on the route between 1907 and 1910.

The First World War intervened and although Holland remained neutral, traffic naturally fell away until the end of hostilities. Several vessels were requisitioned for war service and others became casualties. The *Brussels* was captured in 1916; *Dresden* became *Louvain* and was torpedoed in 1918; the *Copenhagen* was also torpedoed in 1917; *Munich* became the hospital ship *St. Denis* while the *St. Petersburg* was renamed *Archangel*.

Post-war, GER was swallowed into London & North Eastern Railways, who also took over the ferries and built new ones, among them being the 4,220-GT *Prague* and the 4,218-GT *Amsterdam*, both built in 1930. The former was requisitioned at the outbreak of war in September 1939 and after arduous service was refitting in 1947 when a fire broke

The new Stena Superferries *Stena Britannica* and *Stena Hollandica*, 2011. (© Stena Line)

out aboard and she was totally gutted. *Amsterdam* was similarly pressed into service and ended her days as a hospital ship off the Normandy beachhead in 1944 when she was mined and sunk. The Second World War had brought a total halt to traffic and not until 1947 did regular services properly resume.

Among the first of the new ships built in the post-war era was the 4,891-GT passenger-ferry *Arnhem*, built by John Brown in 1946 and which commenced service on the Harwich to the Hook route in May 1947. She was of 114.94 m, overall, with a beam of 15.91 m and a 7.71 m draught, with a speed of 21 knots. She could convey 675 passengers and had 576 berths.

Nationalization in 1948 saw British Rail take control and they built another *Amsterdam*. Of 5,092-GT, she was constructed by John Brown in 1950 and commenced service from Harwich on 10 June that year, remaining on the route until 1968, when she was sold to the Chandris Line and became their *Fiorita*. In 1963 the 6,584-GT *Avalon* was added. Built by Alexander Stephens, Linthouse, Glasgow, she started sailings on the route in July of that year and continued until 1974. During the latter period of her career she was employed by Sealink on cruising. In July 1968 the 7,356-GT Ro-Ro *St. George* heralded the dramatic expansion of the car ferry under Sealink control. She was built at Swan Hunter shipyard on the Tyne and was 128.02 m overall length, 19.97 m beam and 5.03 m draught. She had two 16-cylinder Wärtsilä engines driving two screws for 19.5 knots, and could carry 1,263 passengers and 220 cars. She plied the Harwich to the Hoek van Holland crossing until 1983, when she was laid up at Falmouth, before being sold the following year to become the *Patras Express*.

In 1975 the 8,987-GT Ro-Ro ferry *St. Edmund* began service. She was official built for Passtruck Shipping Company, British Railways Board, London, by Cammell Laird, Birkenhead, especially for the Harwich to Hook run but was delivered several months late in December 1974. She was 130.08 m length, with a 22.08 m beam and 5.284 m draught and was powered by four 8-cylinder 410tm Stork-Werkspoor Diesel (SWD) engines. She had both first-class and second-class accommodation as was standard in those days, and her interior finish and design was notably superior. She continued to run the route until requisitioned by the government for the Falklands Campaign in May 1982 under charter as a troopship, but never saw active service as the war finished before she arrived on station. She was used to repatriate defeated Argentine troops from the islands and then as an accommodation ship at Port Stanley. On return to the UK she was purchased by the Ministry of Defence on 16 February 1983 and became the troopship *Keren*.

In 1984 Sealink's privatization took place and was followed by its sell-off to Sea Containers and, ultimately, to Stena, as already related.

Thus what can be termed the modern era on this route commenced in 1990 when Stena took over Stoomvaart Maatschappij Zeeland and the British operator Sealink. This brought the dividend of further modernization, and in 1992 Linkspan No. 2 was built at Harwich, which could service 200 m long ships. By 1994 the peak of annual traffic movements through Harwich port totalled almost 270,000 vehicles. The coming of the Channel Tunnel followed with further modifications in passenger patterns and such dizzy numbers were never to be seen again.

Between 2002 and 2010 the Stena Line operated two big ferries while two new and much larger ships were ordered and undergoing construction in Germany. These stop-gap vessels were the 55,050-GT *Stena Britannica* which was built in 2003 by Hyundai Heavy Industries at Ulsa, South Korea, for Stena Ro-Ro and chartered across to Sena Line as a replacement for the smaller ship of the same name, which then became the *Finnfellow*. In 2007 she underwent a total refurbishment at Lloyd Werft Yard in Bremerhaven, Germany. She had a best speed of 22 knots and was 240.1 m overall and could carry 900 passengers and 260 trucks.

The 44,372-GT *Stena Hollandica* was built for Stena Ro-Ro in the Spanish shipyard of Astilleros Españoles, at Cadiz. She was chartered to Stena Line BV and in 2007 was also stretched by 50 m at Lloyd Werft, Bremerhaven. Both ships were replaced by the new 'Superferries' that came on stream in 2010, whereupon *Stena Brittanica* was renamed as *Brittanica* and then the *Stena Scandinavica 4*, while *Stena Hollandica* became *Stena Germanica III*.

Current Operators, Ships and Details
Currently Stena Line BV operates a daily 6 hour 15 minute, day and overnight passenger service between Harwich and the Hook of Holland with two Ro-Pax 'Superferries' the *Stena Britannica* (IMO 9419175) and the *Stena Hollandica* (IMO 9499163). These enormous vessels, the largest combined freight and passenger ferries in the world, were built by Nordic Yards, at Wismar, Germany. Both were completed in 2010, the *Stena Hollandica* in May and the *Stena Britannica* in October at a combined cost of £375 million. They each are of 62,000-GT, with overall lengths of 240 m, beams of 32 m and 6.4 m draughts. Engine power for both comprise two 9,600 kW MAN 8L48/60CR and two 7,200 kW MAN 6L48/60CR, with a single 1,500 kW MAN 7L21/31 and three 1,320 kW MAN 6L21/31 auxiliary engines. These give them a speed of 22 knots. There are catalytic converters built in along with a full onboard recycling system for food waste, glass and cardboard, while cabins are fitted with solar-filmed windows and the ship is smoke-free, with the exception of a special smoking lounge on the outside deck. They each also have a pair of fin stabilizers and two bow thrusters. Their capacity is for 1,200 passengers who are offered comprehensive facilities afloat.

The interior design is by Figura and is sumptuous. There is a range of personal accommodation that includes inside and outside cabins and staterooms. Fittings included are a sofa, table, flat-screen satellite TV, wardrobe, telephone and bathroom. There are Comfort-class, Captain-class and Captain suite outside cabins. WiFi internet is available with an internet room. There is a cinema; the Stena Plus lounge; the Stena Shopping outlet, which retails fashion items, jewellery, fragrances, spirits, sweets and toys; a news room and magazine lounge; massage chairs; a *bureau de change*; and a casino. Children have either Teen Town or Kids' Playroom dedicated to their age groups with Curious George entertainment. For good food and other refreshment there are the Metropolitan *à la carte* Restaurant and the Taste Restaurant; the Riva Bar, Taste wine bar and Barista bar. There is also the sundeck for good weather crossings.

DFDS make three to four weekly crossings between Harwich and Esbjerg on the west coast of Denmark with the 22,382-GT Ro-Pax *Dana*

Stena Britannica of Stena Line unloading at Harwich. (© Harwich International Port)

Offshore Ferry Services

The DFDS Seaways vessel *Dana Sirena* at Harwich. (© Harwich International Port)

Sirena (IMO 9212163). During the summer season this increases to one crossing every other day with a passage time of 18 hours.

The *Dana Sirena* was a Ro-Pax laid down by Stocznia Szczecinska im A, Warskiego, Szczecin, Poland, as the *Golfo dei Delfini* for the Italian company Lloyd Sardegna, but late delivery saw the cancellation of the order before completion in 2003. In 2002 she had been bought by DFDS and underwent modifications to make her more suitable for her new area of operations.

She is 199.4 m overall length, with a beam of 25 m and a 6.32 m draught. Her engines are two Wärtsilä 9L46C, developing 18,900 kW, and she has a speed of 22.5 knots. Her passenger capacity is 602, with 195 cabins, and she has three car decks with a 2,510 lane metres capacity and can carry 435 cars and 166 lorries via stern door loading and unloading.

Amenities aboard include Commodore De Luxe cabins on Deck 10 and the Commodore lounge. Sirena-class cabins are on Deck 9 with a range of others on lower decks. All the cabins, except 6-berth ones, have TVs with twenty channels and internet access.

For eating there is a choice of four venues. On Deck 8 can be found the Blue Riband for à la carte, the Seven Seas buffet-style restaurant, and the Explorers Steakhouse. Also on Deck 8 is a smoking room next to reception and the Columbus Lounge with the main bar. The Café

Lighthouse for basic snacks is on Deck 7 and here can also be found a gaming area, toilets and a shop which has a good range of perfumes, clothes, cosmetics, chocolates, cigarettes and snacks. For those rare fine-weather day crossings the ship has ample open deck space.

Harwich Passenger Terminal at Parkstone Quay is reached by car via the M25 or the A12 and the A120, and is signed to Harwich International. Both short- and long-stay paying car parks are available. There are disabled parking bays at the entrance to the terminal and lifts to the travel centres. Trains from London Liverpool Street run to the terminal. Facilities also include a small café, and unisex and disabled toilets on the first floor and the departure lounge. All entrances and exits are level or ramped and wheelchairs are available with advance notice.

Esbjerg Ferry Port is reached via the E20 onto Dokvej and is fully signed. The rail station is connected by the No. 5 bus route from Dokvej with three services per hour. There is only limited seating and a toilet.

The Hook of Holland Ferry Port is reached by car via the E30/E25 motorways and is signed Engeland or Hoek van Holland. There are both short- and long-term paying car parks and disabled driver spaces. The rail lines run to alongside the terminal building. The terminal has a café bar, ATM machines and special needs facilities. There is a minimum 60 minutes check-in time prior to departure.

Contact Details

Stena Office Harwich
Stena Line Ltd, Passenger & Vehicle, Parkston Quay, Harwich, Essex, CO12 4SR
Tel: 01255 243333
Fax: 01255 252249
Email: info@stenaline.com
Web: www.stenaline.co.uk

Stena Office The Hook
Stena Line, Stationsweg 10, 3150 AA, The Netherlands
Tel: + 31 (0)174 315811
Fax: 0174 387045
Email: info@stenaline.nl
Web: www.stenaline.com

DFDS Office Harwich
DFDS Seaways Ltd, Scandinavia House, Harwich International Port, Parkeston, Harwich, Essex, CO12 4SR
Tel: 8705 333 000
Tel: 0871 5229955
Fax: 01255 244 382
Email: info@dfds.com
Web: www.dfds.co.uk

DFDS Office Esbjerg
DFDS Seaways, Dokvej 3, 6700 Esbjerg, Denmark
Tel: +45 7917 1717
Fax: +45 7917 7918
Email: info@dfds.dk
Web: www.dfds.dk

16: Holyhead – Dún Laoghaire – Dublin

Background

Its proximity to the coast of Ireland made 'Haliheved' a natural port of departure for the mails and passengers *en route* from London to Dublin as early as the late sixteenth century. The sailing packets loaded passengers from smaller boats in the lee of Salt Island, which, by 1815, was eventually dignified with the Skerries lighthouse and other improvements, including a second pier.

As in so many places it was the coming of steam and with it the railways and paddle steamers that originated many of the major ferry routes and revolutionized the old-established ones. The Steam Packet Company was in place by 1821, using the Leslie-built *Edith* (749-GT). The postal authorities were persuaded to discontinue with sail and so commissioned two steam-driven vessels, the *Lighting* and *Meteor*, for this task.

In 1847 an Act was promulgated for the construction of a new refuge harbour as the Admiralty Pier had become congested with Dublin steamers. Work on the new facility commenced the next year. This was a major development in the conveying of the mail from London to Dublin via the ports of Holyhead, Isle of Anglesey and Kingstown, Ireland, and the Chester and Holyhead Railway Company became pioneers of both new means of transport in 1848.

So confident were they of winning the lucrative Government contract that they had built no less than four 14-knot iron paddle steamers, the *Anglia* (built by Ditchburn & Mare, 473 tons), *Cambria* (built by Lairds, 590 tons), *Hibernia* (built by Bury, Curtis & Kennedy, 573 tons) and *Scotia* (built by Wigram, 479 tons). All the more of a blow then when the main contract was awarded in 1849 to their bitter rival, the City of Dublin Steam Packet Company. This left these four ships to carry passengers, livestock and general cargo from the stone-built Admiralty Pier to either Kingstown or North Wall, Dublin, a crossing which took them 5 hours. Furthermore, in 1853 the City of Dublin Company built four of their own ships, the 1,421-GT sisters *Connaught*, *Leinster*, *Munster* and *Ulster*, each capable of making the voyage 75 minutes faster.

The City of Dublin Company was soon swallowed up by the London & North Western Railway Company. The LNWR developed the inner harbour with two berths on the west shore in 1866 and later enlarged it further. The dual running of the route continued in the 1880s with a further quartet of new ships coming into service and with CDSPC introducing Laird-built screw ships to replace the paddlers in the 1890s.

The North Wall end of the operation saw harbour dues rise year-on-year, which led L&NWR to think again in 1907, when they recommenced using Kingstown with a new vessel, the 1,569-GT, Vickers, Barrow-in-Furness-built *Rathmore*. They also continued with the elderly 749-GT *Edith*, re-built by Laird in 1892 after sinking and salvaging, and the 1,105-GT *Galtee More*, built in 1898 by Denny, which were in turn replaced on the crossing by the new turbine engined ships, the 1,488-GT *Greenore* built in 1912 by Cammell Laird, and 1,587-GT *Curraghmore* built in 1919 by Denny. During the First World War many of the famous old ships were sunk in Royal Navy service, and the *Leinster* was one, being torpedoed *en route* from Kingstown to Holyhead without warning by a German U-boat just outside the harbour entrance, and going down with a casualty list of 501 from the 615 passengers and

70 crew aboard her. *Rathmore* survived to be sold in 1927 and became the *Lorrain*.

Post-war the L&NWR took over the Irish Mail and more new ships were ordered as a result, taking the old original names. They entered service from 28 November 1920 and the following year, in the order *Anglia*, *Hibernia*, *Cambria* and *Scotia*, before L&NWR was in its turn swallowed up by the London, Midland & Scottish railway. These new ferries took about 3.5 hours to make the crossing to what had become, after the partition of Ireland, Dún Laoghaire, re-named after the legendary seat of the Kings of Ireland.

After the war the *Slieve Bloom* was replaced by the 1921-built *Slieve Donard* on the freight service. After the Second World War and nationalization they continued the service. With the start of the vehicle-ownership explosion the new owners invested in a new car ferry capable of carrying 150 cars as well as 1,000 passengers to which they gave the totally uninspiring and typically bureaucratic title *The Holyhead Ferry 1*. By 1969 the old British Ferries company became Sealink.

Containerization came into vogue in the 1960s, and again the route took advantage by introducing the new *Harrogate* on the crossing, with *Darlington* and *Selby* as reserve ships. A conventionally engined

The HSC *Jonathan Swift* at speed and making short work of the Irish Sea crossing. (© Irish Ferries)

stern-loader, the 4,797-GT *Duke of Rothesay* had operated on the route in the 1965/66 period, but rather more spectacular was the introduction of the Verolme, Cork-built sisters *Brian Boroimhe* and *Rhodri Mawer* in 1970 which could handle 3,000 tons worth of containers. They served until 1989. In the 1970s a new vessel, the 3,333-GT *Lord Warden* was introduced to replace the *Holyhead 1*, which became the *Earl Leofric*. *Lord Warden* commenced work on the route on 7 April 1971. A brand-new terminal was built and modernization continued with the arrival in 1977 of the Ro-Ro *Columbia* with the capacity of 325 cars and 2,400 passengers, being joined four years later by the *St. David* with the capacity of 1,000 passengers, 309 cars and 62 trucks. The last steam turbine ferry, the *Dover* (later the *Earl Siwar* and which was the near sister of *Holyhead 1*) which had first run the route in May 1970, made her final departure in June 1981. Sealink itself was, in its turn, taken over by Stena in 1994 and among many changes, they re-named *Columbia* as *Stena Hibernia* and the 1980-built *St. Anselm* as *Stena Cambria*.

Stena's improvements included again modernizing the shore facilities at Holyhead and equally importantly they brought the new HSS catamaran service to the port, with the *Stena Sea Lynx 1*. She was an aluminium catamaran built by Incat (International Catamarans) Australia Pty. Ltd, Hobart for Buquebus International, Nassau, Bahamas as a new type of car and passenger conveyor. She had a 3,331-GT, was 74.9 m overall, with a beam of 26 m and a 2.4 m draught. Powered by four 16-cylinder Ruston 16RK 270 diesels developing 16,200 kW, she could carry 582 passengers and 88 cars at 35 knots. Delivered in June 1993 she was immediately chartered to the Stena Sealink Line and arrived at Holyhead on 1 July, commencing ferry operations to Dún Laoghaire on the 16th. She ran the crossing for almost a year before moving to Fishguard, returning Holyhead on 18 October 1995 and then, renamed as *Stena Lynx*, again worked the route until 13 April 1996. She later ran many other routes all over the world, from Dover, Stranraer, Malta, South Korea and Tahiti, under the names *Avant*, *Ocean Flower* and *Mandarin*. In 1994 the larger, 78 m, *Stena Sea Lynx II* appeared, under the ownership of Buquebus Uruguay, to operate the crossing until the delayed arrival of the even larger *Stena Explorer*.

The *Stena Lynx III* (IMO 9129328) was an Incat 81 m wave-piercing catamaran (WPC) built by Incat, Hobart, Tasmania in May 1996. She is of 4,113-GT, with a length of 80.6 m, a 26.55 m beam and a draught of 6.12 m. She is powered by four Ruston 16RK270 MkII diesel engines which provide a 40-knot top speed, and can carry 620 passengers and 145 cars. As the P&O *Elite* her first regular operations were across the English Channel in 1998, becoming the *Stena Elite* that same year and briefly working between Rosslare and Fishguard. Operating a summer season service as the *Stena Lynx III*, she was bought outright in 2004 to supplement first the *Stena Europe* and then the *Stena Explorer* and as a relief vessel. Her amenities included the Stena Plus lounge and standard lounges, shop outlets, an arcade, video game arcade and a *bureau de change*. In October 2011 she was renamed as *Sunflower 2* for Asian operations by the South Korean company Dae A Express Shipping of Pohang.

The biggest Stena ship to grace this route over the sixteen years it has been in operation, is the magnificent *Stena Adventurer*, which arrived in the summer of 2003 to replace *Stena Forwarder*, and she continues to operate on the Holyhead to Dublin passage.

Current Operators, Ships and Details
During 2011 Stena Line still, if only just, continued to run the HSS fast ferry between Dún Laoghaire and the east side of the Holyhead Port, on the far west of the Isle of Anglesey, north Wales. They used to run up to four crossings daily which took about 1 hour 40 minutes but which high fuel prices and lower speeds have seen each leg timing increased to

16: Holyhead – Dún Laoghaire – Dublin

2 hours. Passenger numbers have dramatically decreased, with the economic crisis hitting hard in Eire and British Government over-reactive cutbacks also adversely affecting the UK end of the market. The service became summer season only after September 2011, working from 30 March to 11 September 2012 only.

The *Stena Explorer* (IMO 9080194) is an HSS 1500 class catamaran built by Finnyards, Rauma, Finland, at a cost of £65 million in 1996. She is of 19,638-GT, with an overall length of 126.6 m, a beam of 40 m and a 4.8 m draught. Powered by COGAG turbines with a pair each of GE LM2500 and GE LM1600 with four KaMeWa Type S equal-size waterjets, two in

The *Stena Adventurer* operates between Holyhead and Dublin Port twice daily. (© Stena Line)

each hull, she can reach a speed of 40 knots. She can carry 1,500 passengers and has 800 lane metres for 375 cars. Embarkation is via specially-built Linkspans at St. Michael's Pier for faster turnaround times, loading from one pair of stern side doors and disembarking via the others for simultaneous operation. Her amenities include an observation area forward, the Premium Stena Plus business lounge, shops, video games arcade, the Metropolitan bar, the Barista coffee lounge and fast-serve Food City restaurant as well as seating areas, children's play area, and WiFi access, but there are no cabins. She currently operates only in the summer season leaving the smaller *Stena Lynx III* to fulfil the lower winter demand.

The 43,532-GT Ro-Pax ferry *Stena Adventurer* (IMO 9235529) was built by Hyundai Heavy Industries, in Korea for Stena RoRo and operated by Stena Line. She is 211.56 m overall length, with a beam of 29.9 m and a 6.3 m draft. She has four MAN B&W diesel engines developing 6,480 kW apiece, which drive two controllable-pitch propellers and are good for 22.5 knots. She is also fitted with two KaMeWa bow thrusters. She can carry 1,500 passengers with 364 berths in 150 cabins and has 3,400 lane meters of vehicle deck. She has drive-through, two-tier loading utilizing two main decks (3 & 5) and operates a twice daily service from Terminal 2, with an average crossing time of 3 hours 15 minutes.

In 2009 the *Stena Adventurer* (IMO 9235529) was given a £3.1 million upgrade package at Harland & Wolff shipyard, Belfast. Deck 8 was rebuilt with a 202-seat Stena Plus lounge, which includes a family area with MSN stations and dedicated toilets, plus a new business area with WiFi. There is also the Barista coffee house, a new and larger shop, the Teen Town area with MSN stations, the Met Bar & Grill, and for the youngsters the Curious George play area, while the older generation have a dedicated quiet area and reading room. Older features retained include the dedicated drivers' lounge and bars.

Irish Ferries currently operate two different daily services each way with either the Ro-Ro Ferry Cruiser Ferry *Ulysses*, which departs from Dublin at 02.40 and 14.10 and arrives at 05.55 and 17.25 respectively, or the high speed catamaran *Jonathan Swift* Fast Ferry, (promoted as the *Dublin Swift* service) which departs at 08.45 and 14.30 each day and arrives at 10.45 and 16.30 respectively with an average journey time of 3 hours 15 minutes and 3 hours 50 minutes respectively.

The 50,938-GT *Ulysses* (IMO 9214991) was built in Finland at Aker Finnyards in 2001 and is operated by Irish Ferries for the Irish Continental Group plc, specifically for the Holyhead to Dublin route. She has an overall length of 209.02 m, a 31.2 m beam and a draught of 6.4 m. She is powered by four MaK 9M43 engines which give her a speed of 22 knots. She can carry 875 passengers, with 228 berths, and can embark 1,342 cars on 4,076 lane meters of vehicle deck. Her wealth of facilities is spread over Decks 9 to 11 and comprises the following amenities. Deck 9 houses the Cyclops family entertainment video games area; the Volta picture theatre opposite, with two cinemas, Dolby surround sound and a refreshment kiosk; the Travel Galleria shopping outlet; and the Café Lafayette. Further forward is the reception desk, with a *bureau de change* and the Ocean Lift, with, opposite, Boylan's Brassiere. There is Silly Milly's Fun House with a roulette wheel and gaming machines, and Leopold Blooms Casino and bar complex. There is the Surf Box for internet access and WiFi access. Deck 10 has the James Joyce balcony lounge and a luxurious quiet area amidships. Deck 11 has, aft, the Sandy Cove promenade deck, with designated sheltered smoking areas and, forward, the Freight Drivers' Club with an exclusive lounge and restaurant. There is the Martello Club-class lounge with sea views and large TV screens and complimentary refreshments, and the Marino Casino. This deck also has WiFi access.

The 5,992-GT *Jonathan Swift* (IMO 9188881) was built in 1999 by Austral Ships, Australia, for the Irish Continental Group plc and has

16: Holyhead – Dún Laoghaire – Dublin

High-Speed Catamaran *Jonathan Swift*. (© Irish Ferries)

been operated by Irish Ferries ever since. She has an overall length of 86.6 m, a beam of 24.4 m and a 3.2 m draught. She is powered by four Caterpillar 3618 diesel engines developing 28,800 kW and has four Kamewa 112 SII Waterjets, working via a Reintjes VLJ6831 gearbox for a 40-knot speed. She can carry 800 passengers and 200 cars, for which she is fitted with nine main deck lanes and six mezzanine deck lanes as well as having bow doors to facilitate drive-on/drive-off operations and fast turn-around times. Her onboard amenities include a Club-class lounge on Deck 5, with complimentary drinks and reserved seating, and the Trinity Bar, plus an outer upper deck area and toilets; while on Deck 4 there is the Travel Galleria, a shopping outlet, main reception, a *bureau de change*, a TV lounge, the Temple Bar, the Games Zone, Surf Box and on board WiFi. There is also Boylan's Brasserie and the Café Lafayette and toilets fore and aft, plus disabled toilets. In 2012 the *Jonathan Swift* ran a two crossing per day service, departing at 11.50 (arriving at 13.39) and returning at 17.15 (arriving at 19.15).

The ferry port complex is divided between the passenger and vehicle terminals and is reached by car from the A5 or A55. There is a free short-term car park and a paid long-term car park. For Dún Laoghaire there are daily sailings from Holyhead at 10.25 with a return at 13.30. There is a 60 minute check-in deadline. The booking hall has an open lounge with cafés for snacks, a baby-changing room, toilets, disabled toilets, lifts, a *bureau de change* and ATMs. There is a Hertz car rental desk and a tourist information centre. The nearby Holyhead town centre caters for everything else required.

Dún Laoghaire town and harbour is 7 miles from Dublin itself and is accessed by car via the E1 and M50. There are both long- and short-stay car parks with pay and display. There is a currency exchange service, travel information counter, a left-luggage service, internet access, gift and souvenir shops. For physically disabled passengers there are designated amenities and wheelchair access.

Contact Details
Anglesey Office
Stena Line Limited, Stena House, Station Approach, Anglesey,
  Isle of Anglesey, LL65 1DD
Tel: 08705 755755; 0844 770 7070
Freight: 0844 070 4000
Fax: 01407 606604
Email: info.UK@stenaline.com
Web: www.stenaline.co

Dún Laoghaire Office
Stena Line Limited, The Ferry Terminal, St. Michael's Wharf,
  Dún Laoghaire Harbour, Dún Laoghaire Co. Dublin, Eire
Tel: 01204 7700
Freight: 01204 7607
Fax: 01204 7720
Email: info.ie@stenaline.com
Web: www.stenaline.co

Irish Ferries Holyhead Office
Salt Island, Holyhead, Gwynedd, LL65 1DR
Telephone: 08717 300 200
Fax: 01407 760340
Email: bookings@irishferries.co.uk
Web: www.irishferries.com

Irish Ferries Dublin Office
Irish Ferries, Terminal Road South, Ferryport, Dublin 1
Telephone: 01 607 5519; +353 1 607 5519
Fax: +353 1 607 5669
Email: info@irishferries.com
Web: www.irishferries.com

17: Birkenhead – Liverpool – Belfast – Dublin

Background

The ferries between Liverpool and the two major Irish ports of Belfast and Dublin have always been a major passenger and freighting route down the centuries and, despite the alarming decline in recent decades, are still among the busiest crossings still in operation today. There have been a dizzying number of operators and companies that have come and gone on both routes, being absorbed and amalgamated in succession. We can but give the briefest outlines of a complex history here.

In 1822 Charles Wye Williams founded the company that bore his name and which commenced a regular service from Dublin and Liverpool in 1824 with the paddle steamer *City of Dublin*, which was followed by the similar *Thames* in 1826, and further acquisitions quickly followed.

Meanwhile, in 1845 the company had become the City of Dublin Steam Packet Company, and in 1847 the iron paddle steamer *Trafalgar* joined the fleet specifically for use on the Dublin to Liverpool route. She was built by Tod & Macgregor and was of 750-GT, with a length of 57.91 m and an 8.63 m beam. Powered by two 350 bhp cylinder oscillating engines, she was to last for thirty years. In 1860 the 848-GT *Meath* joined the fleet, she was built by Laird Brothers and was 80 m long, and she served for thirty-six years being discarded in 1906.

In the 1890s five new ships were built by Blackwood & Gordon at Glasgow on the Clyde, the *Carlow* (1896), *Cork* (1899), *Kerry* (1897), *Louth* (1894) and *Wicklow* (1895), and served on the overnight crossing and daily return passage for many years, serving right through the First World War to 1919. The *Kilkenny*, which was also built in Glasgow in 1903, survived until 1917 when she was sold to the Great Eastern Railway and became the *Frinton*.

The company suffered what were to be decisive war losses when the second *Connaught*, the *Cork*, and the second *Leinster* were all torpedoed and sunk by German U-boats in 1917–18, the latter with the loss over almost six hundred lives. The financial losses crippled the company and forced it to cease the route in 1919 and sell the ships to B+I. It finally went into liquidation in 1924.

In 1826, one George Langtry, who had started the first steam ship service between Dublin and Liverpool as early as 1819, combined with his brother Robert and another local businessman William Herdman to form Langtry and Herdman, which became the Liverpool and Belfast Steam Packet Company. They introduced the John Ritchie-built wooden paddle steamer *Chieftain*. She was followed by the *Corsair* in 1827. Another wooden paddle steamer, the *Falcon*, entered service on the route in 1835. She was of 229-GT, with a length of 48.33 m, a beam of 6.8 m and a 4.8 m draught. In 1835 the *Reindeer* also appeared, but these ships were to be superseded by iron paddle steamers: the 645-GT *Sea King* built by Rod & Macgregor in 1845 at a cost of £24,000, and the 651-GT, Tod and Macgregor-built *Blenheim*, built in 1848. The former was hardly worth the outlay as she ran aground in fog barely two years later, turned turtle and was a total loss. The firm then absorbed the Cork Steamship Company.

From January 1852 the Belfast Steamship Company was offering competition and in 1859 ended up the sole survivor of five competing companies on the crossing. In 1863 two sisters, *Electric* and *Magnetic*

Offshore Ferry Services

appeared but it was not until 1919 that the company name was finally incorporated into the Coast Grouping.

Between the wars the Belfast Steamship Company ran a string of ships on the Belfast to Liverpool crossing, with the 1,800-GT sisters, *Heroic* and *Graphic*, 99.06 m overall and built in 1906 by Harland & Wolff, and later from the same shipyard, the 2,300-GT *Patriotic*, 100.58 m overall and built in 1911. These all survived the First World War and were still working in 1922. They were finally replaced by the 3,700-GT diesel cross-Channel ferry motor ships *Ulster Queen*, *Ulster Monarch* and *Ulster Prince*, all built by Harland & Wolff towards the end of the decade. During the Second World War these ships were commandeered by the Royal Navy as Auxiliary Anti-Aircraft ships, Landing Ship Infantry (Hand-hoisting) or Fighter-Direction Ships. *Ulster Prince* was sunk by German bombers off Nauplia, Greece in April 1941, while *Ulster Queen* survived the war but her modifications made it too expensive to reconvert her to mercantile service and she was scrapped in 1946. *Ulster Monarch* was, however, returned to service and survived until 1966.

A second *Ulster Prince* appeared in 1946, being the former *Leinster* made-over and updated and she too, lasted until 1966. The Coast Line empire was gradually dismantled piece-meal until the rump was purchased by P&O in 1971. Established as P&O Ferries (Irish Sea Services) the following year, they went after the Ro-Ro market, somewhat belatedly, with the Pandoro (P&O Roll On/Off) brand with the *Bison* and *Buffalo* then added the stretched *Union Melbourne* as the *Puma* later. The new *Ibex* arrived in 1979, but when the company was rebranded as P&O European Ferries (Irish Sea) in 1998, all these ships were renamed, becoming the *European Pioneer* (ex-*Bison*), *European Leader* (ex-*Buffalo*), *European Seafarer* (ex-*Puma*) and *European Envoy* (ex-*Ibex*).

The establishment in Dublin of the British and Irish Steam Packet company in 1836 is perhaps the most consistent thread in this interwoven skein of success and failure. It was as the B+I Line that it was most recognisable and endured as such until as recently as 1992. The first vessels were wooden paddle steamers: the 400-GT *Shannon*, *Devonshire* and *City of Limerick*. They operated initially from Eden Quay, with iron paddle-driven ships taking over then being duly replaced themselves by the iron-built screw-ships *Rose* and *Shamrock*, although these operated to London.

Service was maintained through both world wars although many vessels were commandeered for naval service and others lost. During the First World War and its aftermath many smaller companies were brought into the fold under the umbrella of Coast Lines. Specific to the Liverpool route were ships like the 1,870-GT *Lady Louth* and 1,945-GT *Lady Limerick*, each of which could carry 170 passengers overnight across the Irish Sea in the 1920s; in 1929 the 1,871-GT *Lady Munster*, 1,869-GT *Lady Connaught* and 2,254-GT *Lady Leinster* were bought in.

The depression of the 1930s followed but despite this new vessels were added, including the original 4,300-GT *Leinster* and *Munster*, both built in Belfast by Harland & Wolff, the latter being mined and sunk in 1940. Post-war the *Lady Connaught* became the *Longford* and the *Lady Munster* was renamed *Louth* and this pair plied the Liverpool crossing, while B+I itself survived intact until nationalization in 1965. This sparked off a renaissance of replacing old stock, and new car ferries and freighters were built, including the new Ro-Ro ships with bow and stern doors and ramps. The 5,000-GT German-built *Munster*, which could carry 220 cars and 1,000 passengers, commenced operations in May 1968, while the 4,849-GT *Leinster*, built by Verolme Cork Dockyard, which had space for 280 cars, and was equipped with swing decks for increased vehicle capacity, entered service the following year. Both of these operated the Liverpool crossing from 1969 onward from the newly-built ferry terminal to Trafalgar Dock in Liverpool and totally revolutionized the Dublin ferry scene. Transit times and turnaround

The *Stena Lagan* – Guest Services and the Truckers Lounge. (Courtesy Stena Line)

times were both improved, and the car traffic alone increased from 18,500 in 1967 to 42,400 in 1969. Freight throughput similarly mushroomed. A third vessel, the Ro-Ro Norwegian *Nanomark*, had to be chartered for freight-only traffic in 1972.

Another revolutionary vessel that B+I introduced in 1978 was the *Cuna Mara*, a Boeing Jetfoil which could carry 257 passengers twice a day between Dublin and Liverpool in just over 3 hours. However the weather conditions and lack of passenger interest saw this experiment quickly fail and she was sold off. The 6,800-GT *Connacht*, built at Cork in 1979, with the capacity for 1,500 passengers and 350 vehicles, was used on the Liverpool run in the 1980s, being joined by another *Leinster*, the 6,900-GT Verlome Dockyard-built vessel with the same capacity. In 1983 Trafalgar Dock was closed and the Dublin ferries terminated at Brocklebank Dock instead. But mounting losses soon made this irrelevant and in January 1988 the Dublin–Liverpool route was shut down after 152 years.

Belfast Car Ferries was formed in 1982 at Belfast by Irish Shipping Limited after P&O Ferries had finally abandoned the Liverpool to Belfast crossing in 1981. They chartered the Finnish-built 11,481-GT Ro-Pax *Saint Colum I* (the former *St. Patrick*, ex-*Vacancier*, ex-*Aurella*) on a 9-hour daily passage, leaving Belfast each night and returning next day. They struggled on until 1990 but were forced to close down that October.

The next contender to step up to that particular plate was Norse Irish Ferries, who initially operated the route as a freight-only Ro-Ro crossing between Belfast and Liverpool in November 1991 with the 21,717-GT *Norse Lagan* (built in 1967) and the 5,631-GT (*Transgermania*) built in 1976. Another addition to the fleet included the 20,114-GT *Norse Mersey*, built in 1969; and in 1995 a second Ro-Ro ship of the same name was obtained, she being a 14,820-GT vessel constructed by Cantiere Navale Visentini, in Italy.

In July 1997 two new purpose-built Ro-Pax ships arrived, these being the 21,856-GT *Mersey Viking* and *Lagan Viking*, also built by Cantiere Navale Visentini, each of which could carry 340 passengers and 200 cars on 2,460 lane metres of vehicle deck.

In October 1999 the company was bought by Cenargo, who owned Merchant Ferries, and in February 2001 merged with Merchant Ferries and Belfast Freight Ferries and became Norse Merchant Ferries. In November 2005 the Norse Merchant Group was taken over by Maersk and merged with Norfolk Line, and that same July Norfolk Line was bought by DFDS. This involved a lot of re-naming (and a lot more re-painting) but the transition was not a long one.

In the interim, as described above, P&O Irish Sea had been formed in 1998 with the declared programme of maintaining many services then under threat and purchasing a new Ro-Pax ship from Mitsubishi

The *Stena Mersey*, in new livery after her big refurbishment. (Courtesy Stena Line)

specifically for the Dublin to Liverpool crossing. Unfortunately services were instead shed. The Dublin to Mostyn and the Larne to Fleetwood services went in 2004 along with five ferries, and Celtic Link took over the Rosslare to Cherbourg crossing a year later. After five years the company once more became P&O Ferries, operating a much reduced service but maintaining an all-year route between Dublin and Liverpool with the cargo ships *Norbank* and *Norbay*.

As the economies of the UK and Ireland went into recession and traffic continued to decline, in January 2011 DFDS announced the closure of the Twelve Quays, Birkenhead to Dublin route due to declining passenger numbers. Stena Line took a different approach and announced that they would be taking over the route and, at the time of writing, are currently employing two vessels on charter for the job, pending outright purchase, these being the *Lagan Seaways* (ex-*Lagan Viking*) and the *Mersey Seaways* (ex-*Mersey Viking*) with funnels yet again being repainted, this time in Stena markings. Name changes followed in August 2011 when *Lagan Seaways* became the *Stena Lagan* and *Mersey Seaways* became the *Stena Mersey*. The deal also included the acquisition of the Belfast to Heysham route along with the *Scotia Seaways* (now renamed the *Stena Scotia*) and *Hibernia Seaways* (now renamed the *Stena Hibernia*), as well as the port facilities.

Current Operators, Ships and Details

Belfast Routes

Stena Line Irish Sea Ferry is currently employing the *Stena Lagan* (IMO 9329849) and the *Stena Mersey* (IMO 9329851) on the Belfast to Birkenhead route. There are overnight and daytime passages each day, with a journey time of approximately 8 hours. These sisters are British-flagged Ro-Pax vessels built by Cantiere Navale Visentini at Donada in Italy in 2005. Each is of 26,500-GT, with overall length of 186.4 m, a beam of 25.6 m and a 6.63 m draught. They are engined with two MAN/B&W 9L 48/60B developing 10,800 kW at 500 rpm for a speed of 24 knots. They have a capacity of 980 passengers, with 480 berths in 121 cabins and 38 reclining seats, and have space for 160 cars on 2,245 lane meters on four vehicle decks, with a trailer lane width of 2.7 m that can take 200 lorries and has a free height maximum of 5.1 m.

They have many facilities for passengers, including a cinema and two lounges. The ships have Mezzo hand-held entertainment units that can be hired from the reception or shop, with a range of movies, music, music videos and TV programmes to choose from, with headsets or iPod headset compatibility.

The *Stena Lagan* after modernisation. (Courtesy Stena Line)

For food and drink both ships have the Seven Seas restaurant for evening meals or buffet breakfasts, the snack bar for Grab and Go buffet breakfasts, with night and snack menus, although overnight sailings no longer include meal options.

Stena Lines Belfast terminal is signed as 'Stena Line' from Junction 1 of the M2 at the Fortwilliam roundabout. The terminal building houses a departure lounge, full toilet facilities, the Barista Coffee House, covered check-in area for car passengers, express boarding lane for premium customers and a large paid car park with 300 spaces.

The Birkenhead terminal is reached by road via the M53 Junction 1 exit and the A554, and is signed. Hamilton Square rail station is

5 minutes from the terminal while the Europa Boulevard bus station is 10 minutes away. The terminal houses a cafeteria, lounge, toilet facilities and covered check-in areas.

Contact Details
Office
Stena Line, Victoria Terminal 4, West Bank Road, Belfast, BT3 9JL
Tel: 028 907 47747
Fax: 01407 606811
Email: info@stenaline.com
Web: www.stenaline.com

Freight Office
Stena Line, Victoria Terminal, 1 Dargan Road, Belfast, BT3 9LJ
Tel: 028 9077 9090
Fax: 028 9077 5520
Email: info@stenaline.com
Web: www.stenaline.com

Dublin Routes

P&O operate the Liverpool to Dublin crossing with the conventional ferries *Norbank* (IMO 9056583) and *Norbay* (IMO 9056595). These sisters were built by Van der Giessen-de Noord, at Tamano in The Netherlands in 1993/94, the *Norbank* for Nordzee Verdiensten BV at Rotterdam, the *Norbay* for North Sea Ferries of Hull, both for the freight traffic crossing to and from Rotterdam. *Norbay* was taken over by P&O in 1996 and six years later was transferred to the Dublin to Liverpool route. Similarly *Norbank* was chartered by P&O from January 1997 and started operating on the Dublin to Liverpool crossing a year later. Both ships are of 17,654-GT, with an overall length of 166.77 m, a beam of 23.4 m and a draught of 5.8 m. Their engines are Zgoda Sulzer I ZA40S diesels and they give a speed of 21.5 knots. Cargo capacity is 2,040 m^3 and the ships have space for 125 vehicles depending on type. They have cabins for 114 passengers. Services currently sail at 09.30 and 21.30 respectively and take approximately 8 hours in normal conditions. There is a 60-minute check-in time prior to departure.

Naturally, being cargo ships first, their passenger accommodation and facilities are rather limited in scope. There are cabins with *en-suite* facilities if required. There are the Fables restaurant, two lounges, an open deck, the Poets' Bar, the P&O Sea Shop outlet, a cinema, games arcade and a soft-play area for children. However these ships are currently operated for vehicle drivers, both freight and car, and are not suitable or available for foot passengers. There are no lifts to the main passenger areas, only staircases. The infirm, disabled and young children might well find them unsuitable and great care should be made prior any booking to ascertain whether individual needs can be met.

At Liverpool the P&O Terminal is accessed by road from the M57/M57 interchange and the A5036 and the Seaforth Terminal – Liverpool Freeport entrance is fully signed. Lime Street rail station is 2 miles away with bus connections from Norton street bus station, from which at least 60 minutes transit time should be allowed. Facilities at the terminal are rather spartan but include essential services and snack vending machines.

The P&O ferries sail from Terminal 3, just opposite the O2 Academy, close by the East Link toll bridge and which is signed from the city centre and the Port Tunnel. There is a recommended 75 minute check-in time. It is important to note that as there are not foot passenger services there is no car parking facility at the terminal itself.

Dublin Port has a currency exchange service, ATMs, baby-changing areas, a coffee shop and a convenience store. Toilets and disabled facilities are to be found here as well as short- and long-term pay car parks and dedicated disabled parking.

Contact Details

Office
P&O Ferries Terminal, Gladstone Dock, No. 3 North Quay, Bootle,
  Merseyside, L20 1BG
Tel: 0151 802 1441
Fax: 0151 802 1445
Email: customerservices@poferries.com
Web: www.poferries.com

Freight (Dublin)
Tel: +44(0)845 832 22 22
Fax: +353 1 836 6472
Email: freight.dublin@poferries.com

Freight (Liverpool)
Tel: +44 (0)845 832 22 22
Fax: +44 (0) 151 802 1445
Email: freight.liverpool@poferries.com

18: Douglas IoM – Heysham – Dublin – Belfast – Ardrossan

Background

The Isle of Man Steam Packet Company is claimed to be one of the oldest continuously-operating passenger ferry services in the world following its creation in 1830. However, much earlier than this, in 1767, the government initiated a twice-weekly packet boat crossing to supply the soldiers that garrisoned the island after its purchase from the Atholl family. This service operated between Douglas and Whitehaven. They also built the Red Pier at Douglas which opened in 1801. With the coming of steam the first steam-driven paddle steamers commenced running in 1819.

James Little of Greenock was the agent for the vessels using Douglas as a stop-over on David Napier's Liverpool to Greenock crossing, with a 9 hour, passenger only, three-day-a-week, summer service from Douglas to Liverpool aboard the wooden paddler *Robert Bruce*.

The fare for a cabin and food was 31 shillings and 6 pence; for steerage passengers a mere 10 shillings (50p). Other such ships followed: the *Superb* (1830), the *Eclipse* (three vessels bearing this name were built in 1821, 1826 and 1850), and the *Majestic*.

A Liverpool-based company, St. George Steam Packet Company, also began to run the route from 1822 with Douglas as a port of call *en route*, using the appropriately named *St. George*. A less successful venture was the *Victory*, run by a Mr Coshnahan and which ran between Douglas and Liverpool briefly in 1826. The Mona's Isle Company was formed from public subscription at Douglas in 1829. Their first ship was the first to be named *Mona's Isle* and the company became the Isle of Man Steam Packet Company. She was built by John Wood, Glasgow with a pair of engines supplied by Robert Napier, whose reputation she largely made, and made her maiden voyage on 15 August 1830. She lasted until 1851.

Another vessel with Napier engines was the locally-built, by John Winram, *King Orry*, and she cut the Liverpool crossing time by at least an hour, being once reputed to have made the passage in 6 hours 20 minutes. Another hard steamer was the first *Douglas*, built in 1858 and which was credited with 17.5 knots and a crossing time to Liverpool of 4 hours 20 minutes. Even so, she was sold after just four years service and was employed and sunk as a blockade-runner in the American Civil War. The second *Mona's Isle* followed in 1860, and she had a long career. She was converted to a twin-screw ship after twenty-three years, becoming the *Ellan Vannin*, and was finally lost in a gale in December 1909 with every soul aboard.

Traditional names have become a by-word in the fleet, with *Ben-my-Chree*, named after a famous racehorse, being just one such favourite down the decades. The second ship of the name appeared in 1875 and was a two-funnelled paddle steam which served until 1906. The *Fenella* and *Peveril* were built in the early 1880s as the first twin-screw steamers, but both came to bad ends, both by collision, the *Fenella* in the River Mersey in thick fog in 1929 and *Peveril* off Douglas in 1899.

Paddle steamers continued to be built, including the second *Mona's Queen* in 1885, and she cut the Liverpool journey yet again, this time to 3 hours and 35 minutes. She survived until 1929.

Many of the company's vessels were requisitioned during the First World War and some became war casualties, including the 1887-built

The *Manannan* at sea. (© Isle of Man Steam Packet Company)

Queen Victoria and *Prince of Wales*, both lost in 1915, and the *Empress Queen*, a year later. One, the *Viking*, was converted by the Royal Navy to a seaplane carrier, HMS *Vindex*, and *Ben-my-Chree* and *Manxman* underwent the same alterations. To replace these, and others that were retained by the government or worn-out by hard service, a rebuilding programme began in the 1920s. Included were the 2,586-GT *Ben-my-Cree*, built in 1927 (war service 1939–46) and scrapped 1965; the 3,104-GT *Lady of Mann*, built in 1930 (war service 1939–46) and scrapped in 1971.

The Second World War proved equally hard on the ships. Eight company vessels took part in the 1940 Dunkirk evacuation and two were lost: the 2,756-GT *Mona's Queen* (built 1934) was mined and the 2,376-GT *Fenella* (the second such, built in 1937) being dive-bombed. Additionally the 2,376-GT fourth *Tynwald* (built 1937) was torpedoed off Bougie during the North African landings in 1942.

After the war began another period of construction, including a group commonly known as the 'Six Sisters', the last turbine-powered vessels built by Cammell Laird, Birkenhead. They were all between 2,485 and 2,495-GT and were: *King Orrey*, built in 1946 and taken out of service in 1975; the fourth *Mona's Queen*, built in 1946 and taken out of service in 1962; the fifth *Tynwald*, built in 1947 and taken out of service 1977; the fifth *Mona's Isle*, built in 1950 and scrapped in 1980; and the second *Manxman*, built in 1955 and taken out of service in 1982.

The *Ben-my-Chree* in Douglas Harbour. (© Isle of Man Steam Packet Company)

The pace of change affected all ferry companies, especially with the boom in car ownership. The Isle of Man Steam Packet Company introduced a quartet of unique side-loading car ferries using a spiral stern ramp so that they could load from ports that did not have Linkspans. The initial pair were the 2,724-GT *Manx Maid*, third ship of the name, built in 1962 and taken out of service in 1984, and the fifth *Ben-my-Cree*, of 2,762-GT, built in 1965 and taken out of service in 1984. These were followed by a second pair, the fifth *Mona's Queen*, 2,998-GT, built in 1972 and the first diesel car ferry, not finally taken out of service until 1990, and the second *Lady of Mann*, 3,083-GT, built in 1976 and sold in 2005.

Meantime, yet more problems were in the air. In 1979, the popular and famous motorcycle racing rider Geoff Duke, had headed up a new company with an old name, Manx Line, with the intention of providing a passenger and freight service in the Irish Sea. It would obviously be in direct competition to the Steam Packet Company. They commenced operations with a large Ro-Ro cargo ferry with a multi-purpose mission and very large endurance. She was originally built by S.A. Juliana Gijonesa at Gijon, Spain in 1976, as initially the *Monte Cruceto* and then the *Monte Castillo*, and had a speed of 18 knots. Manx had her modified with fully refrigerated cargo holds in 1978 and she could carry 777 passengers and 130 cars. Renamed *Manx Viking* and as the first Ro-Ro to work from the Isle of Man, she proved a very popular vessel when used on the Heysham route from Douglas where Linkspans were built for her. Although she was initially somewhat prone to breakdowns she settled down and her size made her reliable in even poor weather conditions.

In the interim, in the face of the threat offered by Manx Line, the Steam Packet Company had introduced the 1,975-GT Ro-Ro *Peveril*, which had been built in 1974 as the *NF Jaguar* and was chartered for service. She was followed in 1984 by the sixth *Mona's Isle*, 4,567-GT, and she was sold in 1985. Two further vessels joined the Ro-Ro fleet in 1985, the sixth *Tynwald*, 3,762-GT, built in 1967, and the 3,589-GT *Manx Viking*, built in 1976, which was sold in 1986. In 1990 the sixth *King Orry* arrived, 4,649-GT, built in 1972 and sold in 1998; and the final ship of this type was the 1,599-GT *Belard*, built in 1979 and which joined the fleet in 1993 but was sold in 1998.

A series of HSS vessels have been operated down the years, the first put into service in May 1994, this being the fourth *Snaefell*, built in 1991 and used on the Douglas–Belfast–Dublin circuit; She was followed by the 1991-built *SeaCat Danmark*, which began the Douglas–Liverpool–Belfast–Dublin loop in 1994. In 2000 services began with the *SuperSeaCat 3*, built in 1999, and another newcomer was the 1997-built *Viking*, which operated to Liverpool from March 2003. The 1998-built *Manannan* started working from Douglas to all three major Irish Sea ports in May 2009.

Meanwhile the Manx line had been gobbled up by British Rail's Sealink service but in 1985, after some convoluted negotiations, the Isle of Man Steam Packet Company merged with them. In 1996 the Sea Containers, Bermuda, company took over after a long takeover struggle. In 2003 Montague Private Equity took over the company and then sold it to the Australian Investment bank Macquarie two years later. In 2011 the company was again transferred to new ownership, this time to the Banco Espirito Santo.

A fresh rival to the company's freight traffic and thereby the viability of operations was the establishment of a daily freight ferry route between Douglas and Liverpool in October 2010. The new company was Mezeron, based at Ramsey, and chartered two Estonian Lift-on-Lift-off (Lo-Lo) ships, the 2,658-GT sisters *Kalana* and *Kursk*, (described as 14.5-knot Gearless Dry Cargo ships), along with their crews, from Tschudi Ship Management Tallin Estonia, and offered a direct threat to the future of *Ben-my-Chree*. The cheapness of the new company's service quickly won them contracts from supermarkets Tesco and Shoprite.

The competition forced the Steam Packet Company to increase passenger fares to compensate for the loss of 15 per cent of its freight business and caused a huge furore on the Isle of Man and elsewhere, with allegations of cheap foreign labour and loss of local jobs as a result. The uproar was not dampened when Mezeron director Jörg Vanselow hinted he could not rule out carrying passengers as well as freight in the future. However, in February 2011 Mezeron announced that their service would terminate, with the final sailing from Liverpool arriving at Douglas on the 19th of the month, but they would continue to trade to Glasgow. They continued to operate a freight service from East Quay, Douglas to both Belfast and Glasson Dock, Lancashire, with the 2007-built 3,538-GT *Silver River* (IMO 9359650) (ex-*Langfoss*).

Current Operators, Ships and Details

Isle of Man Steam Packet Company currently operates two vessels from Douglas, since 22 May 2009 the wave-piercing catamaran *Manannan* on a 2 hour 30 minute crossing to Liverpool and the conventional ferry *Ben-my-Chree*, which conducts a weekday 3 hour 30 minute passage to Heysham, Morecambe, Lancashire during the summer months and in winter includes a 4 hour 15 minutes schedule to Birkenhead. A once-a-week service to Dublin takes approximately 3 hours.

The 12,504-GT *Ben-my-Chree* (IMO 9170705) was built in 1998 by Van der Giessen-de Noord BV, Rotterdam and cost £24 million. She is 125.2 m overall, with a beam of 23.4 m and a loaded draught of 14.3 m. She has two MAK 9M32 5,873 bhp kW medium-speed diesel engines which give her a service speed of 18 knots. Her capacity is for 480 passengers, 22 crew and 200 vehicles, including 90 lorries, on 1,235 lane meters of vehicle decking.

The ship has twenty 4-berth *en suite* cabins with TV and there is a sun deck on Deck 8. Other amenities on Deck 7 include, Manannan Premium Lounge, Manannan Executive Club lounge, Niarbyl Reserved Lounge, Legends' Bar, the Coast-to-Coast Café, Ocean Avenue shop, the Junior Shipmates play area and a dog lounge.

The *Manannan* (IMO 9176072) is a 5,743-GT wave-piercing catamaran built by Intercat Tasmania Pty Ltd in 1998. She has an overall length of 96 m, a beam of 26 m and a 4 m maximum draught. She is powered by four resiliently-mounted Caterpillar 3618 marine diesel engines, with 28,800 kW at 1,050 rpm, and four Wärtsilä LIPS 150D water jets for steering and reversing.

The cinema aboard the *Manannan*. (© Isle of Man Steam Packet Company)

The *Ben-my-Chree* at sea. (© Isle of Man Steam Packet Company)

She can accommodate 850 passengers and 200 vehicles. She has a variety of seating areas, two cinema lounges, a large café bar area aft and the Coast-to-Coast café; the Skyberth upper deck lounge has the Niarbyul Reserved Lounge, the Manannan Premium Lounge and the Manannan Executive Club.

Douglas Ferry Port is accessed via the A1, A2 or A5 roads and there is long- and short-term paying car parking near the terminal. The terminal is open 07.00 to 20.00, and in winter 06.00 to 08.00 and 18.00 to 20.00. There is a 45 minute check-in time. The Lord Street bus station is about one minute walk away. There is a café in the departure lounge with toilets and other basic amenities. There are only vending machines at the terminal itself and an ATM.

Heysham Ferry Port is located approximately 6 miles from junction 34 of the M6 and the A683 or A589. The IOMSPC terminal is at South

Quay and is fully signed. There is limited paying car parking near the terminal. The rail station is adjacent to the terminal, with trains to Lancaster and onward. The Combermere Road bus stop is 10 minutes walk away. Terminal opening hours vary but are usually 09.00–17.00 and 22.30–02.30 Mon.–Fri., with a 10.30 opening time on Sunday. It is closed on Christmas Eve and Day and New Year's Eve and Day. There is a 2 hour check-in time. Note that during the TT Race period a different schedule operates so check before booking. There is a café during terminal opening times, and vending machines.

Dublin Terminal No. 1 is shared with Irish Ferries and is open from 04.30 to 22.00 daily, with a 45 min last check-in time. There is long-term paying car parking. There is a café with the terminal itself and a 24 hours waiting room at the port, with vending machines.

Contact Details

Douglas Office
Sea Terminal, Douglas, Isle of Man, IM1 2RF
Tel: 0870 552 3523
Reservations: 08722 992992
Fax: 01624 645697
Email: reservations@steam-packet.co.uk
Web: www.steam.packet.com

Heysham Office
Heysham Port, Heysham, Lancashire, LA3 2XF
Tel: 0871 2221 333
Fax: 01624 645697
Email: enquires@steam-packet.co.uk
Web: www.steam-packet.com

Dublin Office
Dublin Port, Terminal No.1, Terminal Road South, Dublin Port, Dublin 1
Tel: 1 800 55 17 43
Fax: 01624 645697
Email: enquires@steam-packet.co.uk
Web: www.steam-packet.com

Birkenhead
12 Quays Terminal, Tower Road, Birkenhead, Wirral, CH41 1FE
Tel: 08705 523523
Fax: 01624 645697
Email: enquires@steam-packet.co.uk
Web: www.steam-packet.com

19: Larne – Cairnryan (formerly Stranraer)

Background
Although a small port existed at Larne for many years a regular ferry crossing was not forthcoming until the arrival of the railway from Carrickfergus to the new station at Larne Town in October 1862. A paddle steamer link over to Stranraer, at the foot of Loch Ryan, now became feasible, as the Portpatrick Railway opened Stranraer station on exactly the same day. The scheme was, then as now, a seemingly logical route that ultimately would connect London and Belfast via a short sea link. The connecting of Stranraer to the junction with the Castle Douglas and Dumfries railway seemingly cemented the connection, with only the sea passage to complete the plan. Accordingly, The Glasgow & Stranraer Steam Packet Company had been formed in readiness and they had commissioned the Glasgow shipyard of Tod & MacGregor to construct a purpose-built vessel for the purpose. This was the PS *Briton*, a 349-GT ship with an overall length of 53.34 m and a beam of 7.34 m and powered by 2-cylinder, 150 bhp engines. She was launched in June and completed the following month, so was ready to make her inaugural voyage as planned on 2 October 1862. She ran straight into atrocious weather conditions and struggled to make it across in a nightmare debut that took 4 hours to complete. Her maiden voyage was to ultimately reflect the fate of the entire enterprise, which proved too far-sighted for the period. Although she made daily crossings to Larne and back, normally taking 3 hours each way, the route did not pay. After fourteen months of endeavour the inevitable was accepted and in December 1863 the *Briton* was withdrawn and sold to the Bristol General Steam Navigations Company for a southern England–Ireland link to Waterford.

It required the dedicated efforts of a typical Victorian *entrepreneur*, one James Chaine, to re-instate the facilities and thereby the fortunes of the port of Larne. In 1871 the Larne and Stranraer Steamboat Company was set up and another new paddle steamer was built to start the service once more. This ship was the 497-GT side paddle steamer *Princess Louise*, another Tod & McGregor built ship. She was 64.34 m overall with a beam of 7.34 m and a 7.36 m draught, and was launched in May 1872. She commenced service between Larne and Stranraer on 1 July 1872 and this time the enterprise flourished. A mail service was inaugurated in 1875 which continued for a century. This paddler was finally sold to David MacBrayne in 1890, and renamed *Islay*, but was wrecked on Sheep Island, Port Ellen in 1902.

Down through the years various famous ferries maintained this important and busy crossing for both passenger and freight traffic. The ships that followed included the *Princess Beatrice* (1875–1904), *Princess Victoria* (1890–1904), *Princess May* (1892–1910), another *Princess Victoria* (1912–1934), *Princess Margaret* (1931–1961) and *Princess Maud* (1934–1947).

Among the later big ferries were the two more named *Princess Victoria*, which proved an unlucky choice for both came to sad ends. The third ship of the name, after being requisitioned by the Royal Navy as a minelayer was sunk, ironically, by mines of the Humber in 1940, while the fourth foundered in the North Channel during the Great

Storm of 31 January 1953, and brought about the greatest post-war loss of life in British coastal waters. She was a 2,694-GT Ro-Ro ferry, one of the first to be introduced, built in 1947 by William Denny at Dumbarton for the British Transport Commission. She was fitted with sliding stern doors with a protective 'Guillotine' door which could be raised and lowered for extra protection. She ran the 40-mile crossing between Stranraer and Larne uneventfully for five years but the weather proved too much for her that night and she sank with the loss of 133 men, women and children.

She was replaced by the *Caledonian Princess*, a 3,630-GT, steel, twin-screw, passenger/car ferry with stern loading door and ramp, built by Denny of Dumbarton in 1961 for the Caledonian Steam Packet Company (Irish Service) Ltd. She was 107.6 m long overall, 17.43 m in the beam with a draught of 3.66 m. She had two Pametrada steam turbines which gave her a trials speed of 20.9 knots, although she was restricted to 19 knots in service. Carrying capacity was for 1,400 passengers and 103 cars. Due to turbine problems she did not make her delayed maiden voyage until 16 December 1961. She only remained until 1968 when she was fitted with side-loading doors and transferred to other routes.

For a brief period in 1964/65, the *Slieve Donard* [Erse – *Sliabh Dónairt* – Donard's Mountain, the highest of the Mountains of Mourne] operated as a back-up unit. She was a handsome, single-funnelled, 1,569-GT general cargo and cattle vessel, built by Ailsa Shipbuilding Company, Troon, in 1960 for the British Transport Commission. She had a stern door which permitted up to 61 cars to drive straight up onto her main cargo deck, and had a total accommodation of 150 cars, 668 cattle or thirty 6.09 m containers. Her ability to direct-load vehicles in this manner made her a seemingly natural choice at peak summer periods, taking the extra cars across while their passengers sailed aboard the *Caledonian Princess*. However, this proved in practice to be a most unsatisfactory arrangement which was soon terminated.

Other famous ferry ships on this crossing included the *Antrim Princess*, which was built for Caledonian MacBrayne but in 1969 became the very first Sealink drive-through ferry. She was a 3,761-GT vessel, built by Hawthorn Leslie on the Tyne, and powered by Pielstick diesel engines which gave her a speed of 19.5 knots. She could carry 690 passengers and 175 cars serviced by bow and stern ramps. She served the North Channel well until she suffered an engine fire at sea in December 1983, which meant she had to be abandoned, fortunately without any loss of life. She was subsequently repaired but transferred to the Isle of Man Steam Packet Company in 1985 as the *Tynwald*. She shared the route with the similar *Ailsa Princess*, built by Cant. Nav. Breda S.p.A. at Venice, Italy in 1971. She was a 6,177-GT vessel, also powered by two Crossley Premier S.E.M.T. Pielstick diesels, and had a trial speed of 20.7 knots. She made her maiden voyage from Stranraer on 7 July 1971 and served for a decade before being transferred south and becoming the *Earl Harold* in 1985 for Channel Island service.

The final ship of this type was the *Galloway Princess* of 1980. She was built by Harland & Wolff, Belfast, had a GT of 12,175 and also had a pair of Pielstick 16PC2V diesel engines which gave a speed of 19 knots. She could carry 1,000 passengers and up to 280 cars on 850 lane metres. She served with Sealink UK until 1984, then Sea Containers to 1991, before becoming the *Stena Galloway* that year, under which name she served under Sealink Stena, Stena Sealink and finally Stena Line until 2002. After more than two decades working from Stranraer to Larne and later Belfast she was disposed of and became *Le Rif*, working rather more clement Algeciras to Tangier Mediterranean crossing.

Meanwhile the next major development affecting the North Channel crossing had taken place in 1973, when the Atlantic Steam Navigation Company (which had been formed in 1936 and absorbed by European Ferries in 1971) purchased the wartime Military Loading Port No. 2, at the village of Cairnryan on the eastern side of Loch Ryan. Cairnryan was just 5 miles north of Stranraer itself and linked by a custom-built wartime rail line and road. For a nominal sum the company opened up a new ferry route from here to Larne. These two ships, the *Bardic Ferry* and the *Doric Ferry*, both built by Denny of Dumbarton, operated in the livery of the Townsend Thoresen Company (now P&O) from the modern car ferry terminal. At Larne the company reciprocated with the double-deck ramped Chaine Quay, opened in 1978, and the Continental Quay of 1979, helping to make the crossing from Cairnryan via the North Channel the shortest of all Irish Sea crossings. After 150 years of operations the end for Stranraer itself as a ferry port came in November 2011, when Stena Line moved its operations to a new deep water port north of Cairnryan, at the mouth of Loch Ryan, claiming the old route was unsustainable.

The freight service from Larne continued to flourish and led to further improvements to harbour facilities, partly funded by European Regional Fund money, with the opening of the MacKean Quay with two-tier ramps in 1987 and the improved Curran Quay in 1993. The new Freight Centre opened in 1998 and saw the streamlining of freight operations with a 24-hour operating terminal, with vehicles being weighed, registered and organized prior embarkation. Likewise at Cairnryan a brand new terminal, with separate reception areas for passengers and freight, booking offices, information centre, baggage-handling and special facilities for the disabled and children, was opened in 1999. The only retrograde step for the Larne end of the crossing was the 1995 decision by Stena to transfer their Irish terminal down to Belfast. This loss was partially offset by increased investment by P&O with two brand-new 23-knot 'Superferries' in 2000 and 2002, the *European Causeway* and *European Highlander*, which increased capacity and reduced the crossing time to 105 minutes. An even faster summer service had already arrived in 1999 with the 32-knot 'Jetliner', the *Superstar Express*, which made the crossing into a 1-hour service. In 2000 she was replaced by the *Express* and these three vessels currently work the route at peak periods.

Current Operators, Ships and Details

European Causeway (IMO 9208394) is a Ro-Pax ferry that was built by Mitsubishi Heavy Industries, Shimonoseki, Japan and is of 20,646-GT, with an overall length of 159.5 m, a beam of 23.4 m and a 5.5 m draught. She has four Wärtsilä 12V38 engines and a speed of 22.7 knots. Can carry 410 passengers and 315 cars or 84 freight vehicles, and has a crew of 55. She was the first to berth bow-in at the MacKean Quay.

Onboard services include the quiet lounge, Fables restaurant, the Poets' Bar with great ahead viewing, Costa Coffee, SeaShop which sells wines, perfume and gifts, *bureau de change*, two video lounges, TV lounge, commercial drivers' restaurant and lounge, and children's play area. There is ample viewing and seating on the upper outside viewing deck when the climate allows.

European Highlander (IMO 9244116), although owned by Barclays Mercantile Business Finance Ltd, is the P&O Irish Sea Ro-Pax fleet flagship and is an improved and slightly enlarged version of her near-sister, both of which are Nassau, Bahamas flagged. She was built by Mitsubishi Heavy Industries, Shimonoseki, Japan at a cost of £35 million, and completed in 2002, making her maiden voyage on 3 July. She is of 21,188-GT, with an overall length of 162.7 m, a beam of 23.4 m and a 5.5 m draught. She has four Wärtsilä 12V38 engines with a pair of controllable-pitch propellers, and a speed of 22.6 knots. She carries 410 passengers, 315 cars or 84 freight vehicles on a total of 1,825 lane meters, and a crew of 55. She also carries large lifeboats.

Onboard services include the quiet lounge, Fables restaurant, Poets' Bar, Costa Coffee, SeaShop which sells wines, perfume and gifts, *bureau de change*, video lounge, and children's play area.

19: Larne – Cairnryan (formerly Stranraer)

The P&O *European Highlander* operates between Larne and Cairnryan. (© Dave Greer)

Express (IMO 9176046) is one of four wave-piercing catamaran near-sisters built by International Catamarans (Intercat), at Hobart, Tasmania in May 1998. She is of 5,902-GT, with an overall length of 91.3 m, a beam of 26 m and a 3.7 m draught. Powered by four Caterpillar 3618 marine diesel engines with four Lips LJ145D waterjets she has a speed of 40 knots. She can accommodate 868 passengers and 195 cars. Currently registered in Nassau, Bahamas, after a varied career under a variety of names, she was chartered from Los Cipreses S.A. to P&O

Offshore Ferry Services

Irish Sea in place of *Superstar Express* on the Cairnryan/Troon and Larne route. In 2010 an additional call at Douglas Isle of Man was introduced to her schedule.

Onboard facilities include the Fables restaurant for hot meals, the Harbour Coffee Company for hot beverages, sandwiches, and snacks, a newspaper outlet and the SeaShop. She has a passenger lounge and a rearward scenic viewing area.

At Larne P&O's terminal port for Cairnryan is reached from Belfast, 5 miles distant, via the M2 north and then the A8(M) to the ferry port itself. From Monday to Friday the first service leaves at 04.15 and the last at 23.59, while on Sunday the times are 07.30 and 22.59 respectively. There are both short- and long-term car parks. The ferry port has passenger lounges, convenience store, buffet dining, bus and rail stations, tourist information desk, ATM, telephone and toilets including disabled toilets, baby-changing area, all as befits a port with an annual throughput of nearly 1,000,000 passengers and 600,000 vehicles. Foot passengers are driven on board by bus.

At Cairnryan, 5 miles north of Stranraer, the A75 from Carlisle and Dumfries leads to the A77 north to Glasgow, which passes close by the port approach road. On weekdays the first sailing is at 04.15 and the final one at 23.59, while on Sunday the times are respectively 07.30 and 22.59. There is a passenger concourse, toilets, children's play area, baby changing facilities, newsagent, snack-bar and amenities for the physically handicapped. There is limited free car parking at the port. Vehicle check-in times are 30 minutes prior departure with 45 minutes for foot passengers who embark via the gangway.

P&O have up to seven sailings daily, with a 105-minute crossing time. There are computerized check-in and loading systems in place and freight drivers have top-class facilities on board, including a dedicated restaurant, lounge, showers and toilets on board.

Contact Details

Larne
Ferry Terminal, Larne Harbour, Larne, Northern Ireland, BT40 1AW
Tel: 028 2887 2100
Fax: 028 2887 2209
Email: info@portoflarne.co.uk
Web: www.portoflarne.co.uk

Office
P&O Ferries, Larne Harbour, Larne, Co. Antrim, BT40 1AW
Tel: 08716 642121
Fax: 028 2887 2196
Email: enquiries@poishsea.com
Web: www.poferries.com

Freight Office
P&O European Ferries (Irish Sea) Ltd, Freight Terminal Larne, Redlands Estate, Coastguard Road, Larne, BT40 1AX
Tel: 0845 832 2222
Fax: 028 2887 2199
Email: freight.larne@poferries.com
Web: www.poferries.com

Cairnryan Office
P&O Ferries, The Port, Cairnryan, Wigtownshire, DG9 8RF

Cairnryan Freight Office
P&O European Ferries (Irish Sea) Ltd, Freight Terminal Cairnryan, The Port, Cairnryan, DG9 8RF
Tel: 0845 832 2222
Fax: 01776 707901
Email: freight.cairnryan@poferries.com
Web: www.poferries.com

20: Tynemouth – Amsterdam (Ijmuiden)

Background

Founded in 1866, the Danish shipping company Det Forenede Dampskibs-Selskab (The United Steamship Company, or more commonly, DFDS) are now the only passenger ferry operator working from Tynemouth, with their daily service to Amsterdam.

Brief mention should also be made of the now defunct service between Newcastle and Norway the convoluted history of which led to the present-day situation. Ever since the days of sail there had been a service between Norway and the UK, and in 1890 a regular ferry route between Norway and the UK (Newcastle) was established. Much later, Tor Line operated their *Tor Britannia* and *Tor Scandinavia* on a triangular schedule between Felixstowe, Gothenburg and Amsterdam, which was fictionalized in the 1980s by the notoriously awful BBC Television series *Triangle* where both the *Tor Scandinavia* and the *Dana Anglia* were used. The German Prinzen Linien ferries also operated to Scandinavia ports. Tor Line was taken over by DFDS in 1981, as was Prinzen, and the combined group became DFDS Danish Seaways. Former Prinzen ferries operated briefly from North Shields in the 1982–87 period, including the *Prinz Oberon* on the Esbjerg–Newcastle–Goteborg run, and *Prinz Hamlet*, *Prinz Hamlet 2* and *Prinz Oberon* for short periods only. In more recent times the Norwegian Fjord Line was founded in 1993 and is still based at Bergen. In 1998 they obtained the 12,348-GT MS *Jupiter* from Color Line. Fjord Line ran three passenger and freight vessels with three weekly services from Norway, one to Kristiansund, one to Stavanger, which crossing took about 18.5 hours, and another route to Haugesund, also three times weekly, which took about 21.5 hours to complete. In 2004 Fjord Line brought a more useful vessel on-stream, the MS *Fjord Norway*, and *Bergen*, withdrawn as being too small and too slow, was chartered out to DFDS for a year. The summer service between May and September was for the *Fjord Norway* to leave Newcastle each Wednesday afternoon direct for Bergen, while on other occasions she also called at Stavanger and Haugesund.

Back on Tyneside, at North Shields, it was in 1994 that an occasional summer service was commenced to Amsterdam with the 19,292-GT *Admiral of Scandinavia* and the 20,581-GT *King of Scandinavia*, and briefly, in May 1995 the 8,657-GT *Winston Churchill*. This was gradually developed with further ships, including the 21,545-GT *Prince of Scandinavia* and 33,575-GT *Queen of Scandinavia*, which operated daily services across the North Sea.

In 2005 the *Jupiter* was offered up for sale and was later employed in Vietnamese waters; the 31,360-GT *Fjord Norway* along with the route she covered, was sold to DFDS where they renamed her *Princess of Norway*, but she still followed the same itinerary. In 2008 Fjord Line and Master Ferries merged. Seacargo continued to run ships from Kristiansund to Aberdeen but these were freight services only. The Gothenburg, Sweden twice-weekly ferry service run by DFDS Seaways, which took about 26 hours with the *Princess of Scandinavia*, was regarded as uneconomical and ceased all operations at the end of October 2006. In September 2008 DFDS also terminated the service to Norway, due to mounting losses on the route for which many blamed cheap air fares. Currently then there is absolutely no direct passenger ferry between the UK and Norway, incredible though that might seem. DFDS Tor Line, however, continues to run scheduled freight services between Gothenburg and Newcastle and they also run seven 15-hour crossings a week for freight traffic between Ijmuiden and North Shields. In July 2010, DFDS took over Norfolk Line from Maersk and began rebranding their services and ships on all ten routes.

Current Operator, Ships and Details
DFDS Seaways 'Cruise Ferry' make one daily passenger and freight crossing to Amsterdam (Ijmuiden) in The Netherlands, the sailing being at 17.00 and the overnight passage taking approximately 17 hours and arriving at 10.30 local time. The return crossing leaves at 17.30 local time, reaching the Tyne at 09.00. Although a long sea route it enables northern-based travellers to avoid the ordeal of the chaotic British road network to reach the more popular and widely-used ports in the east and south. Two DFDS ships are currently employed on the passage.

King Seaways (IMO 8502406) was built in 1987 by Schichau Seebeckwerft AG at Bremerhaven, Germany, as the *Nils Holgersson* for the TT-Line. In 1992 she became Brittany Ferries *Val de Loire* and then became DFDS *King of Scandinavia* before assuming her present identity in 2011. She was renovated in 2006 and is now of 31,395-GT, with an overall length of 161.45 m, a beam of 27.6 m and a 6.2 m draught. She has four MaK 8M552 diesel engines of 19,580 kW which gives her a cruising speed of 21 knots. She has a capacity of 2,280 passengers, with 1,686 berths in 543 Cabins, and can carry 570 cars on 1,250 lane meters of deck space.

Princess Seaways (IMO 8502391) was also built in Germany by Schichau Seebeckwerft AG at Bremerhaven. Originally christened as *Peter Pan* she served with the German Trelleborg/Travemunde (TT) line plying between those two ports for seven years. In 1993 the TT-Line (Tasmania) obtained her and renamed her *Spirit of Tasmania* based at Melbourne until 2002 when she was chartered to the Fjord Line and

The DFDS ferry *Princess Seaways*, formerly the *Princess of Norway*, which operates on the Newcastle to Amsterdam (Ijmuiden) route. (© DFDS Seaways)

became the *Spir* and then the *Fjord Norway*, working from Bergen. Finally DFDS purchased her in 2006 whereupon she was totally refurbished like her near-sister and became the *Princess of Norway* until 2011 when she was once more renamed, this time as *Princess Seaways*. Her present GT is 31,360 and she has an overall length of 161 m and a

20: Tynemouth – Amsterdam (Ijmuiden)

The bar area on *King Seaways*. (© DFDS Seaways)

The smart restaurant on the DFDS ferry *King Seaways*. (© DFDS Seaways)

beam of 27.6 m with a 6.2 m draught. Her engines are four MaK 8M552 diesels producing 19,876 kW for a 20 knot cruising speed. She has a passenger capacity of 1,600 passengers, with 1,320 berths in 501 cabins and can accommodate 550 cars in 1,410 lane meters on her vehicle decks.

Common to both DFDS ships are the Blue Riband Restaurant with *à la carte* dining and comprehensive wine list; the 7 Seas buffet-style restaurant; international-style dining with eight different dishes; the Explorer's Steakhouse; the Latitude Café; Bake 'n' Coffee café (served from the Latitude on the Princess Seaways); Navigators' Bar; Compass Bar; Neptune Sky Bar on the top deck. There are also wine, beer and whisky tasting sessions; the Sea Shops outlets for wines and spirits, perfumes, toiletries, tobacco, confectionery and toys; as well as the travel retail shop; the Columbus Club; the casino; two cinemas on *King Seaways* and two cinema lounges on *Princess Seaways*; the *Kidz Club* and the Pirates' Club for children; swimming pool and onboard conference facilities. Cabin choices include Commodore Club, with Commodore Plus and Commodore De Luxe, and Seaways-class, with sea view and disabled cabins. There is also accommodation for dogs and other pets.

The international ferry terminal at the Port of Newcastle is situated on the north bank of the Tyne River at Royal Quays, North Shields, Tyne & Wear, NE29 6EG. (Telephone number 0191 296 1313 or 08705

333000). It is 8 miles east of Newcastle-upon-Tyne city centre and handles 700,000 passengers annually. There are covered walkways, a check-in area, and automated baggage handling. Amenities include a café, a *bureau de change*, bar, shop, ticket sales and enquiries office, a games arcade, hot and cold drinks vending machines, toilets and a baby-changing area. There is an ATM at a nearby shopping centre. There is disabled access and toilets in the terminal, and ferry companies offer cabins with wheelchair access. The terminal is reached by car from the A1 (M) via the A194 (M), A19 and A1058, while the central bus and main line rail stations are about 30 minutes away and served by a shuttle bus service. There is a secure paid car park and a short-term paid car park.

Ijmuiden ferry terminal is approximately 30 minutes drive from Amsterdam via the N202, A22 and A9. The terminal itself has limited facilities, with a convenience store for newspapers and periodicals, gifts and such but only vending machines for hot and cold snacks. There is paid, non-secure car parking at own risk. The check-in opens at 14.30, with boarding commencing at 15.30 and ending at 16.15.

Contact Details
Office
DFDS Seaways, International Passenger Terminal, Royal Quays,
  North Shields, NE29 6EE
Tel: 0871 882 0885
Fax: 0191 2936245
Email: enquiries@dfdsseaways.com
Web: www.dfdsseaways.co.uk

Freight
DFDS Seaways, Albert Edward Dock, North Shields, NE29 6EE
Tel: 0871 5229955
Fax: 0191 2936 245
Email: enquiries@dfdsseaways.co
Web: www.dfdsseaways.co.uk

Freight
DFDS Seaways, Felison Terminal, Sluisplein 33, 1975 AG,
  The Netherlands
Tel: 031 255 54 6666
UK: 0870 626 3990; 0844 5760060
Fax: 031 255 54 6655
Email: freight@dfdsseaways.com
Web: www.dfds-seaways-inc.com

21: Tarbert – Islay – Jura – North Uist

Background

The first steam series to operate to Islay were in 1825. The Glasgow company of G. & J. Burns had gradually absorbed most of the individual steamer routes to the Isles and they had a flotilla of eight paddle-steamers on these various routes: the *Curlew, Shandon, Duntroon Castle, Dolphin, Edinburgh Castle,* (later *Glengarry*) *Cygnet, Lapwing* and the original *Pioneer*, all of which were managed by David Hutcheson. In February 1851 these were sold out to his brother and a nephew, David MacBrayne. There followed an enormous expansion of built and purchased steamers, but by 1878 the Hutchesons had also bowed out, leaving the company in sole ownership of MacBrayne. With the arrival of the railways the mail services from their various termini to the islands offered profitable traffic and trade for the company and its rivals.

Their service to Islay commenced in 1876 when the *Islay* sailed twice a week from Glasgow, around the top of Kintyre. The *Islay* was an iron-built paddle steamer made by Messrs. Barclay, Curle, & Co. at Glasgow in 1867, and owned and managed by David MacBrayne, Glasgow. In 1882 she was lengthened to become 62.94 m, with a beam of 7.11 m and a 3.22 m draught, and her tonnage became 169.26-GT. She carried general cargo as well as passengers and had a crew of 23. She had two steeple engines with 145 horse-power combined. She served until she was wrecked.

In 1880 various 'Swift Steamers' operated from West Loch Tarbert to Islay via the tiny island of Gigha to Port Ellen or, alternately to Port Askaig, with laborious connections to the Tarbert to Glasgow on the paddle steamer *Columbia* via Rothesay, Dunoon and Greenock. Built in 1878 by J. & G. Thomson, she was powered by twin cylinder, non-compound oscillating engines; the *Columbia* was of 602-GT and more than 91 m long. She had a huge saloon and a promenade deck, and her facilities included an on-board Post Office, a smoking room and a barber's shop! She served mainly from Tarbert to Ardrishaig.

In 1903, as a brief temporary measure, the *Lovedale* (modified in 1893 from a cross-Channel steamer, *Great Western*, originally built in 1867) operated on the Islay route.

The custom-built *Pioneer (II)* was a 241-GT, 14-knot paddle steam built for David MacBrayne by A. & J. Inglis and was in service as the Islay mail server from 1905 until 1939, when the new *Lochiel* took over her run. She was specially constructed with small paddle wheels and boxes to enable her to operate from the Tarbert Pier. In the 1938 summer season she was still running from West Loch Tarbert, to Jura, Port Askaig, then offloading at Gigha before terminating at Port Ellen three days a week.

By 1928 MacBrayne was the subject of take-over by the London Midland Scotland Railway and associates, who retained the name but modified the routes.

The 577-GT *Lochiel (IV)* was built by William Denny and Brothers, Dumbarton in 1939 for David MacBrayne, and was 55.85 m overall, with a beam of 9.78 m and a draught of 2.31 m. She had a pair of 8-cylinder, 880 bhp Paxman-Ricardo diesel engines with twin three-bladed propellers and was good for 14 knots top speed. Flat-bottomed, but even so the West Loch Tarbert Pier had to be modified to accommodate her. She had a passenger capacity of 600 in two classes, with lounges, saloons and smoking-rooms, and could carry both cars and cattle. She was to be the final MacBrayne mail boat. She served Port Askaig and Port Ellen as well as Craighouse, Jura, while offloading at Gigha. In 1953 she had Colonsay as an additional port of call and in 1958 her route was still advertised by MacBrayne as the 'Islay & Colonsay Mail Services'.

A sister ship, *Loch Seaforth*, was not built until post-war. *Lochiel* herself served until 1970, despite being holed on rocks in October 1962 and finally sinking by the bows with just her bridge and stern deck visible at low water; she was subsequently raised and put back into operation. She was replaced by the *Arran* when Western Ferries began operating competing car ferries from Kennacraig. After various incarnations she ended her days as a floating bar at Bristol and was scrapped in 1995.

Post-Second World War, with the nationalization of the rail companies the LMSR half of MacBrayne became state-owned and remained that way until 1969, when the Scottish Transport Group took part and then total control of the company. Meanwhile private enterprise had returned in the form of the competitive Western Ferries, who foresaw the growth of Ro-Ro and drive-through car services and offered a seven-day service, operating out of Kennacraig to Islay, with more sailings, no subsidy and faster turn-rounds at cheaper cost with a purpose-built vessel, the *Sound of Islay*. Naturally MacBrayne argued that the standard of service was lower and the facilities far more basic, but it did prove popular compared with their slow side-loading operations.

The *Sound of Islay* is a 279.7-GT, Class III, twin-screw, Ro-Ro, passenger/car (Ro-Pax) ferry and was built by Ferguson Shipbuilders, Port Glasgow, in 1968, being 43.39 m long overall, with a beam of 9.53 m and a 2.29 m draught. She was powered by a pair of Bergius-Kelvin TA* 8-cylinder engines. She could carry 93 passengers and 20 cars. She presented a strange appearance on her debut with her superstructure piled up forward and her massive tail-ramp aft, but proved very successful in service. With breaks of service the *Sound of Islay* continued to operate to Islay until September 1981, when she was sold to a Canadian company and is still working forty-plus years later.

Further additions followed with the introduction of the *Sound Of Jura* in 1969 and the landing craft type *Sound of Gigha* (the former *Isle of Gigha*), with the bow ramp and open car deck capable of carrying up to 6 cars, operating between Port Askaig and Feolin on the A846. Unfortunately she capsized in November, which cast some doubts on the viability of the operation! The *Sound of Jura* was a Class III twin screw Ro-Ro drive through passenger/vehicle ferry built in 1969 by Hatl Verksted A/S, at Ulsteinvik, Norway. She had a 557.6-GT, an overall length of 49.35 m, a beam of 11.35 m and a 2.44 m draught, and was powered by a pair of Lister Blackstone EWSL8M 1,000 bhp engines. Her capacity was 250 passengers and approximately 40 cars. She operated three daily crossings until she was sold in 1976.

Eventually the Western service could not compete with the government subsidized operation, which in 1973 had been acquired by the Caledonian Steam Packet Company and re-flagged as the state-owned, Caledonian MacBrayne, headquartered at Gourock. The CalMac *Pioneer* (III) began operating to Islay in 1975 and this proved the turning point.

As for Jura, there has been a summer passenger service in recent years but it has never had its own vehicle ferry, other than the Port Askaig–Feolin crossing. Even the smaller island of Gigha has a dedicated service nowadays. A 2003 plan by the Islay & Jura Ferry Company for a new landing slip at Lagg, Jura, for a 30-minute crossing to Keillmore, Kintyre, 3 miles across on the ancient 'Overland' route to the mainland, was rejected.

Isla SeaSafari, owned by Nichol and Donnie Mackinnon, ran a twice-daily ferry service known as the Isle of Jura Ferry from 2008. It operated from Tayvallich at the head of Loch Sween, via Castle Sween, to Craighouse, the principal settlement on Jura, taking 1 hour to complete the pier to pier crossing. The vessel used was a Redbay *Stormforce 11*, RIB with a protective canopy from the elements and a deep 'v' formed hull form for stability. Passenger capacity was 12 with a crew of 2. This replaced the regular ferry service which had not run for some thirty years.

Contact Details
Isla Sea Safari
Tel: 07768 450000
Email: sailings@isayseasafari.co.uk
Web: www.islayseasafari.co.uk

In April 2011 it was announced in the *Oban Times* that the award-winning Jura Passenger Ferry Service, which the Jura Development Trust had operated over a three-year trial period from Craighouse in the Isle of Jura and Tavyvallich, Argyll, was to close. The Trust had failed to obtain the necessary funding from either Argyll and Bute Council or the Scottish Parliament and was to therefore discontinue services. The route had always run at a loss as a pilot, but so do many other ferry services which receive official funding. At the time of writing, however, there was still some hope that a funding package might be put together to resurrect the service once more.

The ferry service from Lochmaddy, North Uist to Uig to is a fairly recent innovation. Prior to the introduction of the Ro-Ro ships in 1964 there was little but the old outer island mail steamer *Lochmor* to provide a service. Built in 1930 the 543-GT *Lochmor* was a passenger cargo ship, 49 m in overall length, with a 8.8 m beam and 2.7 m draught, constructed by Ardrossan Dock and with Davey Paxman engines. She had a top speed of 12 knots and had to embark cars, and other cargo laboriously by crane alongside. In the main season she plied the 'round-Skye' route from the Kyle of Lochalsh and Mallaig, to Tarbert, Harris, North and South Uist and the small isles, Eigg, Canna, Rùm and Scalpay.

Then the *Hebrides* commenced operations. She was a hoist-lifting car ferry, one of three near sisters built by Hall, Russell & Co of Aberdeen. She had a GT of 2,104, was of 67.1 m overall length with a beam of 13.1 m and a draught of 4 m. She had two SCSA, 8-cylinder engines and a speed of 14 knots. Her passenger capacity was 600 and she could accommodate up to 50 cars which she handled via her hoists, turntables and side-lifts, a cumbersome process. However, *Hebrides* introduced such innovations as bow-thrusters and stabilizers. She was Government subsidized, having a nefarious role as floating control bunker in the event of the Cold War going hot, and was initially leased to MacBrayne. She started service on 15 April and remained in use until November 1985, when she, in turn, was replaced by the *Hebridean Isles*.

Current Operators, Ships and Details
The CalMac ship *Hebridean Isles* operates the main services from the ferry terminal at Kennacraig, south of Tarbert itself on West Loch Tarbert, to either Port Ellen or Port Askaig. The summer service is three sailings a day, with another two sailings each week with Oban as the terminal.

Hebridean Isles (IMO 8404812) is a Ro-Ro vehicle ferry, a half-sister to the same company's *Isle of Arran*. She was built by Cochrane Shipbuilders Ltd, at Selby, North Yorkshire and was launched (sideways) by HRH the Duchess of Kent in July 1985, making her maiden voyage on 5 December of that same year on the Stornoway to Ullapool crossing. She is of 3,046-GT, has an overall length of 85.8 m, a beam of 15.8, and a 3.11 m draught. She was engined by Mirrlees Blackstone Ltd, Hazel

Offshore Ferry Services

The bow visor is raised to horizontal for cargo embarkation while the side loading of passengers also proceeds aboard the *Hebridean Isles*, seen here at Inverary in February 2009.
(© Dave Greer)

Grove, Stockport and her diesels give her a best speed of around 15 knots. She has a passenger capacity of 511, a crew of 24 and can accommodate 68 cars. In addition to her bow and stern ramps, with a bow visor, she is equipped with a vehicle hoist with side ramps aft of the main superstructure.

Facilities aboard include most of the larger ship amenities of the CalMac fleet. There is an observation lounge on Deck Four, and a recliner lounge and a TV lounge on Deck Three with further outdoor seating on both decks for viewing on fine days. The Mariners cafeteria aft on Deck Three serves meals of all types throughout the day, including snacks, packed lunches, vegetarian and children's menus. The Coffee Cabin forward on the same deck serves beverages, alcohol and light snacks, while Shop@CalMac acts as a news agency, bookshop, confectioners and souvenir outlet. The Game-On on Deck 4 has video gaming and machines. There are toilets on both passenger decks with mobility impaired facilities on Deck 3 with wheelchair access as well as a baby-changing area and a dedicated pets area.

Thanks in part to the popularity of Islay whisky, with distilleries at Ardbeg, Lagavulin and Laphroaig, and increased tourist numbers, the *Hebridean Isles* (Gaelic – *Eileanan Innse Gall*) is employed exclusively on an all-year service between the hamlet of Kennacraig in southern Argyll (with the embarkation point just off the A83), down West Loch Tarbert and across to either Port Ellen at the southern end of the Isle of Islay, or Port Askaig, on the Sound of Islay, on the north-east shore. She shares these routes in the summer months with the *Isle of Arran*. The service usually operates on a three or four crossing schedule, Monday to Saturday, with two crossings only on Sundays, but does not operate on either Christmas Day or New Year's Day. Each crossing over to Islay takes approximately 2 hours 20 minutes.

Isle of Arran (IMO 8219554) is a DSMV Ro-Ro passenger/vehicle ferry that was built on the Clyde by Ferguson Ailsa Ltd, at Port Glasgow at a cost of £6,700,000, and made her maiden voyage on 13 April 1984. The vessel is of 3,269-GT, is 84.82 m overall length, with a beam of 15.8 m and a 3.19 m draught. She is engined with two 8MB275 diesels, both developing 2,310 bhp and which give her a best speed of 15 knots in service. She can carry a total of 446 passengers and up to 68 cars and 8 trucks, and has a 20-strong crew. She is equipped with 3 rigid life-boats and a RIB fast rescue craft as well as inflatable life-rafts. She was originally built for the Arran ferry service where the *Clansman* had proved inadequate, but she, in turn, was replaced and took over the Kennacraig to Islay service, again relieving the *Clansman*, and then spent a long period both pioneering and relieving on various services. However, since 2007 she has more-or-less settled down to sharing the all-year crossing from Kennacraig, south of Tarbet, Kintyre, down west Loch Tarbet and across the Sound of Jura to the Isle of Islay, turning either north to the Sound of Jura and to Port Askaig, a 2-hour voyage, or south to Port Ellen which takes approximately 2 hours 20 minutes, routes she shared with the *Hebridean Isles*. After being extensively refurbished in the early 1990s up to full CalMac standards, her Deck 4 facilities now include Mariners cafeteria, Coffee Cabin, Shop@CalMac, Cub Club, Game-On, toilets, baby-changing unit, pet area, mobility impaired facilities and table seating, while there is outdoor open-air seating on Decks 4 and 5. The arrival of the new *Finlaggan* saw her relegated to the position of 'spare vessel' in 2011.

At Port Askaig the ferry terminal has a 6-seat waiting room, with toilets and little else. There are five dedicated disabled car parking spaces but currently no other facilities. There is a 45-minute check-in time prior departure.

The *Isle of Arran* (Gaelic – *Eilean Arrain*) operates a varied schedule on her route, with one ship or the other making three or four voyages daily on weekdays and Saturdays, with just two on Sunday, with two morning sailings and one afternoon sailing to Port Ellen and one early afternoon crossing to Port Askaig. During the summer season there is also a Wednesday crossing to Oban, calling at Port Askaig and Colonsay and which returns from Oban in the afternoon for Kennacraig via Colonsay and Port Askaig. These routes currently do not operate on Christmas Day and New Year's Day. At Port Ellen Ferry Terminal there is disabled access and some parking.

Hebrides (IMO 9211975) is a 5,506-GT passenger/vehicle Ro-Ro ferry used on the Uig to Tarbert and Uig and Lochmaddy services. She was built by Ferguson of Port Glasgow and is a half-sister of the *Clansman* with the same open stern layout, but with improved passenger deck space and interior seating, plus special 'evacuation gaps' for increased safety, all at a cost of £15 million. She was launched by Her Majesty Queen Elizabeth on 2 August 2000, the first of CalMac ships to be named by the Sovereign. She is 99 m overall, with a beam of 15.8 m and a draught of 3.22 m. She is powered by a pair of MAK 8 M32 engines which provide her with a service speed of 16.5 knots and she is fitted with a pair of Ulstein electric bow thrusters. *Hebrides* (Gaelic – *Innse Gall*) was also the first of the fleet to introduce the Marine Evacuation System (MES) of inflatable chutes similar to those used on airliners, as well as pre-packed self-inflating life-rafts. Additionally, three new Linkspans were constructed at Lochmaddy, Tarbert and Uig, while both Tarbert and Uig piers had to be extended, all as part of a £20 million package for the new services. The overflow starboard hoisting mezzanine car deck increases her regular 80 car capacity to 98 at peak months, which she loads via her stern ramp at Uig and bow ramp at her other regular embarkation points. She has a passenger capacity of 612, with a crew of 34.

The Lochmaddy ferry terminal has a 40-seat waiting room, with toilets, disabled toilets, and baby-changing area but no public telephone, vending machine or ATM. There is a bus stop adjacent to the terminal and limited free car parking. It has a 45-minute check-in time prior to departure. The ferry terminal at Uig has a 25-seat waiting room, with toilets, disabled toilets, baby-changing facilities, and a public telephone but no vending machines or ATM. There is some free car parking with a single dedicated disabled parking place. The bus stop is on the main road, 25 m distant. There is no taxi rank.

The passengers aboard the *Hebrides* have the usual CalMac facilities to choose from. The Mariners cafeteria for meals of all types, plus the Coffee Cabin also has light snacks as well as drinks of all types, while Shop@CalMac also dispenses soft drinks and confectionery as well as newspapers, magazines and books. The Game-On gaming arcade and the Cub Club for juniors are both on Deck Four. The ship has TV, observation and recliner lounges as well as open air seating at the rear of both Decks 4 and 5. There are toilets on both passenger decks, and mobility impaired units on deck four. There is a baby-changing area and a dedicated zone for pets.

The majority of her journeys are via Uig, on the Isle of Skye, with only a few direct sailings out of Lochmaddy to Tarbert, and the crossing time of the Little Minch is approximately 1 hour 40 minutes. At Port Askaig the terminal has a small waiting room with 6 seats, and toilets, a car park for which booking is required and with five spaces reserved for disabled drivers. A wheelchair is available and the terminal requires a 45-minute check-in time.

Likewise the ferry terminal at Port Ellen is basic with toilets, an 11-seat waiting room, toilets, a single disabled parking place but little else. At Kennacraig, 5 miles from Tarbert, there is 25-seat waiting room, toilets, including disabled toilets, a 150 place free car park with three disabled slots, baby changing facilities, a wheelchair, a public telephone and a bus stop. However, at the time of writing it is closed for total refurbishment which it badly required and services are currently running out of Port Askaig.

At Lochmaddy the ferry terminal has disabled toilets, access and some parking.

The Tarbert, Harris, ferry terminal has a 52-seat waiting room, with toilets, disabled toilets and baby-changing facilities but no public telephone, ATM or vending machines. There is a free car park some 35 m distant and four dedicated disabled car parking spaces within 10 m of the terminal.

Contact Details

Caledonian MacBrayne, Ferry Terminal, Lochmaddy, Isle of North Uist, HS6 5AA
Tel: 01876 500337
Fax: 01876 500412
Email: Lochmaddy@calmac.co.uk

Ferry Terminal, Port Ellen, Isle of Islay, PA42 7DW
Tel: 01496 302209
Fax: 01496 302557
Email: portellen@calmac.co.uk

Ferry Terminal, Port Askaig, Isle of Islay, PA46 7RB
Tel: 01496 840536.
Fax: 01496 840620
Email: portskaig@calmac.co.uk

Ferry Terminal, Whitehouse, by Tarbert, Argyll, PA29 6YF
Tel: 01880 730253
Fax: 01880 730202
Email: kennacraig@calmac.co.uk

22: Gourock – Dunoon

Background
As with many such ferry ports, Gourock blossomed from a quiet Renfrewshire fishing village into a major crossing with the arrival of the railways and the opening up of Scottish tourism in the early Victorian era. The pierhead building still remains a focus of one of the Dunoon cross-Clyde services. In 1820 a pier was constructed at Dunoon, across the water to the west, a similar community built around two bays and with the distant backdrop of the Cowal Peninsular, from which ran both the short ferry crossing and direct steamer services up the Clyde to Glasgow itself. One of the last traditional carriers to occasionally call was the famous paddle steamer *Waverley*, built in 1946, the last of her long line.

In January 1954 a vehicle ferry was initiated by Caledonian Steam Packet Company, later Caledonian MacBrayne, with a trio of vessels with electrically driven hoist- and side-ramp loading, the *Arran*, *Bute* and *Cowal*. The *Arran* was a 540-GT ship, built by William Denny at Dumbarton, and was 57 m overall with a beam of 11 m and a 2.3 m draught. She was powered by a pair of British Polar engines driving twin screws for a speed of 15 knots. Her original (and austere) passenger capacity was 650 (later reduced to 400) and she could carry 26 cars, with a maximum lift capacity of 5, with turntables, but this total was soon increased to 34. She was, in fact, the lead ship in this latter respect, for the fleet we know today. She was given two major refits in her long life, the second in 1973, converting her to a stern-ramp ship, loading and unloading from a concrete ramp. The hoist was put back again two years later when she acted as a relief ship, conducting a few final journeys between Gourock and Dunoon in 1979 before being laid up and then sold in 1981.

Having led the way, *Arran* was joined by first one, then two similar ships and they continued operations until 1969 when they were temporarily relieved by the *Clansman* in 1970, herself soon relieved by the brand new *Iona*, with the *Glen Sannox* brought in as a stand-by when teething troubles were encountered.

The *Iona* also broke new ground by being the very first Ro-Ro drive-through ferry built for Scottish Transport Group, one of the many forerunners of CalMac. She was built in 1970 by Ailsa Shipbuilding Company and had English Electric Diesel engines which gave her a trial speed of 17.5 knots. Of 1,324-GT, the *Iona* was 74.3 m overall, had a beam of 14 m and a draught of 3 m. A ship of superlatives, she could boast, bow (with visor) and stern ramps, twin rudders, bow-thrust unit and stabilizers, as well as hoists and side ramps. She had two masts, four lifeboats, a fake funnel and two exhausts for her Paxman engines. She had a car capacity of 47 cars and could carry about 400 passengers. She was built to service the Islay route but for many reasons this did not happen and she eventually made her maiden voyage to Dunoon in lieu of *Clansman* on 29 May 1970. Repeated problems saw her relegated from this route very quickly, however, and the new-build *Iona* was replaced by the *Maid of Cumbrae* in the 1972/73 season, but the following year saw the introduction on the route of *Jupiter* and *Juno*, specially built to counter the new competition offered by Western Ferries very basic, sparse but highly functional, Ro-Ro car ferries, the first of which, *Sound of Shuna*, was arriving on the scene.

22: Gourock – Dunoon

On Sunday 3 June 1973 the new company commenced an hourly operation between 07.00 and 22.00 each day on their new designated route between Hunter's Quay, some 2 miles north of Dunoon, and McInroy's Point, on the A770, where new Linkspans had been constructed. The *Sound of Shuna* was the former Swedish ferry *Olandssund IV*, built by A/B Åsi-Verken, Amal, Sweden in 1962. She was of 243.3-GT, had an overall length of 41.91 m, a beam of 9 m and a 2.53 m draught. She began operations across the Clyde in June 1973 and, with an update in 1980, remained in service until May 2001. Her limited car capacity, 25 vehicles in three lanes, soon proved inadequate, and a second vessel, of similar, *Sound of Scarba*, joined in a month later. So successful did this new service prove that a third ship, the former Isle of Wight ferry *Lymington*, was bought and re-christened *Sound of Sanda* and she commenced operations in August 1974. Built by Denny of Dumbarton way back in 1938 for the Southern Railway, she was a 403-GT Passenger and Ro-Ro ship, 45.1 m overall, with a 26.1 beam and a speed of 11 knots. She could carry 516 passengers and 17 cars and she remained in service on the crossing until 1993.

CalMac's response to the challenge were the *Juno* and *Jupiter* which worked the crossing between them, being supplemented by the *Saturn* from 1986 onward, with reserve vessels being the *Pioneer*, *Claymore* and *Coruisk*. The *Juno* (Gaelic – *Iùno*) was built by James Lamont & Co. Ltd, Port Glasgow, and engined by Mirrlees Blackstone Ltd, Stockport with two 4SCSA8 cylinder diesel engines of 1,000 bhp each. These gave her a speed of 13 knots, which earned her the tongue-in-cheek sobriquet of 'Streaker', and this description stuck to the type. She was of 854-GT, was 66.45 m overall, with a beam of 13.8 m and a draught of 2.41 m. Her passenger capacity was 531 with a crew of 10, and she could load 38 cars. The second ship, *Jupiter* (Gaelic – *Iupadar*), was identical in detail but had an improved-vision bridge structure which was later fitted to the *Juno*, and this pair plied the Gourock to Dunoon across the

The Sound of Sanda alongside, with *The Sound of Scarba* in the background. (© Pete McCann)

Upper Clyde route for many years. They had a best speed of 15 knots. Ultimately aspects of this successful design were adapted for a third vessel, the *Saturn* (Gaelic – *Satharn*). She was built by Ailsa Shipbuilding Company at Troon, and with dimensions of 69.5 m overall, 13.8 m beam and 2.45 m draught, she had a tonnage of 851-GT. Compared to her near-sisters she had a higher-level bridge, extra passenger accommodation and the mainmast was positioned forward. This ferry operated mainly on the route from Wemyss Bay to Rothesay. In later years the trio was used on alternate routes, including cruises. With the rationalization of the service, *Jupiter* soldiered on alone but in 2011 was finally sold for scrap.

In April 1985 Western Ferries became Western Ferries (Clyde) Limited and the ex-Sealink, ex-Southern Railways 363-GT ferry *Fresh-*

water was obtained and re-named *Sound of Seil*, starting operations in 1986. Built in 1959 by Ailsa Shipbuilding she had engines by Crossley. Nor was this the end of the expansion as vehicle traffic continued to mushroom, and in 1988 another vessel was added to the fleet, the ex-Dutch river ferry *De Hoorn*, which became the *Sound of Sleat*. She was a Class V double screw steel motor Ro-Ro passenger/vehicle ferry with bow, stern and side ramps, originally built in 1961 by N.V. Scheepswerf en Machinefabriek at Hrdinxvel-Giessendam. She was 40.82 m overall length, with a beam of 15.31 m and a draught of 3.33 m. Her car capacity was about 30, while she could manage 220 passengers.

While CalMac faced up to stiff competition from their drive-through rivals with fast journey times and quick turn rounds with the 'Streakers', behind the scenes considerable political manoeuvring was taking place. The upshot was that CalMac operations were scaled back to become a hourly-crossing with the inevitable reduction in the fleet, with one or another of the trio 'rested'. The *Saturn* worked Bute then became a reserve vessel, while *Juno* was taken out of service in April 2007. Nevertheless a 250 capacity passenger catamaran, the *Ali Cat*, was introduced in 2002 as a charter vessel from Red Funnel Line, to cover peak commuter requirements. Meanwhile Western continued to introduce new ships on their popular vehicle route.

Current Operators, Ships and Details

There currently remain two main operators across this route and the future of the service has become the subject of prolonged and bitter dispute, both companies having their advocates and detractors, and the issue is locally acrimonious in the extreme. However, with two competing services, others think that the users, both passenger and vehicle, have the best of both worlds.

In 2002 the *Ali Cat* (still with no allocated IMO apparently) was chartered to Red Funnel Line but in October 2002 Caledonian Macbrayne were seeking a faster vessel to provide a peak morning and afternoon, passenger-only supplementary service from Dunoon to Gourock during the winter months, and she was contracted to provide this cover. Some initial difficulties were encountered but, with the construction of a breakwater at Dunoon to aid embarkation, the service was extended.

Ali Cat is a catamaran originally built by South Boats of East Cowes, Isle of Wight in 1999 for Solent & Wightline Cruises based at Ryde, IOW. She has a tonnage of 78.2 and an overall length of 19.8 m. She is powered by a pair of Scania DI 14 diesel engines, driving 32-inch propellers, which give her a top speed of 14 knots, although her normal service speed is less. She has a passenger carrying capacity of 250 and a crew of 4. A new Dunoon breakwater built in 2004 considerably improved embarkation in the winter months. There is an open deck aft with an internal lounge served by a bar.

From 30 June 2011 the service became passengers only under the new ownership of Argyll Ferries Ltd, part of the Caledonian MacBrayne group. Also in 2011 the *Ali Cat* was joined on the route by *Argyll Flyer* (IMO 9231016), which had originally been built by OCEA in France in 2011 as the *Banrion Chonamara*. She has a passenger capacity of 224. The two vessels operate 60 services on the Monday to Saturday service and 30 on the Sunday schedule both being 'Pay onboard', and with no service on Christmas Day and New Year's Day.

The CalMac operation at Gourock remains the terminal, on Tarbet Street, next to the rail station and accessed from the A771, which has a large waiting room and facilities including a ticket office, waiting room and toilets. The ferry terminal has toilets with disabled facilities and some paid parking.

The Linkspan and gangway for the Dunoon ships are on the Pier Esplanade at the southern end of town, and there is car parking at the station as well as designated road places. The 50-seat waiting room has a ticket/reservation desk, toilets and disabled toilets, an ATM, public telephone, vending machine and baby-changing area, but no left luggage area. The rail station, bus station and taxi rank are all about 2 minutes walk away.

At Dunoon the old pier has the new Linkspans embedded with passenger waiting areas and vehicle stacking nearby. The Dunoon ferry terminal has thirty free car parking spaces and facilities at the port include a ticket/reservations office, a 50-seat waiting room with disabled access, public telephone, toilets and disabled toilets, but no baby-changing facilities, vending machines or left luggage capacity.

Contact Details
Caledonian MacBrayne, Ferry Terminal Building, Station Road,
  Gourock, Renfrewshire, PA19 1QP
Tel: 01475 650100
Fax: 01475 637607
Email: enquiries@calmac.co.uk
Web: www.calmac.co.uk

The current fleet of Western Ferries (Clyde) Limited comprises four vessels.

Sound of Sanda (IMO 8928894) and the *Sound of Scalpay* (IMO 8928882) are 403-GT double-screw steel motor car and passenger Ro-Ro ferries. *Sound of Sanda* was originally built in Germany in 1963 by Gutehoffnungshulte Sterkrade, Akflengesellschaft, Rheinswerft, at Walsum, as a municipal port for Amsterdam City Council under the name *Gemeentepont 24*. She has an overall length of 48.43 m, a beam of 14 m, a draught of 2.7 m and a speed of 13.9 knots. *Sound of Scalpay* was also built for Amsterdam as *Gemeentepont 23* by the Dutch company Arnhemsche Scheepsbouw Maatschappij N.V., Arnhem and is of the same dimensions. Both of these elderly ladies were purchased by

Stern view of an empty *The Sound of Sanda* which shows to good effect her split accommodation and offset bridge. (© Dave Greer)

Western and fully refitted at James Watt Dock, Greenock in 1996 by the firm of Garvel Clyde, part of the Forth Group, when among other improvements their old machinery was taken out and replaced by a pair of new 480 bhp Caterpillar 3408TA engines and two Holland Roer Propeller Azimuth units, with one fixed pitch propeller at either end. They both have a car capacity of 37, along with 220 passengers and a

Offshore Ferry Services

crew complement of 4, and have a single car deck with bow and stern ramps.

Sound of Scarba (IMO 9237424) is a 489-GT double-screw car/passenger Ro-Ro ferry which was built in 2001 by Ferguson Shipbuilders at Port Glasgow in 2001 and commenced operations in 2003. She has an overall length of 49.85 m, a beam of 15.01 m and a 2.50 m draught. She has Cummins KTA19M3 6-cylinder engines which drive twin Rolls-Royce Aquamaster Azimuth US601 CRP. *Sound of Shuna* (IMO 9289441) is also a 489-GT double-screw passenger/car ferry built by Fergusons Shipbuilders at Port Glasgow in 2003 and is similar in design to the *Sound of Scarba* with the same dimensions, same propulsion and Rolls Royce Aquamaster Azipods for high manoevrability. She started working in October 2003. These ships have side viewing decks and even some passenger cabins with fixed seating and some tables, as well as toilet facilities, but are otherwise basic.

The Western ferry operates 365 days a year, with the first weekday sailing at 06.10 and the last usually around 23.30, but this should be checked beforehand, while weekend services start at 07.00. There are usually four sailings per hour on the 20-minute crossing; booking is not usually required and tickets can be purchased ashore at both terminals or on board. The company transports about 140 cars per hour and there is a reduced service on Christmas Day, Boxing Day, New Year's Day and 2nd January.

Contact Details
Western Ferries (Clyde) Limited, Hunter's Quay, Dunoon, Argyll, PA23 8HJ
Tel: 01369 704452
Fax: 01369 706020
Email: enquiries@western-ferries.co.uk
Web: www.western-ferries.co.uk

The Sound of Scarba near Gourock. (© Pete McCann)

23: Ardrossan – Arran

Background

With the success of the little *Comet*, passenger traffic 'doon the water' had quickly flourished, while the railways, eagerly pushing further into the remoter areas of the country, brought new trade. Soon even the enormous and swelling population of London was within reach of the Western Isles, to those who could afford the journey. Among the ferry routes that became established was that from Ardrossan to the Isle of Arran. Some sources list the Castle Steam Packet Company, founded by J. McColl and A. Patrick in 1832 and owners of the 311-ton, 48.31 m long and 6.14 m beamed, *Inverary Castle*, built in 1839 for D. Hutcheson & Co., Glasgow, and powered by two of David Napier's 80 bhp Steeple Engines, as having initiated the Ardrossan, Ayrshire to Brodick, Isle of Arran, ferry service. However, as far as can be ascertained she never served this route but operated solely between Glasgow and Inverary.

The more likely contender was the Ardrossan Steamboat Company, which was established in 1839 and in 1847 operated the paddle steamer *Isle of Arran* until 1860. In the latter year she was replaced by the 144-GT *Earl of Arran*, a wooden paddle steamer, was built and engined by Blackwood and Gordon of Paisley, with double steeple engines. She plied between Ardrossan and at Lamlash and Brodick until 1872, but lack of suitable landing facilities meant that both passengers and cargo had to be transhipped to smaller vessels at both ends of the route until the wooden piers were erected.

She was followed by the *Lady Mary*, from the same builders in 1868, built for the Duke of Hamilton's Commissioners for the Ardrossan to Arran route. It is recorded that she proved so popular that by 1870 traffic indicated the need for a larger and faster vessel to cope. This resulted in 1871 with the arrival of the 271-GT, iron-hulled steam paddle boat *Heather Bell*, with 2 cylinder single diagonal type propulsion, yet another Blackwood and Gordon built vessel, owned by Sir C.E. Scott, Bart. Reputed to be speedy but uneconomical she was sold after just a few seasons on the crossing, and served off the coast of southern England until 1903. The shipbuilders had taken the *Lady Mary* in part exchange for the replacement and had, in turn, sold it to a Mr Watson of Skelmorlie, and the Commissioners were forced to charter her back for service on her old route for a couple of years before she was again sold to the Marquis of Bute in 1873.

Captain W. Buchanan, the Clyde shipping magnate, operated the 1865-built *Rothesay Castle*, a 61.87 m long, 5.86 m beam, iron paddle steamer, constructed by Henderson Coulborn and Co. of Renfrew, on the crossing between 1874 and 1878, and then had the *Brodick Castle* specifically built by H. McIntyre & Company of Paisley, for the Arran crossing in 1878. *Brodick Castle* was a 283-GT iron paddle steamer, fitted with the single diagonal engines transplanted from the 1864-built *Eagle*, and was the largest ferry used on this route up to that time. Alas the combination of old engines and large size did not work; *Brodick Castle* proved an uneconomical ship and by 1887 had been sold out.

The *Ivanhoe* was a 282-GT paddle steamer built in 1880 by D. & W. Henderson and Co. She was 68.65 m overall and had a beam of 6.75 m. Engines were 2-cylinder diagonal oscillating 2×43-inch in a single working crank. She was built for the Frith (*sic*) of Clyde Steam Packet Company and was used by them to ply to Arran via the Kyles, being managed by Captain James Williamson. In 1892 she was fitted with new boilers and then chartered out before returning to Scotland in 1897 as part of the Clyde Steam Packet fleet and served throughout the First World War before being scrapped.

The Caledonian Steam Packet Company Limited appeared on the route in 1890 with the 553-GT, 76.2 m long, and 9.14 m beamed paddle steamer *Duchess of Hamilton*, built by William Denny & Bros and captained by Robert Morrison. She had the capacity to carry 1,780 passengers for which she had a huge saloon, and full promenade deck. Her arrival coincided with the opening of the Lanarkshire and Ayrshire Railway and she was, by contrast to her immediate forebears on the route, such a success that she stayed in service here until 1906. Another new vessel for this company was the smaller 295-GT, 61 m overall, with a 7.31 m beam, *Marchioness of Lorne*. She was engined by Rankin and Blackmore of Greenock, with 4-cylinder triple-expansion two crank diagonal. She had to be re-boilered in 1897 and was mainly used for winter service on the Arran route then as a summer excursions boat in the high summer seasons between 1891 and the outbreak of the First World War when she was taken over by the Royal Navy for minesweeping and base duties in the Mediterranean, before being scrapped in 1923.

Their fierce rivals, the Glasgow and South Western Railway Company, had the 241-GT Paddle steamer *Glen Sannox* built and engined by J. & G. Thomson, on Clydebank in 1892, as part of the cut-throat competition of the time as a direct challenger to the *Duchess of Hamilton*. She proved to be a speedy (19.23 knot) vessel as well as being one of the largest in the country at the time. She proved popular and, apart from a very brief requisitioning by the Royal Navy in 1915, she remained in service right through the First World War and until 1925, when she was sold and scrapped. The same company's *Glen Rosa* was a paddle steamer of 306-GT, with a large passenger capacity of 1,035 and again

Caledonian Isles is one of Caledonian MacBrayne's largest vessels. (© Dave Greer)

principally employed as the winter period mail steamer to Arran, remarkably surviving until 1938 before being laid up and scrapped a year later. Finally the G&SWR had the 486-GT twin-screw, turbine steamer *Atlanta* built by John Brown & Co, Clydebank in 1906 at a cost of £21,000. She was built around her Denny/Parsons turbines; a kind of trial set for the trans-Atlantic giant liner *Lusitania*, and, as a result, featured an extra wide beam. She was used on the winter mail service from Ardrossan to Arran but was not really satisfactory; she rolled heavily in these conditions, and her boilers were replaced after only a brief period to induce better speed for this service. She was used for mine-sweeping by the Royal Navy during the First World War and soldiered on until 1936 and even saw further war service during the Second World War before going to the breakers in 1947.

Although not a regular on the crossing, the 394-GT Glasgow & South Western Railway Company paddle steamer *Jupiter* significantly carried the first motor car to Arran in 1897, the precursor of what was to become the ferries' mainstay cargo.

Meanwhile Caledonian SPC had introduced the *Duchess of Argyll*, a very large turbine powered paddle steamer of 593-GT built by William Denny & Bros at Dumbarton in 1906. She had a best speed of 21 knots. Between 1906 and 1915 she sailed the Arran to Ardrossan route until requisitioned by the Royal Navy as a cross-Channel troop transport. She saw subsequent service elsewhere, lasting as an Admiralty test facility at Portland as late as 1970. A close-sister to the *Duchess*, also a 21-knotter and christened as the new *Glen Sannox*, appeared on the scene in 1925; a turbine steamer also built by William Denny & Bros, Dumbarton, she had three Parsons geared turbines and a GT of 664. She was actually built for the LMS Railway but transferred to the Caledonian Steam Packet Company in 1935. She operated on the Ardrossan to Arran service in the summer months carrying passengers on her long promenade decks and cars below during peak periods, and mixed cargo, including cattle and sheep at other times. She was also used as a troop transport during the Second World War and was eventually sold in 1954.

The London, Midland & Scottish Railway Company, who actually owned the Caledonian Steam Packet Company, decided that there was a need to reinforce the *Glen Sannox* with her limited capacity and replace the aging *Atlanta* on the Ardrossan to Arran route and commissioned the shipbuilding firm of Fairfield, Govan, to come up with the answer to both quandaries. The result was the *Marchioness of Graham* which appeared in 1936. She was a 500-GT twin-screw passenger/cargo carrying steamer and specifically designed with car space from the onset. She was fitted with 8-cylinder 4Sa steam turbine engines, German-built, supplied by Masch Augsburg-Nurnberg and which gave her a 15-knot speed. She had an overall length of 67 m, a beam of 10 m and a 2.74 m draught. Pre-war she briefly served on the Arran crossing but post-war only conducted intermittent back-up services on this route until withdrawn in 1958 and sold abroad.

With Caledonian Steam Packet company expansion and impending metamorphosis into Caledonian MacBrayne, a dedicated Arran ferry was required due to the boom in post-war motoring which revitalized the Western Island routes beyond the capacity of the then existing vessels to maintain, a pattern that has constantly repeated itself since. The 1,269-GT vehicle ferry *Glen Sannox* had an overall length of 78 m, a beam of 14 m and a 2 m draught. Built in the Ailsa shipyard at Troon in 1957, at a cost of £468,000, she was powered by Swiss-built, Sulzer Bros Winterthur 2 Oil 2SCSA 8-cylinder diesel engines, which gave her a speed of 16 knots. She had a bow rudder for manoeuvrability and side lifts, with a car capacity of 55, which at the time was deemed excessive! She featured a large 7-ton crane astern, which proved largely a redundant feature in usual practice, had an open main cargo deck, high headroom for larger vehicles, a satisfying large, squat funnel, with piled-up superstructure forward with commodious seating, lounges and even a tea room. She could claim to carry over her more than a thousand passengers with a good degree of immunity from the unpredictable Minches weather, despite the absence of stabilizers.

She conducted her maiden voyage on 29 June 1957, and by mid-July had largely replaced the *Marchioness of Graham*, the *Jupiter* and *Clyde* and also the Campbeltown Shipping Company's *Kildonan* on the route. She had various modifications made during her long and illustrious career, but was eventually replaced on the route in 1970 by the *Caledonia*, and (disastrously) converted for cruising before being sold abroad.

The *Caledonia* had been built by A/S Langesuns Mek Versted, at Langesund, in Norway, in 1966 for the Stena Line as a basic Ro-Ro vehicle ferry and employed on the route London to Scandinavia, with the name *Stena Baltica* and was taken over by the Caledonian Steam Packet Company in 1970, being extensively modified by Scott Lithgow, Greenock. As the Caledonia she made history by being the first drive-through ferry operating on the Clyde, but, even so, her car capacity of 40 proved far too small for the Isle of Arran crossing. In the summer months the old *Clansman* had to replace her, and she was transferred during that time to the Mull route. Finally she was withdrawn totally in 1982, and six years later was sold abroad and again re-named as *Heidi*, being finally broken up in 2005. The *Clansman* herself was a David MacBrayne hoist-loader car ferry built by Hall, Russell & Company, Aberdeen, with power plant by Crossley Brothers, Manchester, comprising two SCSA 8-cylinder engines which gave a 14 knots best speed. She was completed in 1964, making her maiden voyage in June, and was of 1,420-GT, had an overall length of 71.6 m, a beam of 14 m and a 2.7 m draught, one of three near-sisters. She could carry 50 cars. The hoist, turntable and side-lift arrangement proved awkward and slow, so in 1972 she was converted to a drive-through vessel with bow and stern ramps, which involved a 11 m increase in her length, the fitting of a bow-thruster and twin rudders, higher headroom and other internal improvements. She operated various routes and only served on the Ardrossan to Arran crossing between 1982 and 1984 before being replaced by the *Isle of Arran* because of major mechanical failures and was sold abroad. This new vessel proved far more successful and serviced the Arran journey for nine years, but in 1993 she in turn was replaced by the current ferry, although she is still in service on another route.

Current Operators, Ships and Details

Caledonian Isles (IMO 9051284) at 5,221-GT, a length of 94.3 m, breadth of 15.8 m and a draught of 3.2 m is one of the biggest ships of the CalMac flotilla. She is a steel Double Screw Motor Vessel (DSMV) that was built in 1993 by Richards Shipbuilders, Lowestoft, Suffolk, being christened by the *Princess Royal*, and with engine supplied by Mirrlees Blackstone Ltd, of Stockport, Cheshire and has a top speed of 15 knots. She is well equipped and is fitted with a Caterpillar Diesels 700 bhp bow thruster to aid manoeuvring in confined harbour space. With bow and stern watertight ramps giving Ro-Ro loading access via a Linkspan, nominally she has a totally enclosed 110-car capacity plus 10 trucks. She has two hoistable mezzanine decks to port and to starboard as extensions, and when both are deployed her car capacity is 25 lane meters in addition to 99 car-only spaces. Her passenger capacity is 1,000 and she has a crew of 26.

On board facilities include the observation lounge and recliner seating and a TV lounge plus an open air deck area. For refreshment there is the Mariners cafeteria with catering for most tastes including special vegetarian and children's menus, the Coffee Cabin, which in addition to beverages and light snacks also dispenses newspapers and periodicals. The Still is an onboard bar which in addition to a range of

23: Ardrossan – Arran

The *Caledonian Isles* (Gaelic – *Eileanan Chaledonia*) operates a five-crossing schedule on the Ardrossan to Brodick (Isle of Arran) run which takes just under 1 hour and is one of the most popular tourist and day tripper CalMac routes. On Friday nights during the summer season there is an additional late round trip crossing leaving Ardrossan at 20.30.

The ferry terminal at Winton Pier, Ardrossan has over 500 paid car parking spaces both long term and short term with just three disabled spaces. There is a car check time of at least 30 minutes prior to departure. The rail station is within a short distance. The 65-seat waiting room has toilets, disabled facilities and baby changing but little else. At Brodick Pier there are paid car parks, both long and short term, including three disabled spaces. There is a 30-minute check-in time prior to departure. The train is a one minute walk away, with a bus stop nearby and a taxi rank at the foot of the gangway. The 65-seat waiting room has toilets and disabled toilets and a baby-changing area.

Contact Details
Caledonian MacBrayne, Ferry Terminal Building, The Harbour, Ardrossan, Ayrshire, KA22 8ED
Tel: 01294 463470
Fax: 01294 601063
Email: david.cannon@calmac.co.uk
Web: www.calmac.co.uk

Caledonian Isles alongside at Ardrossan. (© Dave Greer)

whisky and local ales has coffee and light snacks. Teenagers are catered for at Game-On, an arcade with video games and quiz machines, while younger passengers have Cub Club, a supervised juvenile play zone and there is a baby-changing area. There is a wheelchair access lift and a special disabled toilet. For the family friend there is also a dedicated pet area.

24: Oban – Tiree – Coll – Lochhosidale – Castlebay – Islay – South Uist – Skye – North Uist – Tarbert

Background

Long before the unfortunate Jacobite Pretender Charles Edward Stuart was conveyed 'over the sea to Skye' equally valuable cargoes and persons had for many years made the short passages from mainland Scotland to the Hebridean Isles and had also made both commercial and covert crossings between the scattered communities. While today the 'Bonnie Prince' would most likely have been smuggled away from the searching Redcoats concealed in a truck across the Skye bridge, for many others in the twenty-first century the little ferries that continue to ply these, often dangerous, waters are still a major life-line and essential service, even in these days of universal air travel. The Hebridean ferries still constitute 'The road to the Isles.'

Perhaps the most ancient such sea passage was that linking the world with Iona (*Chaluim Chille*) where Saint Columba founded the monastery in 563 after exile from Ireland and which became a famous seat of learning and brought scholars and mystics alike to the tiny island. The sea passage from Oban or across from Mull, were much-used down the centuries, from the marauding and pillaging Vikings of Magnus Barelegs and Haakon, to the burial parties of many Scottish and Irish Kings at Rèilig Odhrain as well as providing the continuous link that kept monk and pilgrim alike fed and catered for. Today the traditional small boats are as much in use as ever, but now they take tourists to Fingal's Cave at Staffa, or for bird, seal and whale watching and sea angling, as much as anything else.

Ancient ferry houses abound, still giving positive memory links back to the 1700s when locals and early visitors from the south, like Doctor Samuel Johnson and his companion James Boswell in 1773, found much to wonder at and admire in the remote communities. The beginnings

CalMac's *Finlaggan* against a typical Hebridean backdrop. (© Dave Greer)

24: Oban – Tiree – Coll – Lochhosidale – Castlebay – Islay – South Uist – Skye – North Uist – Tarbert

Loch Striven against a wintry Highland backdrop. (© Dave Greer)

of regular ferry crossings began long before this period, and continually spread with ports like Ullapool (which did not exist prior 1788) becoming major ports in the region in a very short time scale. With the arrival of steam at sea with the little *Comet*, individual ownership companies ran paddle steamers on an *ad hoc* basis to many of the Western Isles during the early 1800s. One of these owners was William Campbell, an Islay man who ran a pioneering service between Isla, Skye, Iona and Staffa to West Loch Tarbert from 1825 with the *Maid of Islay*. By the middle of the century, however, many of these had been absorbed into the G. & J. Burns empire of companies, which, in turn, were sold to David Hutcheson & Company, one of whom, David MacBrayne took over in 1879. Under this succession of thrusting businessmen a whole network of steam sea services spread up the Hebridean chains.

Paddle steamers of the early Victorian age are represented by such ships as the 229-GT *Mountaineer*, built for David Hutcheson in 1852 by J. & G. Thomson. She was distinguished by a long flush deck and a wide passenger lounge. She gave sterling service for thirty-seven years, initially on the Ardrishaig passage and then working out of Oban to Iona and further afield. She was lengthened twice in her long life but ran aground and broke in half off Oban in 1989.

The railway boom of the nineteenth century mainly confined itself to the mainland ports, only the Island of Mull actually having its own rail line, while the proposed Dingwall to Skye Railway, as just one example, ended at Strome Ferry in 1870. A decade later the Glasgow to Oban rail link reached Oban, while the Callander and Oban Railway opened the Connel Ferry station in 1880. Another decade on and it had pushed on to Ballachulish, while the proposed Hebridean Light Railway Company down from Uig would have had a terminal at Isleornsay, at the southern tip of Skye, but, this was never built. This extension of reach via the steam paddle boats saw a flowering of ferry services at that later period.

The existing ferry operators, gained the contracts to carry the mail from these railheads out to the islands, and this became a lucrative operation. They also operated the so-called 'Royal Route' between Tarbert and Ardrishaig and the most famous of all such paddlers was the 602-GT *Columba*, built by J. & G. Thomson for David MacBrayne in 1878, and whose attributes included her own onboard post office.

More typical of the paddle steamers of this era was the 357-GT *Grenadier*, built on the Clyde for MacBrayne by J. & G. Thomson for service on the Oban to Iona and Staffa summer route and then running the mail service to Ardrishaig in winter. She had an overall length of 222.9 m, a beam of 7.035 m and a 9.276 m draught. She served as the minesweeper HMS *Grenade* during the First World War but was burnt out at Oban in 1927.

The 241-GT paddle steamer *Pioneer* was built by A. & J. Inglis, Pointhouse, Glasgow in 1905, for David MacBrayne, specifically to carry the Royal Mail to Islay, and had a speed of 14 knots. She made her maiden voyage in April of that year and served Gigha, Jura, then Port Ellen and Port Askaig with five weekly passages, until 1939 when she moved to Oban.

In the aftermath of the First World War the brief period prior to the Wall Street crash saw some resumption in passenger traffic for which turbine ships like the 796-GT *King George V* were built to cater for in addition to the mail service. Built by William Denny and Brothers at Dumbarton in 1926, she was innovative in that she had no less than seven Parsons Marine turbines, which, with two high-pressure boilers, gave her a speed of 16 knots but quite a lot of problems and she required re-boilering twice. She had an overall length of 79.4 m, a 9.8 m beam and a draught of 2.1 m. She could carry 1,432 passengers. Her owners were Turbine Steamers Limited, before being absorbed by David MacBrayne in 1935. She survived the Second World War and she

24: Oban – Tiree – Coll – Lochhosidale – Castlebay – Islay – South Uist – Skye – North Uist – Tarbert

The Caledonian MacBrayne *Clansman* stern loading at the massive concrete pier at Barra Island. (© Dave Greer)

The TSMV *Western Isles* approaching beautiful Inverie across Loch Nevis.
(© Undiscovered Scotland)

served on the Oban to Iona (Staffa ceased being a port of call by 1967) journey as late as the 1970s and was not finally scrapped until 1984.

The paddle steamers lasted a long while in the Western Isles but gradually modern types were introduced to replace them. One well-known vessel on the 'between-the-wars' run between Ayr, Troon and Ardrossan was the 795-GT *Duchess of Hamilton*. She was built for the Caledonian Steam Packet Company in 1932 by Harland & Wolff, Govan and was powered by twin-screw, triple direct-drive turbine engines which gave her a speed of 18 knots. She took over from the old *Juno* and served until 1939 After being used as a wartime troopship, she continued service from Larne and was not finally withdrawn from service until 1970.

During the war the 1939-built *Lochiel* ran the West Loch Tarbert to Port Ellen and Port Askaig, Islay passenger service. She was built for David MacBrayne by William Denny, and was of 577-GT, with an overall length of 55.95 m, a beam of 9.78 m and a 2.31 m draught. Her engines were two 8-cylinder Paxman-Ricardo diesels driving twin three-bladed propellers for 12 knots and she could carry 600 passengers. She was joined post-war by a sister, *Loch Seafort*, but was taken out of service in 1970 and scrapped in 1995.

Post the Second World War the Royal Mail service to the Inner Isles from Oban was initially serviced by the 1947-built *Loch Seaforth*, a 1,126-GT vessel first used on the Stornoway route. She was holed on a rock between Coll and Tiree in March 1973 and, although salvaged and brought into harbour, was subsequently broken up. The Inner Islands mail service to Barra, Call, Mull, South Uist and Tiree was taken up by the MacBrayne vessel *Claymore*. She was built in 1955, and proved the last of the conventional ferries constructed for the company. Of 1,024-GT, she was 58.52 m overall length and could carry 500 passengers. As such she served for twenty years, being one of those ships retained when the company became Caledonian MacBrayne in 1973, before she was sold to Greece in 1976.

What was to prove to be a second flowering was initiated by the arrival of the new breed of car ferries, the first of which was the 2,104-GT *Hebrides*, launched from the shipyard of Hall, Russell in 1963. This ship and her two sisters, *Clansman* and *Columba*, still used the hydraulic lift and side-ramp methods of loading, methods that were slow and clumsy, but had the merit (as the operators and Government

Small ferries such as *Loch Striven* provide an essential lifeline to remote island communities. (© Dave Greer)

The *Isle of Mull* in harbour. (© Alastair Gardiner)

viewed it) of not requiring much in the way of modernization of the embarkation ports themselves. In fact, *Hebrides* and her ilk were quickly to prove themselves obsolete by their own success and the Ro-Ro concept soon foresaw their demise. Also, revolutionary as they seemed, she and her kind had actually been pre-dated by thirty years by the car ferry service that operated across the Kylerhea Narrows from Glenelg since 1934, but which was interrupted by the war. (Happily a community-owned ferry still maintains this 550 m crossing during the summer months. In fact, during the winter of 2011–2012 the Glenelg ferry was brought out of winter retirement to cover a temporary route from South to North Stromeferry on Loch Carron due to a landslide on the main road.)

In October 1953 the first free passenger and vehicular ferry in Scotland opened between Luing Island across Cuan Sound. The post-war booming of car ownership opened new avenues of tourism to the Western Isles, as had the coming of the railways a century earlier. However, although the car brought welcome finance, it also brought with it more urban customs that did not sit well with the islanders themselves, like the violation of the hitherto sacred observance of the Sabbath, which as late as 2006 the citizens of Lewis and Harris were fighting a hard rearguard action to maintain, in spite of mounting commercial pressure. Even the opening of the Skye Bridge in 1995 failed to dent the continuing popularity of the ferries, despite dire warnings to the contrary, but right up to today the Government funding of these services remains a constant battlefield in times of shrinking coffers and ruthless pruning of subsidies.

Juno (IMO 7341063), *Jupiter* (IMP 7341051) and *Saturn* (IMO 7615490), were, until recently the three oldest vessels in the CalMac fleet. The former was scrapped at Rosneath between May and July 2011; the *Jupiter* was sold for scrapping, also in 2011, leaving just the *Saturn* forlornly awaiting her fate at Rosneath at the time of writing. They were commonly known as *Streakers* and were introduced in the 1970s on the Clyde estuary as Roll-on/Roll-off services began via Linkspans at Gourock and Wemyss Bay. They were Steel DSMVs and had a stern ramp which led into a open car deck concentrated aft, with twin funnels on either side along with a gantry-style mast, known as a 'tetrapod'; while the bridge, passenger and crew accommodation were all to the fore end of the vessel. On either side of the ship at the forward end of the car deck were additional, and wider, vehicle ramps able to accommodate trucks.

The growth of the Ro-Ro can be typified by Uig which, prior to 1964, was not considered a ferry port. The arrival in 1964 of the *Hebrides* changed all that and she served through until 1985 when the 62-car capacity *Hebridean Isles* took over operations. Since 2001 a new *Hebrides*, with a car capacity enhanced to 98 vehicles, now runs a 105-minute route to Lochmaddy and back, two to three times daily.

Current Operators and Routes

Caledonian Macbrayne (or CalMac as it is more popularly known) is by far and away the largest ferry operator in Scotland and runs a fleet of thirty-two ships of various types, which connects the mainland with twenty-two of West Coast islands. There is also, since 2006, a subsidiary, NorthLink Ferries Limited, which is covered separately in this book, although both are part of the David MacBrayne Group (DML) and responsible to the Scottish Parliament's First Minister to provide a good reliable service to the outlying island communities, known as lifeline ferry services. As few of the routes it operates are profitable in themselves the company receives some support from the Scottish Government. The restructuring of October 2006 saw Caledonian MacBrayne renamed Caledonian Maritime Assets Ltd (CMAL) who own all the ships of the fleet, and these vessels are leased to, and operated by, CalMac Ferries Ltd (CMF). Both companies are wholly owned by Scottish Ministers. Caledonian MacBrayne and CalMac remain as the trading names of CalMac Ferries Ltd.

Argyle (IMO 9365178) is a 2,612-GT, steel-built, DSMV, constructed on the Motlawa River by Stocznia Remontowa at Gdansk, Poland in 2006 at a cost of £9 million pounds and which entered service in May 2007. She is a half-sister to the *Bute* but slightly modified internally with second car deck lift and enlarged passenger accommodation, and has an overall length of 72 m, a breadth of 15.3 m and a draught of 4.2 m. She can carry 450 passengers and 60 cars and she has a crew of 10. She has both bow and stern access plus a car ramp situated towards the stern on the starboard side as the port-of-call at the Rothesay end initially lacked full Ro-Ro provision, but the end-loading Linkspan at Rothesay, also built by Remontowa in December 2007, obviated the need for this facility. She is powered by two MAK engines and has a top speed of 14 knots. Facilities include two internal lounges separated by a kiosk and toilet area, while the upper deck has seating between the funnels to abaft the bridge.

Argyle (in Gaelic *Earra-Ghàidheal*) is currently employed on the Upper Clyde Wemyss Bay to Rothesay crossing which is of approximately 35 minutes duration. The Rothesay ferry terminal has a 35-seat waiting

24: Oban – Tiree – Coll – Lochhosidale – Castlebay – Islay – South Uist – Skye – North Uist – Tarbert

The *Argyle* of the Caledonian MacBrayne fleet in Wemyss Bay, November 2009. (© Peter McCann)

room with toilets, disabled toilets and a public telephone, but no baby-changing facilities, vending machines or ATM. There is no car parking other than paid parking in the town itself.

Bute (IMO 9319741) was one of two Class IV Pax/Ro-Ro ferries built in Poland to an enlarged specification to replace the 1970s built *Streaker* class vessels which only had a 40 car capacity. The new pair of vessels, of which *Bute* was the lead ship, increased car stowage by a third. Constructed by Stocznia Remontowa at the Northern Shipyard at Gdansk, she is powered by a pair of MAK engines, the after 8M20 engine developing 1,520 kW at 1,000 rpm (2,038HP) and the forward 6M20 engine developing 1,140 kW at 1,000 rpm (1,528 HP), with twin Disc Slipping clutch gearboxes, 3000-6-HD aft and 3000-3-HD forward. Her propulsion is via Azimuth thrusters with aft Schottel twin Propeller, STP 12/12, and forward Schottel twin propeller STP 10/10. She has as her main generators two Scania D1 12 15 of 200 kW apiece at 1,500 rpm and a SISU Diesel 634 DSBIG 130 kW at 1,500 rpm as an emergency backup. This outfit gives the *Bute* a top speed of 14 knots. *Bute*'s car capacity is currently 60, and passenger capacity 450 with a basic crew of 10, with some shift reliefs. The passenger areas include onboard TVs linked to the ship's Sat TV system, there are toilet facilities and the central café dispenses tea, coffee and other beverages as well as soup, sandwiches, fruit and cake.

The *Bute*, (her Gaelic name is *Eilean Bhoid*) sailed on her maiden voyage on 11 July 2005, relieving the twenty-eight-year-old *Saturn* on this 35-minute crossing.

Clansman (IMO 9158953) is a near-sister to the *Hebrides* and was built in 1998 on the Torridge River estuary by the then Appledore Shipbuilders, Devon and was built as a specific replacement for the aging *Lord of the Isles* to work from Oban to Castlebay, Lochboisdale and Coll, Tiree routes but was still too large to service Tobermory. Of 5,499-GT, she is 99 m overall, with a beam of 15.8 m and a 3.22 m draught. *Clansman* (Gaelic – *Fear-Cinnidh*) is powered by a pair of MAK 8 M32 engines which give her a service speed of 16.5 knots. She is equipped with two Electric Ulstein bow thrusters of 90TV, each 7 tonnes thrust. Her passenger capacity is 638 served by a crew of 28. She can carry up to 90 cars on her main vehicle deck, and 9 trucks, but she also has a starboard adjustable mezzanine deck which, when in place, can stow a further 10. There are two rigid lifeboats, one RIB fast rescue craft, a rigid launch and inflatable life-rafts. She made her maiden voyage on 4 July 1998.

147

The Caledonian MacBrayne ferry *Clansman*, seen here making speed in 2009. (© Dave Greer)

On-board facilities include an observation lounge, a recliner lounge and a TV Lounge and since 2003 her deck area has been extended also. The usual CalMac amenities for their larger vessels include Mariners cafeteria with a wide range of menus including vegetarian and children's choices, and the Coffee Cabin which also serves snacks. There is Shop@CalMac for souvenirs and essentials alike, Game-On for Teens, Cub Club for juniors and a dedicated pet area. The afloat mobility impaired facilities include lift access for wheelchair users and a disabled toilet.

The *Clansman* currently operates services to Coll and Tiree, but additionally has a six-days-a-week service to Barra and a weekly service to Lochboisdale. During the winter months she operates as relief vessel for Arran, Lewis, Mull and the Uig area.

At Castlebay ferry terminal the 20-seat waiting room has toilets and disabled toilets, but no baby-changing facilities. There is some free car parking near the terminal building itself and a bus stop within 200 m. The Tiree ferry terminal has disabled toilets, access and baby-changing facilities. There is no public telephone, ATM or vending machine but there is free car parking. There is a taxi rank 2 minutes walk away. The Royal Incorporation of Architects in Scotland (RIAS) in 2003 dubbed the building the 'best new building in Scotland', while the locals were rather more reserved in their judgement, it being described by them as 'two walls and a telephone box with no phone'.

Coruisk (IMO 9274836) is a 1,599-GT Ro-Ro vehicle ferry of a new type known as sheltered water vessels (as distinct from sea-going) for summer operations in the Sound of Sleat and winter relief work in the Upper Clyde, replacing the existing *Pioneer*. She is fitted with both bow and stern ramps, the former protected by an open visor, but with an additional side ramp to port forward, so that she can be employed at some Clydeside piers at Wemyss Bay and Rothesay which have more restricted facilities. New European regulations came into force around the time of her design which called for a 5.1 m car deck clearance for vehicles and that the car decks be higher out of the water, and with the two passenger decks added on top she presents a very tall, ungainly appearance.

Another product of the Devon yard of Appledore Shipbuilders, she cost £6,750,000 when she was completed in 2003. Of 65 m length and 14 m beam she has a draught of 3.05 m. She is powered by two 6M20 engines rated at 1,000 kW at 1,000 rpm, and propelled by two Schottel SPT 1010 rudder propellers. These rotating pods to which the propellers are attached, (Azipods) give combined steering and propulsion which in theory should result in better manoeuvrability. She is also fitted with stabilizers and her power plant gives her a maximum speed of 14 knots. She has a passenger capacity of 249 and space for

40 vehicles. She has an overall length of 65 m, a 14 m beam and a draught of 3.05 m

The *Coruisk* made her maiden voyage on 10 August 2003 but almost immediately suffered technical problems, and then on 24 August, she lost one Azipod when a loss of power and steering saw her scrape a reef off Mallaig harbour. It was winter before she was deemed fit for service once more. Her high superstructure caused some difficulties in windy conditions and there was the need for several modifications, including detachable 'lugs' fitted for operations with the new electrically-operated gangways introduced at the piers at Wemyss Bay and Rothesay, and modified upper decking and accommodation.

The passenger facilities on the *Coruisk* include a seated table area, with the Coffee Cabin serving hot beverages and alcohol, as well as light snacks, and a retail area for newspapers, souvenirs and the like. There are toilets, including a mobility impaired unit and there is also a baby-changing facility. With the current enormous cost of petrol, the fact that the Skye Road Bridge is now toll-free has not dramatically affected the popularity of the ferry which can compare favourably in terms of time.

The *Coruisk* (Gaelic – *Coir 'Usig*), is currently employed on the Mallaig to Armadale summer route, with a single journey time of approximately 25 minutes, where she operates eight services daily between Monday and Saturday with a reduced five trip service on Sundays between 1 May and 25 September. She also acts as a relief vessel in the Clyde in winter months when she in turn is relieved by the *Lochnevis*.

Armadale ferry terminal has a 24-seat waiting room, disabled facilities, toilets and a baby-changing area; there is bench seating with a bus stop 2 minutes walk away. There is limited paid parking in the Council car park but no dedicated disabled parking places. There is a 30-min check-in time prior to departure.

Eigg (IMO 7340411) is one of the four surviving vessels of the eight-strong Small Island class of basic passenger car ferries, built by James Lamont & Company at Port Glasgow in 1975. Their design was a simple one, influenced by the Landing Craft Mechanized (LCM-7) built for the Royal Navy between 1943 and 1944 which could carry a single 40-ton tank or 60 troops and put them ashore on enemy-held beaches, but refined for mercantile usage. As such she is equipped with a double-jointed bow ramp, which itself has a ventral protection bar below it, with a gantry carrying the mainmast. This gives access to an open vehicle deck of 12 lane meters, a turntable, and, extreme aft, the bridge

The tiny *Eigg* is based on military landing craft designs. (© Dave Greer)

with funnel, engine exhaust and radar mast located above a small sheltered passenger space. Designed to service small landing slips on little-used routes they were cheap to build, run and service. They required only small custom-built slipways or firm shelving beaches to load and unload either passengers, vehicles or livestock. After initial use of the first pair, the type was lengthened by 1.524 metres and later the wheelhouse was raised by several metres to give better visibility.

Her power plant was originally twin M6cy 300 bhp diesel engines supplied by English Electric Diesels, Kelvin, Glasgow, but she was re-engined by Timbacraft, Shandon, on Gare Loch, with Scania D9 93M35 turbocharged 6-cylinder diesels, which give her a best speed of 8 knots. She is a Class IV, VI and VIA vessel and is of 69-GT, having an overall length of 22.5 m, a beam of 6.4 m and a draught of 1.40 m. She has capacity for 75 passengers with space for 5 cars and has a crew of 3. She made her first voyage on 25 February 1975 and despite her age is currently still one of the last pair remaining in use with CalMac. Her facilities are necessarily limited, being confined to a small passenger lounge and a toilet, space precluding anything grander. All but two of these vessels have been phased out with the introduction of the Loch class ships, although two others remain in use, but serving other masters.

Eigg (Gaelic – *Eilean Eige*) is currently still employed on the Oban to Achnacroish (on the south-east side of the Island of Lismore) crossing, a journey time of approximately 1 hour. The summer timetable currently runs across Loch Linnhe from 25 March to 22 October, with four crossings daily on Monday–Saturday with an extra Request crossing on Saturdays, and two crossings on Sundays.

Finlaggan (IMO 9482902) is one of the newest ships in the CalMac fleet. Caledonian Maritime Assets Limited announced the order for a Ro-Ro Euro Class B, vehicle/passenger ferry built to serve the Isle of Islay. She was built in the Remontowa shipyard at Gdansk, Poland and

Finlaggan is one of the newest of the Caledonian MacBrayne fleet. (© Dave Greer)

was launched in the summer of 2010, and following a week of sea trials, was delivered in May 2011. She is of 5,209-GT, has an overall length of 89.9 m and a draught of 3.4 m. Her total cost is £24.5 million and she is being financed by a loan from the Scottish Government with interest and capital repayments being made by CMAL. She has a passenger capacity of 550 and room for 85 cars, or the equivalent trucks or coaches. Power is from two Wartsilla 8L32 at 4,000 kW at 750 rpm which gives her a top speed of 16.5 knots. She is fully fitted with stabilizers. As part of the same improvement package Kennacraig Pier on the Mull of Kintyre has been upgraded by the fitting of a £3.44 million new berthing dolphin by Granham Construction, plus repairs to the existing sheet piled walls, re-proofing of the fixed concrete ramp, and upgraded fuelling facilities, water supply and lighting. There is a 25-seat waiting room with toilets and disabled toilets, baby-changing, vending machines and public telephone, but no ATM. There is a 150-space free car park with three dedicated disabled places, with a nearby bus stop. There is a 30-minute minimum check-in time prior departure.

The MV *Finlaggan* (Gaelic – *Fionnlagain*) has all the usual CalMac facilities, including three passenger decks, an observation lounge, recliner seating, a quiet lounge, restaurant, shop, children's play area, large areas of external fixed seating, with two lifts serving the mobility impaired passengers. She operates the service between Port Ellen on Leodamas Bay, Islay and Kennacraig.

Isle of Cumbrae (IMO 8219554) is a 201-GT Steel DSMV Ro-Ro Car Ferry built by Ailsa Shipbuilding Ltd, at Troon specifically for the Largs to Cumbrae crossing, a route which she operated for nine years, before moving to the Sound of Mull where she plied between Fishnish and Lochaline for a further eleven years, later briefly working to the Kyles of Bute.

With a passenger capacity of 139 concentrated down her starboard side and a crew of 3, her three-lane car deck, with folding ramps fore

The Caledonian MacBrayne ferry *Isle of Cumbrae*. (© Peter McCann)

and aft, has space for 18 cars. She is 32 m overall with a beam of 10 m and a 1.4 m draught. She has 6-cylinder Gardner Engines, with a pair of Voith Schneider Propellers which make for a best speed of 8.5 knots. She carries a single inflatable launch as well as life-rafts and made her maiden voyage on 4 April 1977.

The *Isle of Cumbrae* (Gaelic – *Eilean Chumraigh*) has since 1999 operated on the Tarbert on Loch Fyne route, working from a concrete slipway on East Loch Tarbert, Kintyre, to Portavadie, Cowal, on the eastern shore near Tighnabruaich, crossing Loch Fyne in just approximately 25 minutes. She runs an hourly service in the spring/summer schedules, with the *Loch Riddon* and other CalMac ferries relieving her during the winter, when services are fewer and include a run up to Lochranza, Arran.

Isle of Mull (IMO 8608339) is a passenger car ferry and still one of the larger vessels of the CalMac fleet. She was originally built in 1988 by Appledore Ferguson, Newark, Port Glasgow on the Clyde, and was designed for the Oban to Craignure, Isle of Mull crossing, although she also works between Oban and Colonsay, where she replaced the *Caledonia*. She is of 4,719-GT, and now has a 90.3 m overall length after being lengthened by 5.4 m by Tees Dockyard in an effort to overcome a 100-ton over-weight problem created by a British Steel computer system during the hull plating manufacture, and which had to be rectified shortly after her maiden voyage in April of that year. The work also required re-adapting her loading piers at her destination ports. She now has a beam of 15.8 m and a draught of 3.19 m. Her Diesel engines are of the Mirrlees Blackstone 8MB 275T type and give her a service speed of 15 knots. She was launched by Princess Alexandra, The Hon. Lady Ogilvy on 8 December 1987, was refurbished ten years later then underwent a third embellishment in 2005, setting what is now the CalMac standard for range of facilities which have been adopted by the majority of the larger ships of the company.

Her current amenities include, on Deck 3, the Mariners cafeteria, the Shop@CalMac, the Still Bar, as well as a TV lounge and recliner lounge, Game-On area, with the usual pets area and baby-changing area, while on Deck 4 there is the Coffee Cabin and the observation lounge. Toilets are on both decks as are mobility impaired facilities, while the *Mull* is famous for the impressive extent of open-air seating.

At Craignure ferry terminal the 8-seat waiting room has no amenities but adjacent to the terminal there are toilets, disabled toilets and a public telephone, while 50 m away at the local Post Office there is an ATM, but there are no baby-changing facilities or vending machines. There are sixteen pay-and-display car parking slots, with two dedicated disabled spaces. There is a bus stop 30 m distant and a taxi rank.

Isle of Mull (Gaelic – *An T-Eilean Muileach*) has a passenger capacity of 968 passengers, spread across two decks, and accommodation for her 28-strong crew and a fully-enclosed car deck that, after modifications, reduced her accommodation to 70 cars and 20 trucks, for which she has 4.7 m headroom. Vehicles embark/disembark via folding stern and bow ramps that open out onto the Linkspan, and the bow has a protective visor. For safety she is equipped with three rigid boats, one RIB fast rescue craft as well as inflatable life rafts.

The Oban to Craignure summer crossing takes her approximately 46 minutes with currently six Monday sailings, seven Tuesday to Thursday sailings, seven Saturday sailings at different times, and four

The CalMac ferry *Isle of Mull* (© Alastair Gardiner)

24: Oban – Tiree – Coll – Lochhosidale – Castlebay – Islay – South Uist – Skye – North Uist – Tarbert

or five Sunday sailings, all of the above with some seasonal limitations which require carefully checking. There is a reduced service in the winter. At the time of writing there is an ongoing debate about a possible larger replacement vessel and consultation regarding a Mallaig to Lochboisdale to Barra route for which she may be deemed suitable.

Loch Alainn (IMO 9147722) is a 396-GT Steel DSMV built by Buckie Shipyard Ltd on the east of the Moray Firth, Aberdeenshire, and has an overall length of 43 m, a beam of 13.4 m and a draught of 1.73 m. Loosely based on the design of the smaller *Loch Bhrusda*, she is powered by a pair of Cummins KT38M Diesel engines, rated at 800HP at 1,800 rpm, which drive Voith Schneider propulsion units. These revolutionary systems feature axially paralleled vertical blades, rotating around inside a flush fitted casing, and can be directionally positioned from the bridge to give thrust in any direction across the whole spectrum. Ships thus equipped can almost spin around in their own length and make for versatility in confined waters, ideal for small and remote CalMac terminal operations.

Loch Alainn (Gaelic – *Loch Àlainn*) has an operating speed of 10 knots. She has a passenger capacity of 150, a crew of 4 and can carry 24 cars on her four-lane (each of 6 cars) open vehicle deck with her bridge structure suspended above. She has jointed-section bow and stern ramps for basic embarking/disembarking of vehicles onto concrete slipways. She is equipped with a single inflatable launch and life-rafts. She has strictly limited on-board facilities: just a single passenger lounge to starboard with on-deck fixed seating above, and toilets. She made her maiden voyage on July 1997 but suffered a number of engine failures and mishaps early in her career before she settled down and became reliable. She has served on various routes, mainly the Largs to Cumbrae slipway and later in the Outer Hebrides, based on the Sound of Barra in the summer and working as a Barra relief ship in the winter.

The approximately 40-minute crossing from Barra to Eriskay operates both a summer and winter service Monday to Sunday, with the latter being a request service not always operating, so checking is essential.

Loch Bhrusda (IMO 9129483) is a Ro-Ro car ferry. She was built by McTay Marine, Bromborough, Merseyside, to another modified Loch design adapted to operate in the shallow and hazard-strewn waters of the Sound of Harris between Otternish on North Uist and Leverburgh. This 246-GT ship has an overall length of 35.4 m, a beam of 10.8 m and a 1.4 m draught. She is powered by Cummins Diesels, which give her an operating speed of just 8 knots, and have saddled her with the reputation for being the nosiest ferry in the Highlands. She was the first CalMac ship to incorporate the SPU132 505 kW Schottel Water Pump Jet, which is an Azimuth thruster system that provides good manoeuvrability and does away with underwater extensions below the hull and is ideal for shallow water operations.

Loch Bhrusda (Gaelic – *Loch Bhrùsta*) has a passenger capacity of 150, a crew of 3 and vehicle deck with capacity for 18 cars. She entered service in June 1996, but the service she introduced proved so popular that in a short time she was deemed inadequate for purpose and was replaced by the purpose-built *Loch Portain* with twice her capacity, whereupon she was relocated to the Isle of Eriskay crossing to Ardmhor, Barra across the Sound of Barra. However, since 2007 when she was relieved by the *Loch Linnhe*, she has been reduced to the status of reserve ferry on the Clyde.

Loch Buie (IMO 9031375) is a Ro-Ro vehicle ferry with a tonnage of 295-GT and was built by a J.W. Miller & Sons Ltd, St. Monans [Monance], Fife. She is a cousin to the smaller 'Baby Loch' quartet of the late 1980s but she has an overall length of 30.2 m, a beam of 10 m and a 1.6 m draught. She is fitted with both bow ramp and an extended stern vehicle ramp and can convey 250 passengers with a crew of 4 and space on an open deck for a maximum of 9 cars in two lanes. She carries an inflatable launch and life-rafts. She was equipped with Swedish Volvo-Penta 6-cylinder diesel engines, and also fitted with two of the Voith-Schneider vertically-mounted rotary propellers for manoeuvrability. She has a speed of 9 knots and entered service in July 1992. She was built specifically to replace the *Morvern* on the crossing to Iona from Fionnphort, on St. Ronan's Bay, the Isle of Mull and here she has mainly stayed with only a few brief excursions elsewhere.

Her facilities include three passenger lounges, one either side of the bridge structure with a third straddling her bow deck, which restricts vehicle heights and deck seating above. This extra facility was built in as her passengers usually consist of an unusually large percentage of tourists and day-trippers, with the Nunnery and Abbey attracting 140,000 visitors and pilgrims annually.

Loch Buie (Gaelic – *Loch Buidhe*) continues to operate the daily mile-long, 10-minute, journey from Fionnphort, Isle of Mull to Baile Mòr, Iona at frequent intervals, with a reduced service on Sundays, carrying cars issued with Iona Vehicle Permits and service vehicles but *only* for the benefit of the islanders themselves; tourist cars are *never* embarked.

Loch Dunvegan (Gaelic – *Loch Dùnbheagan*) (IMO 9006409) is a 549-GT Steel DSMV, double-ended, passenger and car ferry, with her design following the outlines of the earlier *Loch Striven*, and these two became colloquially known as 'Super Lochs' because of their enhanced dimensions. She has a length of 54.2 m, a beam of 13.41 m and a draught of 1.6 m. She is equipped with two TAMD 162 4SCSA oil engines developing 448 bhp apiece with the Voith Schneider propulsion units which give her a top working speed of 9 knots. Her capacity is 200 passengers, with accommodation concentrated into a high and narrow superstructure ranged down the starboard side of the open car deck, with a crew of 4, and she can carry 36 vehicles arranged in four lines of 9 cars each. She has two identical gantry type masts over either end of the deck.

Built by Ferguson Shipbuilders Ltd, Port Glasgow especially for the Kyle of Lochalsh to Kyleakin service, she first commenced operations in May 1991, even though the planning for the Skye Toll Bridge (as it was then termed) was already under way. Other than some initial long vehicle offloading difficulties with her ramps, soon rectified by modifications, she and her sister operated successfully together as a team during daylight hours and one or other continued operations during the hours of darkness.

With the Skye Bridge opened in October 1995 she and her sister were put on the sales list, but after a two-year period laid up at Greenock, *Loch Dunvegan* was re-utilized on the Lochaline to Fishnish crossing of the Sound of Mull briefly before breaking down, and later operated the Mallaig to Armadale route before another period of idleness. With the construction of a suitable pier and the widening of the concrete slipway at Colintraive in the Kyles of Bute, in 1999 she took over from the *Isle of Cumbrae* and also worked briefly between Tarbert and Portavadie. Her facilities are basic, with two passenger lounges one above the other, with limited open deck space above.

The Colintraive ferry terminal has limited free car parking with a bus stop 30 m away. There is no waiting room and only local toilets with no baby-changing, disabled toilets, vending machines or public telephones.

The *Loch Dunvegan* currently continues to work on the 5-minute Colintraive to Rhubodach crossing, which is called 'Britain's Shortest Sea Journey'. The vessel was refitted with new, improved, wider two-section vehicle ramps in 2004, although mainly she operates with these unfolded to save time on this busy route.

The *Loch Fyne* (IMO 9006411) is a sister ship to the *Loch Dunvegan* and shares most of her details and early history, and when her sister failed

24: Oban – Tiree – Coll – Lochhosidale – Castlebay – Islay – South Uist – Skye – North Uist – Tarbert

CalMac's *Loch Fyne* in a misty haze. (© Dave Greer)

on the Lochaline (in south Morvern) to Fishnish (on the Isle of Mull) crossing, she replaced her and made that particular route her own from 1998. Although the single track roads that make up the last half of the road journey from the Corran Ferry can make this journey an additional hour in travelling time, the overall saving is cost and time is still attractive and *Loch Fyne* (Gaelic – *Loch Fine*) makes the 30-minute sea journey across the Sound of Mull frequently. She has ample lounge space, and there is also a small café and public toilets at the Fishnish slipway. In her summer schedule, which in 2012 ran from 25 March to 22 October, she makes about twelve crossings in each direction per day, with eight on Sundays.

Loch Linnhe (IMO 8512308), *Loch Striven* (IMO 8512293), *Loch Ranza* (IMO 8519887) and *Loch Riddon* (IMO 8519875) were a class of four 260-GT new-concept Steel DSMV Ro-Ro ferries which were improvements to the *Isle of Cumbrae* design. They were built in pairs in 1986/87 by Richard Dunston (Hessle) UK, Ltd, Hessle (Damen Shipyards) on the Humber River near Hull, shortly before they closed down, and designed specifically for the routes from Largs to the Cumbrae Slip, from Colintraive to Rhubodach, the Lochranza to Claonaig crossing and the Fishnish to Lochaline route, where they principally replaced the older bow-loading vessels then in use. They were designed right from the offset to carry many more passengers in two accommodation areas,

Offshore Ferry Services

The *Loch Striven* of the Caledonian MacBrayne ferry company lowering her bow ramp to begin unloading. (© Dave Greer)

The Caledonian MacBrayne ferry *Loch Riddon*. (© Peter McCann)

with lounges ranged on either side of their narrow, two-line car decks. Each line is capable of accommodating just 6 cars, restricting their overall car-carrying capacity to just 12; even so this was an improvement on the previous vehicle numbers.

They are of 30.2 m overall length, with a beam of 10 m and a 1.50 m draught. Their engines are two Swedish Volvo-Penta 6-cylinder fore and aft, which drive Voith-Schneider propellers,. and give a best speed of 9 knots. They also feature two electrically-driven general service pumps for bilge emptying, fire main supply and the transfer of ballast water, and an emergency diesel pump. Their passenger capacity is 203 passengers and 12 vehicles and they have a crew of 3. They are equipped with a single inflatable launch and life-rafts. They have a small wheelhouse to starboard carrying their mast for Deck 4, while Deck 3 is the passenger deck with bow and stern ramps, open decks to port with a central exhaust, and also forward on the starboard side, with the lifeboat astern. Deck 2 is the Car Deck.

The Largs ferry terminal has a 10-seat waiting room, with toilets, disabled toilets and baby-changing facilities but it has no vending machine, public telephone or ATM. There is paid car parking 2 minutes walk away but no dedicated disabled places.

24: Oban – Tiree – Coll – Lochhosidale – Castlebay – Islay – South Uist – Skye – North Uist – Tarbert

Loch Linnhe made her maiden voyage on 4 July 1986 and up to 1997 was principally employed on the Largs. Ayrshire, to Cumbrae Slip on Great Cumbrae, maintaining this crossing during the summer months and then, up to 1995, saw service in the winter period on the Lochaline to Fishnish crossing among others; but she has served on practically all her sister ships' routes at one time or another.

Since 1999 the *Loch Linnhe* (Gaelic – *An Linne Dhubh*) has been chiefly used on the 35-minute route between the slipway at Tobermory, Isle of Mull to the Mingary Pier, close to Kilchoan, Ardnamurchan, but only in the summer season, when *HopScotch* combination ferry fares are popular, and in the winter she is relieved by the smaller *Raasay* in order to maintain a limited, all-year round service. The Tobermory ferry terminal is a very small terminal building with just 4 seats and nothing else. From Monday to Saturday between late March and late October, approximately seven round trips are made, while the Sunday May to August only service, operates five crossings in each direction. The Tobermory ferry terminal has disabled access only but no facilities whatsoever. There is a 10-minute check-in time prior to departure.

The *Loch Striven* original served principally on the route between Largs and Cumbrae, and later operated winter services at Tarbert to Portavadie and also Claonaig to Lochranza before settling down on her present schedule in 1997. Currently during the summer period, 25 March to 22 October in 2011, *Loch Striven* (Gaelic – *Loch Sroigheann*) plies from the slipway at Sconser, on the southern shore of Sligachan, Isle of Skye, where the only facilities are a small waiting room and toilets, but with the Sconser Hotel close by. The route is across the Narrows of Raasay, to the Raasay landing about a mile from Inveraish village on Raasay itself, and which has no pubic transport of its own. Both embarkation points have small areas set aside for a limited number of waiting vehicles. On weekdays there are up to ten crossings per day, with one additional Saturday only service, but on Sundays this reduces to just two passages in the morning and afternoon. Reliability cannot be faulted, for example, of 492 operated sailings in the month of September 2010, there were no diversions, no cancellations, and each crossing was made right on time.

Originally used exclusively as a summer ferry on the Claonaig to Lochranza, Arran, route until 1992, today *Loch Ranza* (Gaelic – *Loch Raonasa*) is used on the Tayinloan to Gigha all-year round ferry crossing. Made famous by the renowned Achamore Gardens which is an unexpected tropical paradise off the west coast of Scotland, an illusion reinforced by dolphin sightings from the ferry itself on occasion, Gigha itself is run by a Heritage Trust.

Tayinloan, Kintyre, is around 4 miles from Muasdale, 12 miles south of Tarbert, and is just off the A83 between Glasgow and Campbeltown and is signposted. At the waiting area near the slipway, which is within walking distance of the village itself and where one should arrive at least 10 minutes before departure, there are a number of car waiting spaces and as usual, payment is made aboard, including the pre-bookable *HopScotch* tickets. The summer timetable, between 25 March and 22 October in 2011, sees hourly services between 08.00 and 18.00 and six crossings on Sundays. The journey time is approximately 20 minutes.

From her commissioning this ferry was used on the Colintraive to Rhubodach crossing but in 1997 moved to service the Largs to Cumbrae Slipway route, with winter work between Tarbert and Portavadie. However, at the time of writing, *Loch Riddon* (Gaelic – *Loch Raodain*) is now only employed as a spare vessel.

Loch Portain (IMO 9274824) is a Steel DSMV Ro-Ro vehicle ferry which was constructed specifically for the crossing of the Sound of Harris from Leverburgh, Harris to the northern end of the Berneray Causeway, North Uist, replacing the *Loch Bhrusda* which had pioneered the original route to Otternish in 1996, but which had only half the vehicle capacity. She was built by McTay Marine, Bromborough, Merseyside, to a specially modified design whose main deviation from the Loch type was brought about by the shallowness of the waters in the Sound, which has a large number of islets, submerged skerries and projecting rocks, sandbanks and similar hazards which call for the utmost caution. To allow for a system of propulsion and manoeuvrability that obviates this underwater risk, a special water-jet propulsion unit was adopted in place of the more usual Voith Schneider units of earlier vessels. The two SPU132 Schottel Water Pump Jets, of 505 kW, each comprises a pump which draws in water at a very slow rate of intake via a gridded access aperture in the hull bottom, which prevents any debris influx. The system then pushes the water into a diffuser which in turn charges it with energy by increasing static pressure before it is ejected at high velocity which accelerates it through ducts and the concentrated flow out through outlet nozzles set at a 15-degree angle, via an egress aft. As the water is expelled astern an equal and opposite reaction is generated to the hull. This Azimuth thruster system allows for good turning abilities and obviates the need for propellers, shafts, brackets and rudder as underwater protrusions. It has an added advantage of being a very low noise system.

The *Loch Portain* is of 950-GT, has an overall length of 49 m, a beam of 14.4 m and a 3 m draught. Her propulsion system gives her a top speed of 10.5 knots, but she is restricted to 9 knots working speed on her necessarily convoluted and densely-buoyed route. She can accommodate 195 passengers and 31 cars and has a 5.1 m head clearance. She commenced service in June 2003. Her facilities are limited for her size, with just fixed seating areas, which in good weather afford a unique seabird observation platform, and an information display, vending machine catering and toilets.

The route from Leverburgh is close to many islets off Harris and then south towards the north-eastern extremity of North Uist, turning acutely to starboard off Grodhaigh and then west to Berneray. Currently the summer timetable between 25 March and 3 September has four crossings each way per day, reducing to three, and (since 2006 amid some controversy over observance of the Sabbath) Sunday services of three, reducing to two, Sunday services, the first such in the northern Western Isles. The winter schedules also vary considerably according to the month and should be double-checked carefully, with two, later increasing to three crossings. There are no services on 25 December or 1 January. The journey takes approximately 1 hour 10 minutes.

Loch Shira (IMO 9376919) is a fairly new DSMV Ro-Ro passenger/car ferry of 230-GT built in 2006 by Ferguson Shipbuilders, Port Glasgow, for the Largs to Cumbrae Slip crossing at a cost of £5,800,000. She is one of the largest vessels of the CalMac fleet and has a length of 54.27 m, a beam of 13.9 m and 1.8 m draught. Her motive power are two Caterpillar 559b kW main diesel engines developing 1,800 rpm which drives her at a top speed of 10 knots, along with two Cummins/Stamford 113 kW auxiliary generators. She has a pair of German-built 540 kW at 625 rpm Voith-Schneider 16 R5 propulsion plants set diagonally opposite to each other for high manoeuvrability. She has a carrying capacity of 250 passengers, which are accommodated to starboard on three levels including two lounges, a 60-capacity lower and a cross-deck upper, with the bridge structure and mast offset above it, plus an open upper deck space, and 32 cars on a single, open, three-lane, (with a wider central lane for small commercial vehicles) deck although due to traffic congestion at both terminals of her route she is generally restricted to just 24 vehicles. She loads/offloads via bow and stern folding ramps onto slipways. She is fitted with inflatable life rafts and is fully equipped and certificated to carry all types of hazardous cargo. She made her maiden voyage on Saturday 2 June 2007.

24: Oban – Tiree – Coll – Lochboisdale – Castlebay – Islay – South Uist – Skye – North Uist – Tarbert

Loch Shira near Largs. (© Peter McCann)

Loch Shira (Gaelic – *Loch Siora*) still currently operates the 10-minute journey across the Firth of Clyde from the specially re-built pier opened in September, 2009 by HRH The Princess Royal at Largs, Ayrshire. At the ferry terminal there is a 10-seat waiting room with toilets, physically-impaired toilets, baby-changing facilities and limited wheelchair access, with a car park, rail station and bus station all within under 10 minutes walking time while at the Cumbrae Slip on Greater Cumbrae Island, there are only toilets, a public telephone and bus stop; all other amenities can be found at Millport itself. The summer schedule between 25 March and 22 October in 2011, has regular sailings from 06.45 onwards and a later starting Sunday service, and has enhanced sailings, with the assistance of *Loch Riddon*, between 22 May and 28 August, and a winter service with no sailings on Christmas Day or New Year's Day. All have a 10-minute vehicle check-in time.

Loch Tarbert (IMO 9039389) was one of the last ships built by J.N. Miller & Sons at their St. Monans facility in the East Neuk of Fife on the Firth of Forth. She is a 211-GT, Steel DSMV, Ro-Ro passenger/car ferry with an overall length of 30.2 m, a beam of 10 m and a draught of 1.6 m. Her design is heavily influenced by the *Isle of Cumbrae* layout.

She has a pair of Volvo Penta 6-cylinder engines and German Voith Schneider propellers and has a top operating speed of 9 knots. This ferry now has a passenger capacity of 147, accommodated in a lounge on her starboard side, and toilet facilities, two outer open-deck seating areas and a crew of 3. She has space for 17 cars on her three-lane open car deck, for which she has bow and stern ramps. Her prominent wheelhouse is offset to port and her large funnel to starboard on either side of her open vehicle deck and she carries a single inflatable launch and life-rafts. She first entered service on 25 July 1992 and has basically stayed put, although from 1994 she has also found limited employment as the Largs to Cumbrae Slip relief ship when *Loch Shira* is unavailable as well as working at Fishnish and Colintraive and on the Otternish to Leverburgh crossing as a reserve ferry.

Loch Tarbert (Gaelic – *Loch an Tairbeirt*) still plies the same 30-minute end of March to late October summer route as she was built for, between Claonaig, south of Tarbert, on the Kintyre Peninsula, to the slipway adjacent to the pier just west of Lochranza, on the northern tip of the Isle of Arran. This is a viable alternative to the main southern crossing and this seven-day service has a maximum of nine daily sailings, seven days a week, but, other than via the useful *HopScotch* tickets, these are not bookable. At both slipway terminals there are

Offshore Ferry Services

Loch Tarbert showing her folding bow ramp. (© Dave Greer)

eighteen numbered car waiting places for the non-bookable service but there are few other services. In the bleaker winter months a required bookable daily service is operated from Lochranza and Tarbert.

Lochnevis (IMO 9209063) is a revolutionary vessel that was built to fulfil a very special rôle by Ailsa Shipbuilding in Troon in 2000 at a cost of £5,500,000 and was the last ship built at that yard. She is a Steel DSMV, stern-ramp only, Ro-Ro ferry but one that is not used as a commercial car carrying ship but only to convey service vehicles to the 'Small Isles' of Eigg, Muck, Rum and Canna–Sanday from Mallaig. Because of the limited facilities at her destinations she has many unique features and is also unique in that she is the only CalMac ship to carry more passengers in the winter months than in the summer!

She is of 941-GT with an overall length of 49.2 m, a beam of 11.4 m and a draught of 2.7 m. She has three 12-cylinder Cummins KTA-38-M2 vee type engines, and she is fitted with a triple 3,039 bhp stern-mounted Azipod multi-directional propeller system (which obviate stern rudders) and two bow manoeuvering, thwartship thrusters, and has a speed of 13 knots. In order to shield her Azipods in the shallow water, her most conspicuous feature is her huge, folding, stern ramp which enables her to lower it, back inshore and offload at a safe distance from the hazards. She also has an exceptionally large (for her normal usage) vehicle deck, of 17 lane meters, with 5 restricted car spaces, insisted upon in her design, for her winter tasks. She carries too, a passenger gangway on her starboard side especially for use at the Isle of Canna.

She has a passenger capacity of 190, can carry 14 cars and has a crew of 10. Her passenger accommodation is located forward of the car deck, with the large Coffee Cabin cafeteria located on the starboard side forward of Deck 2, serving hot beverages, alcohol of all types, snacks and light food options. As with all the CalMac fleet there is ample provision of toilets on both Decks 2 and 3, with baby-changing facilities, mobility impaired facilities, including toilets, and lift from the vehicle deck to Deck 2. A notable feature is the large observation lounge forward with obliquely arranged seating for views that are, uniquely, for once not obscured by any bow ramp blocking the view ahead. There is table seating on Deck 2 and a baggage area and much side-deck open seating. Her large wheelhouse with its wide-scope viewing design is located atop the lounge amidships, with her large funnel offset to starboard. She has embarked a single RIB fast rescue craft on her port side, as well as inflatable life rafts, and she also carries a single HIAB hydraulic crane for offloading heavy cargo which can be conveyed on her boat deck for offloading at Canna Pier. Once nervous passengers were disembarked offshore by transfer to local island 'Flitboats' a practice done away with as the various onshore terminals, piers and slips

24: Oban – Tiree – Coll – Lochhosidale – Castlebay – Islay – South Uist – Skye – North Uist – Tarbert

were created as part of the CalMac improvement packages, following her introduction into service on 20 November 2000 when she replaced the *Lochmor*.

Lochnevis (Gaelic – *Loch Nibheis*) operates a variable weekday service in the summer months to all these islands in a 7-hour cycle but there are no Sunday services. In the winter months from October to March she also works from Mallaig to Armadale. Island permits are required for all vehicles so in effect tourism is limited to either round-trip sightseeing or passenger-only island hopping and services are not always possible. Not every departure covers every island: Kinloch, Rum, Galmisdale Bay, Eigg, and Port Mor, Muck, tend to alternate on the rotas, so strict advance planning is required and timetables should be rigorously checked for last-minute changes, while it must be borne in mind that many destinations have only tiny populations and strictly limited on-shore facilities. In the early and late weekdays sailings are also conducted by the *Lochnevis*, (which was all along designated to operate winter vehicular traffic) to Armadale, Skye, and stern loadings and unloadings from the slipways and Linkspans at that port and Mallaig itself.

Lord of the Isles (IMO8710869) is a Class IIA and III, 3,504-ton Steel DSMV passenger/car ferry and one of the largest vessels of the CalMac fleet. She was built by Appledore Ferguson Shipbuilders, Port Glasgow on the Clyde, as a replacement for both the Western Isles ships, the *Claymore* operating from Oban to Castlebay and Lochboisdale, and the *Columba* out to Coll and Tiree from the same terminal. She is 84.63 m overall length, with a beam of 15.19 m and a draught of 3.127 m. Her Mirrlees Blackstone engines are diesel and she has two electric bow thrusters of 7 tonnes thrust for manoeuvering. She has a best speed of 16 knots and is equipped with three Rigid Boats, a RIB fast rescue craft and inflatable life rafts. She also has a vehicle hoist astern of her twin funnels.

Her capacity is 506 passengers, served by a crew of 28, and can convey 54 cars and 16 trucks on her 130 lane meters of car deck, plus 7 restricted car spaces. She made her maiden voyage on 22 May 1989 and was based at Oban for the next ten years, with relief work to Craignure, Uig, Ardrossan and to Skye among other ports of call.

Her on-board facilities feature all the CalMac range, with, at the bow end of Deck 4, the comfortable and spacious Mariners cafeteria, which can provide everything from breakfasts to full lunch or dinner, or light snacks and packed lunches, including dedicated children's servings and vegetarian choices. At the other end is the Coffee Cabin with coffee and other hot beverages, ales and malt whisky and light snacks. Next to it is Shop@CalMac with a range of soft drinks, confectionery, books, magazines and newspapers along with local produce. For entertainment nearby can be found Game-On for the latest video games and quiz machines. For a more restful crossing LOTI (as she is affectionally known) offers a large observation lounge to the rear of Deck 5, while on Deck 4 is a comfortable recliner lounge and a TV lounge. Should the weather be clement there is ample outdoor seating on Deck 5. There are toilets on both decks, with mobility impaired facilities on Deck 4 and a disabled lift from the vehicle deck up to Deck 4. There is a baby-changing area on Deck 5 and dedicated pet areas on both decks. She was originally built with cabins and sleeping berths as she was to operate a 24-hour service to cover both routes, but these were seldom used in practice and have been converted to more usable passenger space.

At Coll ferry terminal the 20-seat waiting room has toilets, seating and disabled facilities but no baby-changing area, public telephone or vending machines. There is an ATM at the nearby Post Office. There is limited free parking with two dedicated disabled parking spots.

At Lochboisdale the terminal has a 10-seat waiting room with toilets, disabled toilets and access and baby-changing facilities but no vending machines or public telephones. There is an ATM at the Royal Bank of

Offshore Ferry Services

With bow doors open the Caledonian MacBrayne *Lord of the Isles* approaches Colonsay terminal in 2009. (© Dave Greer)

Scotland 300 m distant. There are six free car parking spaces but no dedicated disabled spaces. Bus drop off points and a taxi rank are adjacent to the terminal.

Lord of the Isles (Gaelic – *Righ nan Eilean*) currently operates from Oban, Argyll, to Colonsay, Coll, Tiree, Barra and Lochboisdale (South Uist), working in conjunction with the new *Clansman* to provide a *LifeLine* service and occasionally joined by a third vessel when there is a peak in demand. Day Sails are another popular recent addition to the already crowded itinerary. Services are very varied and in some months an alternate route from Kennacraig, Argyll, is in operation. Very great care and checking is required when planning a journey on these routes.

At the Oban terminal there is the main ticket office, a 150-seat waiting area with toilets, disabled toilets, baby-changing area, vending machines and public telephone, but no ATM. There is no car parking on the pier, but at the Scotrail terminal about 50 m away there is paid parking but currently no dedicated disabled space. Passenger boarding is via Linkspans with connecting walkways from the terminal building itself, and there is a large, two lane car assembly area.

At Colonsay there is the Pier and a Linkspan on Scalasaig, with a passenger gangway and adjacent car waiting areas. Journey times from Oban are approximately 2 hours 20 minutes with six crossings in summer and three in winter.

At Coll there is a pier and Linkspan at Aringagour with toilets and ticket office close by. The crossing takes around 3 hours.

At Tiree there is a ferry office with facilities, with a car waiting area, and embarkation is via the pier, Linkspan and a passenger gangway. The journey time from Oban is approximately 4 hours 5 minutes according to weather conditions and other variables.

At Castlebay, Barra, there is a terminal office with a waiting area, ticket office and facilities with a Linkspan and pier. The journey time from Oban is approximately 6 hours 45 minutes.

Colonsay ferry terminal is only open 2 hours prior to sailing and the 25-seat waiting room has toilets, disabled toilets, seating, baby-changing facilities, but no vending machine, ATM or public telephone. There are six free car parking spaces with disabled parking opposite the terminal building.

Muirneag (IMO 7725362) is a Steel DSMV Ro-Ro vehicle ferry currently on charter to CalMac for the Ullapool to Stornoway vehicle-only service. She was originally built by Frederikshavn Vaerft, at the Danyard in Frederikshavn on the north-east Jutland coast of Denmark (since closed down) on the Kattegat, as a Class FV 256 TEU Ro-Ro ship. She was built in April 1979 for Merc-Scania KS and was christened *Mercandian Carrier*. She cost £3.2 million and at 3,350-GT she has an overall length of 105.5 m, a beam of 18.8 m and a draught of 5 m. She was engined with a MaK 12M453AK diesel of 3,310 kW output which drives a single VP propeller, and her maximum speed is 15.5 knots.

Down the years she has worked for several companies: P&O Irish Sea, Isle of Man S.P. Co, Aabrenaa Rederi, Kingston, St. Vincent, Northern Ireland Trailers, Exxtor Ferries and Ferryways among others, and ultimately Harrisons (Clyde), Glasgow, and she accordingly carried a variety of names, including *Alianza* in 1984 and *Belard* and *Carrier II* in 1985. In September 2002 CalMac took up her charter and renamed her after a mountain on the Isle of Lewis. She was extensively modified, including being fitted with Vec Twin rudders, and a 2,000 HKs Elliot White Gill Jet bow thruster unit was fitted to aid manoeuvrability in restricted areas. The original hoist which serviced her upper freight deck was removed and a new internal vehicle ramp fitted. She has 756 lane meters capable of carrying 12 trucks; she carries 12 passengers and is fitted with two rigid lifeboats and inflatable life rafts.

Offshore Ferry Services

Muirneag runs an overnight service between Ullapool and Stornaway. (© Dave Greer)

In June 2008 Caledonian Maritime Assets Limited (CMAL) started the tendering process to commission a Scottish Transport Appraisal Guidance (STAG) to review her future, CalMac being obliged to a twice-daily return sailing on the route for passengers and vehicles.

The *Muirneag* (Gaelic name for the highest point [248 m] on the Isle of Lewis) is, at the time of writing, still employed exclusively as an overnight goods and provisions ferry working between Ullapool and Stornoway. She sails from Stornoway every evening at 23.30 (save for Sunday when she departs at 00.30 on the Monday due to the strict Sabbath observance), docking at 03.00 in Ullapool, and returns at 08.00 next day. It is expected that, due to age, wear and tear, the *Muirneag* will no longer be viable on this service beyond October 2013 when she will finally be withdrawn.

The Stornoway ferry terminal has a 110-seat waiting room, with toilets, disabled toilets, baby-changing area, but no public telephone, vending machines or ATM. There is a 40-space short-stay free car park, with a free, 120 space, public car park just a minute distant, with a bus stop adjacent to the terminal itself. At Ullapool the terminal has a 78-seat waiting room with toilets, disabled toilets and baby-changing facilities but no public telephone, vending machine or ATM. There is no car parking other than in the town itself, but there is a single dedicated disabled car space in the terminal assembly area.

Raasay (IMO 7340435) was the last of the 'Small Island' ferries to be built. She was a passenger/car ferry, built by James Lamont & Company at Port Glasgow in 1976. Their design was based upon the Royal Navy's Landing Craft Mechanized (LCM-7) but adapted for mercantile usage. Designed to service small landing slips on little-used routes, they were cheap to build, run and service. She is equipped with a double-jointed bow ramp, which itself has a ventral protection bar below it, with a gantry carrying the mainmast. There is an open vehicle deck of 12 lane meters, a turntable, and, extreme aft, the bridge with funnel, engine exhaust and radar mast located above a small sheltered passenger space.

Her power plant was originally twin M6cy 300 bhp diesel engines supplied by English Electric Diesels, Kelvin, Glasgow, but she was re-engined by Timbacraft, Shandon, on Gare Loch, with Scania D9 93M35 turbocharged 6-cylinder diesels which give her a best speed of 8 knots. She is a Class IV, VI and VIA vessel and is of 69-GT, having an overall length of 22.5 m, a beam of 6.4 m and a draught of 1.40 m She has a service speed of 8 knots and capacity for 75 passengers with space for 6 cars and a crew of 3. She made her first voyage on 30 April 1976 and saw most of her long life operating between Sconser on the Island of Skye and Raasay, until replaced by the larger *Loch Striven* in 1997. Despite her antiquity at the time of writing she is currently still part of CalMac fleet. Her facilities are necessarily limited, being confined to a small passenger lounge and a toilet.

Raasay (Gaelic – *Eilean Ratharsair*) is one of only two surviving ships of this class and is currently used only rarely as a spare or relief vessel, being moored at either Oban or Tobermory until called upon.

Contact Details
Head Office
Ferry Terminal, Gourock, PA19 1QP
Tel: 01475 650100
Fax: 01475 650336
Email: david.cannon@calmac.co.uk
Web: www.calmac.co.uk

Inter-Island
Aran Island Ferries of Rossaveal, County Galway, have a fleet of modern luxury, purpose-built ferries that ply the Aran Island routes to Inishmor, Inis Meáin and Inisheer. All the vessels have wheelchair

access and the majority have a snack bar serving light refreshments and alcoholic beverages during the journey. The principal vessels in use are the 234-ton sister ships *Ceol na Farraige* (*Music of the Sea*) and *Draíocht na Farraige* (*Magic of the Sea*), both being 37.4 m Wavemaster monohulls, with 8 m beams, and capable of speeds up to 20 knots, with a passenger capacity of 294/272 respectively; *Glór na Farraige* (*Voice of the Sea*) was built by Alfa Naval, France, with a passenger accommodation for 244 persons.

There is also the *Banríon na Farraige* (*Queen of the Sea*) (MMSI 250007000), built by Societe Francaise de Constructions Navales, France. She has a length of 23 m and a beam of 6 m, with a top speed of 16.6 knots, and can carry up to 188 passengers.

The 172-ton *Banríon Chonamara* (*Queen of Connemara*) (IMO9231016), formerly the *Queen of Aran II*, is also of French construction and was built in May 2001 by OCRA, at Les Sables d'Olonne. She has an overall length of 39.9 m, a draught of 2 m and a 244 passenger capacity, with 120 main deck saloon seats and 30 more on the after deck. There is a PA system installed and vent heating system in the passenger area, with both open and sheltered upper deck areas and wheelchair accessible toilet facilities and a lift for wheelchairs and buggys. She has a top speed of 19 knots.

Finally there is the smaller *Sea Sprinter* (IMO 9423657) built by Lochin Marine, East Sussex with a passenger capacity of 35.

Contact Details

Aran Island Ferries, 37–39 Forster Street, Galway, County Galway, Irish Republic
Tel: (353) 91 568903
Fax: (353) 91 568538
Email: islandferries@eircom.net
Web: www.aranislandferries.com

Argyll & Bute Council

The Council operates a number of vessels. For the short crossing of the Cuan Sound between Oban and the Isles of Luing and Seil in the Firth of Lorn, the *Belnahua* (DG) operates several times a day. She was originally constructed by the Campbeltown Shipyard for the Seil to Luing service, being transferred in 1975 to Strathclyde Regional Council and then in 1996 to her present managers. With a top speed of only 8 knots, the favoured operating option is to cross at right angles to the 15 km/hr main tidal flow.

When *Belnahua* undergoes her annual refit she is replaced by her much smaller relief vessel, *Grey Dog*, which has a 12-passenger capacity, with a maximum of 3 cars. With the *Belnahua* requiring more care and attention as she ages, the *Grey Dog* is used quite frequently, operating for five weeks in 2010.

The 93-ton *Easdale* was likewise originally built in 1996 to ply the Ellenabeich to Easdale passenger service for the Strathclyde Regional Council, before being taken over by Argyll and Bute Council in 1996. She has a passenger capacity of just 11 and a top speed of 6.5 knots. Although there are now less than sixty inhabitants of this 'Slate Island', the all-year service is still maintained, subject to the weather. During daylight hours the ferry can be summoned by means of a klaxon and after dusk by the operation of light buttons, both of which are housed in the Gerry Waiting Shed on the Ellenabeich Pier. On the annual Stone Skimming World Championship Day little *Easdale* comes into her own.

The 86-ton *Eilean Dhiura* (DG) is used for the short crossing between Port Askaig, Isle of Islay and Feolin on the Isle of Jura. This ship was originally built in 1998 at McTay Marine at Bromborough, Merseyside for Stirling Shipping, Glasgow, and was managed initially by Serco Denholm and then ASP Seascot. This vessel replaced the *Sound of Gigha*. She was fitted with a new bow ramp in 2002 and has a 50 passenger capacity and space for 13 cars and 1 lorry.

When she is under refit or has technical problems with her engines, the *Eilean Dhiura* is replaced by her relief vessel, the *Margret Sinclair*. This latter is a Coastal Landing Craft, built by Nobles of Girvan in 2006. She has an overall length of 21 m, a beam of 7.25 m and draught of 2 m with a 14.5 m deck length and a hydraulic bow loading ramp 4.1 m wide. She also has a 60 m^3 hold and a 32-ton crane. She has a passenger capacity of 12, and has a 2-man crew but can accommodate four with centrally-heated accommodation, shower, mess room and galley. She is owned by the Inverlussa Shellfish Company Ltd.

The even tinier vessel, *The Lismore*, is a 12-ton, 9.7 m ferry built in 1988 which can carry a total of 20 passengers along with bicycles (which are carried free of charge). She operates between Port Appin and The Point at the north end of Lismore Island (the 'Great Garden'), crossing the mile-wide narrows at a top speed of 8 knots in 10 minutes at approximately hourly intervals. This is both the shortest and cheapest crossing and the ferry can be reached from the mainland off the main coastal road, between Ballachulish and Connel, at Appin, where it is signposted to the landing stage at Port Appin.

The Council also subsidized the ferry to Jura via a *Stormforce II* RIB. Argyll Ferries Ltd was awarded a six-year contract to operate this service, commencing 7 June 2011.

Contact Details
Argyll and Bute Council, Kilmory, Lochgilphead, Argyll, PA31 8RT
Tel: 01546-602127
Email: enquiries@argyll-bute.gov.uk
Web: www.argyll-bute.gov.uk/transport-and-streets/ferry-travel

Aran Islands Direct, (Báid Arann Teoranta) from the Irish Republic operated a ferry service from Rossaveal, Connemara, to Aran, with a summer service also to Mór, Inis Oir and Inis Neaiw. In 2011 this company went into receivership. Two of the ferries, *Clan Eagle* (known to locals as *Clan Empty* due to low bookings) and *Clann Na Noileáin* were taken into receivership. The fate of a proposed third vessel, a 40 m catamaran prospectively named *Aran Princess* ex-*Harbour Lynx*, ex-*Phillippine Kvaerner Fjellstrand Singapore Flying Cat*, which never ultimately materialized in Irish service, is unclear. She was to have been refitted by her original builders, Fjellstrand, AS, at Omastrand, Hardangerfjord, Norway.

Arranmore Ferry (Báid Farantóireachta Árainn Mhór), Irish Republic, is a long-established car and passenger ferry service company with a quarter of a century operational experience. It is an Irish Government organization supported by The Gaeltacht Authority (*Roinn na Gaeltachta*) which supports tourism in Irish-speaking areas of the Republic. The company runs two 69-GT passenger car ferries, the *Coll* and the *Rhum*, from Burtonport Pier, 5 miles from Dungloe, Rosses, West Donegal, to Leabgarrow Pier, Arranmore Island, passing Rutland and Inishcoo Islands. In the summer period they run on an approximately hourly basis, depending on weather conditions. There are also additional evening sailings from Burtonport and Arranmore on Fridays only.

Both vessels were part of a class of eight originally built for Caledonian MacBrayne in 1973 by James Lamont & Company, Port Glasgow, being that firm's Yard Nos 421 and 422 respectively, and each was engined by English Electric Kelvin Division, Glasgow with a pair of 4SCSA6 cylinder engines, each of 150 bhp, driving two screws via reverse reduction gearboxes. They have an overall length of 25.23 m, with a 8.66 m beam and an extreme draught of 1.36 m. Both ships were purchased in 1998.

The two ships are able to accommodate 6 cars apiece and each has a passenger accommodation of 86. The journey time is approximately 15 minutes.

Offshore Ferry Services

Contact Details
Arranmore Ferry, Bridge House, Leabgarrow, Arranmore,
  County Donegal, Irish Republic
Tel: (353) (0)7495 20532
Fax: (353) (0) 7495 20750
Email: arranmoreferry@arainnmhor.com
Web: www.arranmoreferry.com

Bruce Watt Cruises operates a twice-daily Knoydart Ferry Service between Mallaig and Inverie on the Knoydart Peninsular on the northern shore of Loch Nevis on Monday, Wednesday and Friday, with the afternoon sailing calling Tarbert on the southern shore of Loch Nevis (only between May and September). A new pier was opened in August 2006 to serve the 60 or so inhabitants and tourists. There is currently no other access to the village nor are there any weekend services. The service utilizes the TSMV *Western Isles*, a 46-ton twin-screw motor vessel, with an overall length of 19.5 m and capacity for 81 passengers. She leaves from the Knoydart Steps at Mallaig and the average journey time is 45 minutes. The Mallaig ferry terminal has a 14-seat waiting room with toilets, disabled toilets and baby-changing facilities, but no public telephone, vending machine or ATM. There is limited free car parking adjacent to the terminal with a single dedicated disabled car place in the company car park. The rail station, bus stop and ATMs are 5 minutes walk away.

The TSMV *Western Isles* of Bruce Watts Knoydart Ferry Service. (© Undiscovered Scotland)

Contact Details
Bruce Watt Cruises, The Pier, Mallaig, Inverness-shire, PH41 4QG
Tel: 01687 462320
Email: brucewattcruises@aol.com
Web: www.knoydart-ferry.co.uk

25: Aberdeen – Shetland Isles – Scrabster – Orkney Islands

Background
The history of services to the Orkneys and Shetlands are here principally considered individually, although some ships overlapped to both destinations as will be seen.

Orkneys
The story is that in the reign of King James IV of Scotland, a Dutchman by the name of Jan de Groot settled in the area that now bears his name and that, in 1496, he was granted the Royal Sanction to run a ferry service to the subservient fiefdom of Orkney that had passed to the Crown from Norway as recently as 1468. His enterprise was successful and enduring and he lies buried close by at Canisbay Kirk.

Both Kirkwall and Wick had steamer services to Inverness and other mainland Scottish harbours in the early decades of the nineteenth century. In 1828 the Aberdeen, Leith, Clyde & Tay Shipping Company used their wooden paddle steamer *Velocity*, built in 1821, to make a test crossing from Aberdeen to Wick, and in 1833 she commenced a regular service. In 1832 another steamer, the P&O's 206-GT *Fowett*, built by Caleb Smith at Liverpool and equipped with 60 bhp engines, also arrived at Shetland. The *Velocity* herself was later wrecked at the entrance to Aberdeen harbour in October 1848 but in the meanwhile a new vessel, the paddle steamer *Sovereign*, had taken over the run in 1836, when she commenced a summer sailing schedule from Leith via Aberdeen, Wick and Kirkwall to Lerwick. This was supplemented by a limited winter service between 1850 and 1861, with cattle far outnumbering any passengers aboard her. In September 1860 the *Sovereign* replaced the *Prince* on the Orkney and Zetland passage but this ship was sold in 1861. The predominant company serving the islands, the Aberdeen Leith and Clyde Shipping Company, became The North of Scotland & Orkney and Shetland Steam Navigation Company of Matthews' Quay, Aberdeen. In 1890 it took over the Shetland Islands Steam Navigation Company, Lerwick, and was yet later to become the North of Scotland, Orkney and Shetland Shipping Company Limited (not surprisingly, more usually known as the 'North Company').

The first regular steam ferry service across the Pentland Firth to Orkney was originated by John Stanger, who in 1856 commenced a route from Scrabster to Stromness with the locally-built *Royal Mail*. Another vessel, the *Earl of Caithness*, also had appeared on the scene, operated by a James Bremner. The *John O'Groat Journal* of 11 June 1858 announced that, 'The *Royal Mail* will sail daily between Orkney and Caithness.' By 1861 the *Prince Consort* was running a service from Caithness to Orkney and Shetland and she was later replaced by *The Queen* of the Aberdeen, Leith and Clyde Shipping Company. This route later became known as the Long Sea Crossing. Another, more direct, route became known as the Short Sea Crossing and this ran from Gills Bay to Stroma, Swona and Orkney. In 1864 Captain George Robertson set up an inter-island service by purchasing the wooden steamer *Quarry Maid*, which he renamed as *Orcadia* and she commenced a four-day-a-week inter-island service in February 1865. She was replaced four years later by a larger vessel built at South Shields of the same name and on 1 January 1868 his company became the Orkney Steam Navigation Company, with the new *Orcadia* serving for more than two dozen years,

The Northlink ferry *Hamnavoe* docked in Stromness in the Orkneys. (© Northlink Ferries)

being herself lengthened by 6.096 m and given new engines in 1884. In 1892 a second ship, the *Fawn*, joined her. The incredible *Orcadia* was to be refitted twice more, in 1905 and 1919, and lasted sixty-three years, but *Fawn* was sold in 1917.

In the interim, in 1877, with the railway link north having previously reached Thurso, Stanger obtained a contract for carrying the mail and so operated a paddle steamer, the second *Royal Mail*, on the route to Stromness. This latter harbour became something of a backwater for a brief period once the Scapa Pier at Kirkwall was built in 1880, but when the North Company built the *St. Olaf* in 1882 especially for the Pentland Firth passage it came back into vogue once more. Other operators attempted to make a viable competition on the crossing. George Robertson's *Express*, the 1876-founded McCallum and Co's *John O'Groat*, and the Argyll Steamship Company Limited with the 224-GT iron-built steamship *Argyll*, built by R. Duncan & Co at Port Glasgow, all appeared for short periods. The *Argyll* was to be wrecked at Milleur Point, Wigtownshire on 17 September 1893, and due to her indifferent performance *St. Olaf* herself only endured until 1890.

Other vessels on the route in the late nineteenth century included many that were noted for their longevity, such as the 787-GT *St. Nicholas* which was an iron-built screw steamer built at Whitinch in 1871. She was notable as the first ship on the direct Aberdeen to Lerwick route in 1891 but in June 1914 she grounded and broke her back off Wick harbour. The 961-GT *St. Sunniva* was a steel hulled, clipped bowed steamer and was originally one of the first cruise ships. Built by Hall, Russell & Company of Aberdeen, she was of 960-GT, with an overall length of 71.9 m and a beam of 9.2 m. She had triple-expansion reciprocating engines of 189 bhp which drove a single screw for a speed of 15.5 knots. She had accommodation for 142 passengers. After long service in her designed role she was converted in 1908 to a ferry ship, with a cargo hold and other modifications, and she served Lerwick from Aberdeen and Leith, until wrecked in thick fog on Mousa Island, Shetland in 1930. The the first *St. Rognvald* joined the fleet in 1883; she was of 984-GT with an overall length of 73 m and could carry 90 passengers.

The *St. Ola* was built in 1892 at a cost of £11,000 and she served on the Scrabster to Stromness service, faithfully criss-crossing the Firth with six return runs per week for almost sixty years, being withdrawn in 1951. Other vessels included *St. Ninian*, 1895–1948 and the second *St. Rognvald*, 1903–51. In 1905 the first pier was built then a harbour followed and the North Company withdrew from cruise traffic to Scandinavia to concentrate on ferry services with the *St. Sunniva*, which

Hjaltland arriving at Hatston at night. (© Northlink Ferries)

in 1908 began carrying the Royal Mail from Aberdeen and Leith to Lerwick, Shetland. The second *St. Magnus* was a 809-GT, single-funnelled steamer, built by Ramage & Ferguson at Leith in 1912. She was of 65.5 m overall with a 9.4 m beam and a draught of 4.6 m, and powered by a 206 bhp triple expansion engine. She served on the Lerwick to Aberdeen crossing. She was highly thought of but unfortunately she was sunk by a German torpedo off Peterhead on 12 February 1918.

During the First World War, service was supplemented by the vast numbers of Royal Navy officers and men on passage to and from the enormous British battle fleet assembled at Scapa Flow. After the First World War and before the depression set in, the third *St. Magnus* joined the fleet in 1924 and served through to 1960. The 1,368-GT *St. Sunniva II* was a steam passenger and cargo ship built in 1931 and she was distinguished by her clipper bow and high, white freeboard. She was advertised as a 'First-Class Passenger Steamer' sailing from Leith to Aberdeen and Shetland four times a week and from Aberdeen to Shetland five times weekly as well as summer cruising. She was requisitioned by the Admiralty at the start of the Second World War and became a convoy rescue ship, but on 22 January 1943 she became a war casualty, being lost with all hands off Sable Island, due, it was assumed, to the sheer weight of ice on her upper decks and superstructure making her suddenly turn turtle.

The second *St. Clair*, 1937–1960, became *St. Magnus IV* and between 1960 and 1967 was employed on the Leith and Edinburgh service to Stromness, Orkney and on the Lerwick, Shetland services. Of 1,641-GT, she was 88.07 m overall length and could carry 174 passengers plus 206 on deck. The 548-GT *Earl of Zetland II* ran between 1939 and 1975 mainly on the Lerwick, Shetlands to North Isles and was 50.59 m overall. The *Highlander* was purchased from the Aberdeen, Newcastle & Hull Steam Company in October 1939 to replace vessels requisitioned by the

View from inside the bridge of the Shetland ferry *Dagalien*. (© Shetland Islands Council)

Admiralty. Attacked by bombers on 2 August 1940 she was credited with shooting down two, some of the debris from the crashing aircraft being reputed to have fallen on her decks. Re-named as *St. Catherine II* three weeks later, she was again bombed that same November and this time sunk with the loss of 14 lives.

Post-war re-construction commenced with the *St. Clement II* built in 1946 and surviving until 1976, while the second *St. Ninian* ran between 1950 and 1971. She was a 2,242-GT vessel built by Caledon, Dundee as the workhorse of the Leith, Aberdeen, Kirkwall and Lerwick passage, which she did until February 1971 before being sold to Atlantique Cruise Lines, Nova Scotia. The 750-GT *St. Ola II* was built by Alexander Hall and Company, Aberdeen and launched in March 1951. She had an overall length of 54.254 m and was powered by diesel engines which gave her a speed of 13 knots. She had a capacity for 360 passengers and 30 cars. She worked the Scrabster to Stromness crossing until 1975. A third *St. Rognvald* was built in 1955 and served for over twenty years. The 3,302-GT *St. Clair III* was built at the Ailsa shipyard, Troon in 1960 and, although she cost one million pounds she was in many ways already something of an anachronism. She was the final vessel built for the North Company to feature both first- and second-class accommodation, and the last ship of the fleet that was not of Ro-Ro capability. She was fitted with anti-roll stabilizers and she also had chilled and refrigerated cargo holds. She had an overall length of 90.52 m and a 12.19 m beam. She became part of P&O Ferries and made her final voyage from Lerwick to Aberdeen in April 1977 before being sold to Kuwait as the *Al Khairat*.

The *St. Magnus IV* served between 1960 and 1967 and meanwhile, in 1961, the North Company was absorbed by Coast Lines. The following year the old Orkney Steam Company Navigation Company became the Orkney Islands Shipping Company Limited. Also in 1962 a new *Orcadia*, the third ship of the name, was built at government expense for the Secretary of State for Scotland, being constructed at Hall, Russell and Company at Aberdeen in 1962. She was of 896-GT, with an overall length of 50.02 m, a beam of 10.98 m, a 4.14 m draught, and had 1,230 bhp engines that drove her at 12 knots. She replaced the *Earl Thorfinn* and served as the mail and passenger ship in conjunction with the cargo carrier *Islander* at Kirkwall between 1962 and November 1982 and was then chartered to P&O. She was sold in 1994 to LeSea Global Feed, registered under the name of *Louisa* and flagged at Kingstown, St. Vincent & the Grenadines, in the Caribbean.

The following decade saw several new vessels appear; the *St. Magnus V* arrived in 1966 and served for over a decade, the *St. Clair IV* (ex-*Peter Pan, SF Panther* built 1965) and fifth *St. Clair* (ex-*Travemünde*, of Njegos, Tregastel, Barakat built in1971); the fourth *St. Ola* (ex-*Svea Scarlett, Eckerö*, built 1971) and the third *St. Sunniva* (ex-*Djursland, Lasse II, nf Panther, Faye*, built 1972). In 1971 P&O took over Coast Lines and, as the

The *Good Shepherd IV* heels over as she loads the single car she can carry.
(© Shetland Islands Council)

parent company of North of Scotland Orkney and Shetland Shipping Company, announced a new Ro-Ro ferry for the Pentland Firth crossing. By 1975 the company had been rebranded as P&O Ferries (Orkney & Shetland Services). In January of that same year the 1,344-GT Ro-Ro *St. Ola III* arrived with the new Scrabster Pier Linkspan facility on stream to cope with her. Built by Hall, Russell, she could carry 400 passengers and 98 cars to Orkney. She served until 1992.

The 1971-built, 3,575-GT Ro-Ro car ferry *ROF Beaver* served P&O Scottish Ferries between April 1975 and 1987, including duty on the Pentland Firth route. Built by D.W. Kremer Sohn GmbH in Germany, she was of 80.7 m overall length, with a 12.91 beam and a 4.15 m draught and was powered by an Alpha 16-cylinder engine for 13 knots. The *St. Clair IV* was obtained as the car ferry from Aberdeen to Lerwick, Shetland, being the former *Peter Pan* built for Travemunde-Trelleborg Linie in 1965 by Lubecker Flender-Werke and which in 1973 had been sold to Southern Ferries (then part of P&O Group) and renamed *SF Panther* for the Southampton to San Sebastian route. Withdrawn in 1975, she was then chartered as *Terje Vigen* of the Oslo-Aarjis Romoe (Da-No Linje) fleet and finally transferred to P&O's North of Scotland, Orkney & Shetlands Shipping Co, Aberdeen to Lerwick as *St. Clair IV*. She was again transferred to P&O Ferries in 1978 on the same route until 1992, and renamed *St. Clair II*. In 1989 the company became known as P&O Scottish Ferries.

In 1984 there was a brave attempt to re-open the moribund passenger sea link between the Orkney and Shetland groups, closed since the withdrawal of the *St. Ninian* by the North Company in 1971, and the mainly cargo-carrying *St. Rognvald* and the later *St. Magnus* had only limited capacity and had no firm timetable to rely upon.

Chris Marrow formed Norse Atlantic Ferries Limited with the former *Scillionian II*, *Devonia* and *Devoniun*, which he purchased for £110,000 and renamed *Syllingar*. She was built by J.I. Thornycroft at Woolston, Southampton in 1954 and was of 921-GT, was 63.55 m overall, with a beam of 9.37 m and was powered by two 6-cylinder Ruston & Hornsby 4-stroke engines driving twin screws for 15.5 knots. The plan was to run a twice-weekly crossing between Kirkwall, Westray and Scalloway, Shetland, 6 miles from Lerwick.

In 1985 operations commenced but unfortunately the little vessel continually suffered problems with her crankshaft which caused the cessation of sailings at the height of the summer season. The losses this caused proved insurmountable and in August the company ceased trading. The *Syllingar* made a final voyage in November before she was laid up and then sold to Greece in 1986 being renamed *Rennvi*. Ironically the *Orcadia* then had to be chartered to keep the service going until she was replaced by the new *St. Sunniva* (ex-*Lion*).

The *St. Clair V*, 1992–2002, was originally built as the car ferry *Travemünde* in 1971 by Schiffbau-Gesellschaft Unterweser AG, Bremerhaven for Moltzau Line A/S, Gedser, Denmark, for use on the Gedser to Travemünde route. After several ownership changes, in 1991 she was sold to P&O Scottish Ferries and became *St. Clair V* for the Aberdeen to Lerwick crossing. Extra cabins were added at Bremerhaven in 1992 and she also operated briefly at weekends from Lerwick to Bergen. In 2002 she worked to Shetland and Orkney for NorthLink and, as *St. Clair*, was sold to Saudi Arabia to become *Barakat*. Another vessel of this era was the *St. Magnus VI* a car ferry which ran between 1978 and 1989. The fourth *St. Ola* served between 1992 and 2002. She was a car ferry and had originally been built in 1971 by Meyer Werft, Papenburg-Ems for Skandinavisk Linietrafik as *Svea Scarlett*, on the Landskrona to Tuborg Havn service. In 1980 she was sold to A/S D/S Öresund, Denmark for Malmö to Tuborg Havn, then sold 1982 to Rederi Ab Eckerö, Eckerö, Finland, as *Eckerö*. Rebuilt with extra accommodation, in 1991 she was sold to P&O Scottish Ferries and in 1992 became *St. Ola IV* on the Stromness to Scrabster passage. In 2002 the service became NorthLink, and in October she was again sold, this time to Estonia, and the *Hebridean isles* took over her run, but proved too small and was not a popular choice and was later replaced in her turn by the new *Hamnavoe*.

The car ferry *St. Rognvald IV* served between 1989 and 2002 having originally been built in the late 1960s as the *Rhonetal* for Rhienecke of Hamburg. In May 1974 she became the *Norcape* with North Sea Ferries on their Hull to Zeebrugge run, but reverted to *Rhonetal* and in May 1975 was sold to Co. Meridionale de Navagition (CMN) of Marseille, and became *Rhone* running between Marseille and Bastia. In 1977 *Rhone* was sold to Societe Slibaila, Marseilles then, in 1987 was sold to Compagnia Navigazinone del Tirreno Conatir S.p.A. as *Marina Torre*. Chartered by P&O Ferries in 1989 for the Aberdeen to Lerwick route and bought outright in 1990, she was renamed *St. Rognvald IV*. In 2002 she was chartered to North Island Ferries, formed by Caledonian MacBrayne and Royal Bank of Scotland, for the Aberdeen to Kirkwall service.

The Car Ferry *St. Sunniva III* was used on the Aberdeen, Stromness to Lerwick, via Kirkwall service between 1987 and 2002. Built in 1972 for Jydsk Faergefart as *Djursland II*, in 1974 she was transferred to the Juelsminde-Kalundborg Line as *Lasse II*. Sold to Normandy Ferries for the Dover to Boulogne route in 1979 she became the *nf Panther*. Normandy Ferries sold her to the European Ferries Group, which then became Townsend Thoresen. She sailed with them until June 1986 before being laid up at Chatham, when she was then sold back to P&O Scottish Ferries in 1987 as *St. Sunniva*. She could carry an impressive 220 cars and was handy enough not to be retired until 2002 when the Shetland and Orkney were all taken over by NorthLink.

In the late 1980s Orkney Ferries initiated a project to re-introduce a regular crossing from Burwick on South Ronaldsay. A Linkspan and a terminal building were constructed at both ends of the proposed route and a new ferry was bought. This was the 928-GT Ro-Ro ferry *Varagen*, built by Cochrane Shipbuilders, Selby. She had an overall length of 49.85 m, a beam of 11.4 m and a 3.006 m draught. She was powered by two Caterpillar 790 kW engines for a speed of 14.5 knots. She had a 92/142 passenger capacity, a crew of 9 and could carry 28 cars. While Burwick was still under development the service was commenced using Houton, near Orphir, the maiden voyage being on 15 August 1989. It was a bitter blow then that the Linkspan at Gills suffered heavy weather damage almost immediately, causing the new ferry to be virtually stillborn and it ceased functioning on 16 September after just one month's operation. The ferry was taken out of service and in 1991 taken on by Orkney Island Council on the inter-island service and there the first attempt lay in ruins.

Two new ships were built for the Council in 1990, the sisters *Earl Sigurd* and *Earl Thorfinn*, which were 771-GT vessels with an overall length of 45 m, a beam of 11 m and a 3.155 m draught, built by McTay Limited of Bromborough, Merseyside and fitted out at St. Monas, Fife. They were powered by two Mirrless 743 kW engines which gave them a speed of 12 knots. Capacity was for 91/190 passengers, with 9–10 crew and 22 cars which they embarked and disembarked with a 7-ton crane.

Finally, after some very confusing and sometimes acrimonious dealings and negotiations, NorthLink took control of P&O Scottish Ferries in 2002 and, for the time being at least, some period of calm descended on these traditionally stormy waters!

Shetlands

The first regular ferry to the North Isles was the *Janet*, which began operating from Lerwick on 12 June 1838. Another early reference to a regular ferry service relates to Alexander Sandison of Unst, who owned a pair of fishing vessels in the 1850s in which he conveyed goods and passengers to the mainland. With the growth of ferry traffic elsewhere he bought a larger screw steamer in 1868 for £2,100, *Chieftains Bride*, and

Offshore Ferry Services

Hrossey with Shetland lighthouse in the background. (© Northlink Ferries)

set up the Shetland Steam Navigation Company. The route was from Tyree to the mainland across some of the roughest waters in the world. As an example, in October 1866 conditions were so bad that the crew and passengers had no option but to ditch the unfortunate livestock cargo of 54 cattle and sheep in order to regain control of the vessel.

In 1876 a service between Lerwick to the North Isles was maintained by the steamer *Lady Ambrosine*, and the following year the 253-GT *Earl of Zetland* arrived and she became a legend in herself. This vessel was built by the John Fullerton Yard, Paisley, and was of 44.09 m overall length, with a beam of 6.14 m and a 2.94 m draught. She was powered by a single Howden 250 bhp compound triple expansion engine with three coal fired furnaces, with a working pressure of 70 lbs and which gave a speed of 9 knots. Working out of Balta Sound she made a twice weekly crossing from Lerwick to Unst, plus once a week visits to the outer skerries and the harbours in Yell Sound, although from 1932 the ports of call fell away due to competitive services. This gallant old lady served with diligence no less than seventy years on this route, surely some sort of record. She was well past her retirement date in

1938 when it was planned to replace her, but the onset of the Second World War saw her retained in service until 1946. During the war she was twice attacked by enemy aircraft but survived, before she was finally retired.

The new 548-GT *Earl of Zetland* was built by Hall, Russell and Company Limited at Aberdeen in 1939. She was 50.6 m long overall and was powered by a single 6-cylinder Polar Diesel M46M engine giving 840 bhp at 220 revolutions. She spent most of her operational life working between Shetland and Orkney as the inter-island ferry for the North of Scotland, Orkney & Shetland Shipping Company. This service was for many years subsidized by the Department of Agriculture and Fisheries to the tune of £100,000 per year. Her scheduled route was three weekly sailings (always with weather allowing of course) to Yell, Unst and Whalsay, and a weekly service to Fetlar and Skerries. With only a single derrick, loading and unloading was a time-consuming operation, and, conversely, due to her size she was unable to dock at the smaller islands of Fetlar, Skerries and Symbister. Passengers from such outposts had to be rowed out to her by dedicated 'Flit Boats' from Brough, Houble and the like, each contributed by the local communities. Although not as long-lived as her predecessor, she survived until 1975 until taken out of service. She lingered on as a floating restaurant at various locations.

For inter-island ferry routes between the smaller islands, for many years sailing vessels remained the only option. Typical of these was Mr Blance's service from Ossbank and Ulsta. In later years small motor vessels like the *Viking* worked to Yell Sound, the *Tystie* from Ulsta Pier and the *Osprey*, which was the relief boat, crossed Bluemull Sound from Gutcher and Bellmont, and this continued until the early 1950s. At Yell Sound for the half-century from the 1920s until as recently as the early 1970s, similar conditions prevailed. Essential services were supplied by small boats like the *Tirrick* (ex-*Norseman*) between Burra and Scal-

Earl Sigurd tied alongside. (© Dave Greer)

loway, the *Tystie*, later replaced by the *Shalder*, the *Puffin* and the *Osprey*. The Black and Williamson ferries *Norna* and *Brenda* worked on the Bressay crossing in the 1930s through to the 1960s, and then continued working along with the *Viking Queen*, for Kirkpatrick and Moncrief, and finally, Kenneth Manson, until 1973. With the advent of Ro-Ro ferries like the *Geira* and the *Fivla* at Bluemull and Bressay Sounds these little boats continued running for some years after that. Foula was for many years served by the sailing and rowing craft *Advance* across the 16 miles separating her from the mainland. A crane had to be used to lift the boat out of the water between crossings as a precaution against the stormy seas. In 1950 a new boat, the *Island Lass*, was built as a replacement, but was wrecked 6 miles north-east of Mull Head, Papa Westray, in 1962. She was replaced by two boats named *Westering Homewards*, neither of which lasted long on the route. In 1996 Richardson's Boatyard at Stromness, Orkney, built the present vessel, the *New Advance*, which can carry twelve passengers as well as general cargo, and since 2006 has been operated by Atlantic Ferries owned by Gains Brothers of Whitness. She runs twice weekly in winter and three times a week in summer between Foula and Walls, with occasional runs to Scalloway. The catamaran *AliCat* acts as a reserve unit, but in 2011 there were threats to the subsidy paid by the Council for this service which caused grave concern.

This old-fashioned method of working had already been put under the microscope by several surveys initiated by Zetland County Council in the early 1960s. Eventually a whole new fleet of Norwegian-influenced ferry boats based on the *Rovdehorn*, with associated Linkspans, were built. These being the 146.98-GT stern-loader Ro-Ro sisters *Fivla* and *Geira*, which were constructed from 1973 onward by Thorshavnor Skipasmidja at Thorshavn in the Faroe Islands and were of 23.15 m overall length, with a beam of 7.85 m and a 3.2 m draught. They were powered by a pair of Kelvin T6 engines of 13 kW at 1,000 rpm for a speed of 12 knots. They could carry 10 cars or 2 lorries, had a crew of 5, and could carry 100 passengers. They replaced the *Shalder* between Lerwick and Bressay, and the *Tystie* at Yell and Bluemull, between Gutcher, Yell and Belmont, Unst, respectively. They were very successful, too successful for their own good, for traffic increased so rapidly that within a decade they were deemed too small for the job and were sold in 1982 and 1986 respectively, when they were renamed as the *Island Joiner* and the Orkney Island Shipping Company ship *Hoy Head*.

The Shetland Islands Council replaced the Zetland County and Lerwick Town councils in 1975 but they continued with the programme from the same shipbuilder; the 146.98-GT *Grima* was not Faroe-built but constructed to roughly the same specifications at Bideford Shipyard, Bideford, Devon in February 1975. She had an overall length of 23.89 m, a 7.71 m beam and a 2.28 m draught. She was powered by two GEC engines developing 268.56 kW. *Grima* was initially chartered by North Company as a substitute for the *Earl of Zetland* between Lerwick and Whalsay, and then worked to Bressay. She served until a final voyage in October 2004 before, with the arrival of the *Leirn*, being sold to Manson Marine. The 146.98-GT *Fylga* entered service that same year, replacing the *Earl* on the Whalsay crossing but subsequently on Bluemull Sound

Ship's bridge of the Shetland ferry *Dagalien*. (© Shetland Islands Council)

and was finally sold to M.M.W. Marine Services Ltd (Trawl Systems (Shetland) Ltd) in 2005. The last of the class, *Thora*, arrived in September the same year as the second Yell Sound ship, and became a reserve ship in 2009. Finally, a different class of ferry was bought in so that the Whalsay service had a back-up vessel. This was the *Kjella*, which had been built in Harstad, Norway by the Kaarbos, Mek, Verstad, back in 1957 for Torghatten TS. She was of 1,471-GT and had an overall length of 28.8 m, an 8 m beam and a draught of 2.47 m. She was powered by a single Kelvin TSCC8 375 kW 1,350 rpm engine for a speed of 12 knots. She had a bridge positioned above her open car deck with a single mast and twin engine vents to port and starboard aft. She retained her Norwegian name but was modified for work in the more open waters of the Shetlands, with her side passages plated in and made into extended lounges and a bow visor fitted to her forward car door. She could carry 100 passengers. She served until 1998 when she was sold to Quest Underwater Services.

Between 1974 and 1976 both car and passenger traffic increased still further and even these vessels were found insufficient. Subsequently, during 1972 to 1992, four larger replacements appeared on the scene, the first of these being the 225-GT *Hendra*, built by McTay Marine at Bromborough, Merseyside, in 1982, which replaced the original *Fivia*. She had a capacity for 18 cars and later worked Yell Sound and then to Vidlin, Whalsay. The second *Fivla* was built by the Ailsa Shipbuilding Co of Troon, in 1985, which replaced the first *Geira* on the Bluemull Sound passage. The second *Geira* was built by Richard Dunston at Hessle in 1988 and was initially used on the Laxo to Symbyster crossing, but in 2005 was moved to the Bluemull Sound route. The *Bigga*, built by J.E. Miller & Sons, St. Monans, in 1991, was the first three-lane ferry in the Shetlands and she worked the Toft to Ulsta service until 2004, before becoming a reserve boat. Finally the 420-GT *Leirna* was built at Ferguson Shipbuilders of Port Glasgow in 1992. She has a pair of Kelvin Diesels which power twin Voith-Schneider propulsion units, giving her a speed of 9.3 knots. The *Leirna* has a capacity of 96 passengers and room for 19 cars, and is notable for being the first double-ended vessel in the Shetland Islands Council fleet. She replaced the *Grima* on the Lerwick to Bressay passage.

Meantime the turbulent and unpredictable 25-mile Fair Isle passage continued to be looked after by the fourth *Good Shepherd* which was built in 1986. A 76.38-GT custom-built vessel, she was manufactured by James Miller & Son at St. Monans, Fife, and put together by McTay Marine at Bromborough. She is 18.3 m overall length, with a beam of 5.8 m and a 2.63 m draught and has a single Volvo TMD 121C engine developing 238.6 kW. She plies the 2 hour 30 minute route between Grutness and Fair Isle when the seas allow, with additional summer service to Lerwick. Her maiden voyage took place on 24 May 1986. Capable of carrying only a single car, which is craned on and off, and just 12 passengers, constrained in belted seats in a passenger cabin abaft the wheelhouse, this sturdy little vessel is the main sea link between Fair Isle and Grutness, and also makes Lerwick calls in summer. Between crossings she is hoisted out of the water at North Haven and stowed in a special storm-free resting place on Buness. During winter months a Tuesday-only service is operated, when conditions allow. She replaced her namesake, the former inshore trawler *Good Shepherd III*, which had been operating since 1972 and this vessel became the *Koada*. The 34.56-GT *Koada* was originally built at Bideford Shipyard, Bideford in 1969 and was of 14.55 m overall length, with a beam of 4.72 m and a 2.4 m draught. She was mainly used on the Papa Stour service until relieved and sold in 2004.

By the 1990s the Marine Operations Department of Shetland Island Council was running the ferries and they used the 73.62-GT former Navy Motor Fishing Vessel *Ashgrove*, built in 1947 by Herd & Mackenzie. As the *Spes Clara*, she worked out to the Skerries until she was replaced by the 130-GT custom-built *Filla*, built by Iversen, at Flekkefjbrd, Norway and making her maiden voyage on 28 November 1983. The *Filla* could carry 20 passengers in summer, 12 in winter, as well as 1 car or 1 lorry which were loaded via a stern ramp. She worked from Vidlin or Lerwick. She in her turn was replaced by a second ship of the same name in 2004 with an increased passenger capability of 30 and which can carry 9 cars, whereupon the original vessel became the *Snolda*. The new *Filla* was built at Gdansk, Poland. Her engines are two Mitsubishi diesel engines of 617 kW with 1,600 rpm. Her facilities include a capacious passenger saloon with two wide-screen televisions and toilets that include baby-changing facilities. For general cargo she has a pair of refrigerated holds and a 19-tonne freshwater tank. She entered service on 19 June, at which time the Shetland Islands Council ordered the building of two brand-new vessels based on the Polarkonsult design. These double-ended sisters, the *Dagalien* and the *Daggri*, are now currently running the Yell Sound passage.

In September 2002 a rival to NorthLink was initiated, this being Norse Island Ferries, which was a freight and livestock shipping company set up by three haulage companies and two shipping lines to provide a cheaper alternative. The first route was Lerwick to Aberdeen for which two vessels were readied, the 6,056-GT Ro-Ro Cenargo ship *Merchant Venture*, credited with 17 knots but one of whose engines was in a chronic state so that she was only fit for 9 knots in practice; and the 2,645-GT *St. Rognvald IV* (ex-*Rhonetal*, ex-*Rhone*), originally built by Orenstein & Koppel at Lübeck, Germany. She was 103.76 m overall, had a beam of 18.75 m, a capacity for 26 cars and she was chartered from P&O, as she had become surplus to their requirements. The company barely lasted six months, the *Merchant Venture* soon breaking down and never re-entering service; she later became the Panamanian-registered *Warsan* and then the Lebanese *Sunlight Bey* and was constantly in trouble with the regulation authorities. Cenargo itself went bust soon afterward. By 7 June this abortive challenge had petered out in total failure and the *St. Rognvald* was sold to Indian shipbreakers for scrapping in 2003.

A new summer service to the Orkney Islands was initiated in 1997 by Andrew Banks, who re-founded Pentland Ferries by purchasing the former CalMac ship *Iona* in October and renaming her *Pentalina-B*. Banks also took out a 99-year lease on the old Gills Bay, Caithness, site, located some 3 miles west of John o' Groats and developing the terminal in conjunction with its opposite number at St. Margaret's Hope, on South Ronaldsay, Orkney Islands. In the face of well-established routes like those operated by Caledonian MacBrayne and NorthLink, the new operator eventually succeeded in establishing a popular and non-subsidized Pentland Firth crossing where an earlier attempt in 1989 had failed. Between May 2001 and 2007 *Pentalina-B* worked the route successfully without problems. During off-peak seasons the ship was chartered out as an English Channel cattle boat, and in 2008–2009, back to CalMac itself on the west coast once more before being finally sold. Meanwhile another former CalMac vessel, the *Claymore*, was purchased in October 2002 with the intent of opening a second crossing, from Invergordon, but this did not catch on and instead *Claymore* worked on the *Pentalina-B*'s route until March 2009 when she was sold and became CT Offshore's *Sia*.

A very different approach followed, with the establishing of a unique 1-hour crossing being made by the Ro-Pax catamaran ferry *Pentalina*, especially built for Pentland Ferries in 2008, and she started operations in March 2009.

NorthLink Ferries currently operate three purpose-built Class LR+100A1 car and passenger Ro-Ro ferries between Aberdeen and Lerwick, these being the *Hamnavoe*, *Hjaltland* and *Hrossey*. All three were custom-built at Aker Finnyards, Rauma, Finland and cost from £35 million upward apiece; all entered service in 2002–03.

NorthLink also operates two freighting ships out of Aberdeen to the Shetlands and Orkney Islands. The *Helliar* was built in 1997 by Astilleros de Huelva SA at Huelva, Spain, for the Estonian Shipping Company, Tallinn, and christened as *Lehola*. In 2005 she became the Greek *RR Triumph* of the Elmira Shipping Company and was chartered to P&O Ferries on the Liverpool to Dublin crossing before working out of Spain. In 2007 Seatruck Ferries, Heysham, bought her and renamed her as *Clipper Racer*, chartering her to Condor Ferries on the Portsmouth to the Channel Islands route and then to the Isle of Man Steam Packet Company on the Heysham to Douglas crossing. She was in turn used on the Liverpool to Dublin route, and in 2009, by Baleària, Spain before being charted in January 2001 to NorthLink as *Helliar*.

The *Hildasay* was also built by Astilleros de Huelva SA at Huelva, Spain, for the Estonian Shipping Company, Tallinn, in 1999, and was originally named *Leili*. She served from 2002–2005 as the *Port Everglades Express* under charter to Crowley Maritime, before being sold to Greece as the *RR Shield*, becoming *Shield* in 2008 with Seatruck Ferries at Heysham and finally being chartered to NorthLink Ferries in January 2010 who gave her the current name.

The essentialness of the 'Lifeline Links' that are the islands ferry services have long been recognized by the Government, both before and after devolution, and have led to the payment of the Tariff Rebate Subsidy (TRS) in 1960. At the time of writing the services for the Northern Isles from 2012 are undertaken by NorthLink Ferries Ltd, while those of the Clyde and Hebrides are undertaken until 2013 by CalMac Ferries Ltd, and the Gourock to Dunoon ferry service is undertaken by Cowal Ferries Ltd. Public subsidy is also provided to four local councils: Argyll & Bute Council, who runs the routes to Easdale, Lismore, Luing and Jura; the Highland Council, who runs the Corran Ferry between Corran and Ardgour; Orkney Islands Council, who run the inter-island services; and Shetland Council, who operates the inter-island routes in that group. Other routes are commercially serviced. In March 2011 the Scottish Government completed the Scottish Ferries Review, and published the Draft Ferries Plan for consultation, the outcome of which, with European Union involvement, will decide the ultimate future of all these routes.

Current Operators, Ships and Details

NorthLink Ferries

A new contract confirmed from 5 July 2012 and they currently operate three, seven-deck, purpose-built car and passenger Ro-Ro ferries between Aberdeen and Lerwick, these being the *Hamnavoe* (IMO 9246061), *Hjaltland* (IMO 9244958) and *Hrossey* (IMO 9244960). Of these the smaller *Hamnavoe* normally runs the 90-minute Scrabster, Caithness

The Northlink ferry *Hjaltland* arrives in Lerwick. (© Northlink Ferries)

Hamnavoe leaving Stromness. (© Northlink Ferries)

to Stromness, Orkney crossing three times daily, while *Hjaltland* and *Hrossey* work a daily schedule from Aberdeen to Lerwick and Kirkwall. These schedules are likely to change under the new contract terms.

The smallest of the trio is the *Hamnavoe* at 8,780-GT, and she has an overall length of 112 m, a 18.5 m beam and a 4.4 m draught. Her engines are two Krupp MaK 9M32C, each developing 4,320 kW at 6,195 bhp, driving three Voith Schneider propellers for a top speed of 24 knots. She has two 900 kW bow thrusters as well as Mitsubishi stabilizers. Her capacity is 600 passengers, with a crew of 28, and she can carry 95 cars on 450 m of vehicle deck. She carries two lifeboats, two RIB fast rescue craft and inflatable life rafts.

Facilities on board include: passenger lounges; bars with a selection that includes Orkney and Shetland beers like Red Macgregor, Skull Splitter, Simmer Dim and White Wife; the Ladeberry *à la carte* restaurant; the Braebrough self-service restaurant; the Northern Isles shop selling snacks, gift items and travel products; a cinema lounge; a children's play area; a sun deck; a games room and internal telephones. There are twelve passenger *en-suite* cabins with both 2- and 4-berth accommodation, with hairdryers, shaver points and air conditioning, plus two specially-adapted cabins for disabled with wheelchair access, while the ships themselves are specially designed with wheelchair and disabled access throughout. There are several toilets and baby-changing facilities

The 8-deck sisters *Hjaltland* and *Hrossey* are of 11,720-GT, with an overall length of 125 m, a 20 m beam and a draught of 5.4 m. Powered by four MAK 6M43 engines developing 5.40k each, they have two CP propellers and two bow thrusters, and have a best speed of 24 knots. Capacity is 600 passengers in 117 cabins, with a crew of 37, plus 140 cars on 650 m of vehicle deck.

Facilities on board include: passenger lounges with total seating for 600; the Lönabrack *à la carte* restaurant; the Shoormal self-service restaurant; the Northern Isles shop selling snacks, gift items, and travel products; bars that include Orkney and Shetland beers like Red Macgregor, Skull Splitter, Simmer Dim and White Wife; a cinema lounge; toilets including disabled toilets; baby changing facilities; a children's play area; a sun deck; a games room; internal telephones. Passengers are accommodated in 356 berths with 117 *en-suite* cabins, both 2- and 4-berth, all *en-suite* with hairdryers, shaver points and air conditioning, and there are two specially-adapted cabins for the disabled, allowing easy wheelchair access, plus disabled lifts and wheelchair access throughout.

Hrossey and Shetland landscape. (© Northlink Ferries)

Offshore Ferry Services

Contact Details
NorthLink Ferries, Stromness Ferry Terminal, Ferry Road, Stromness, Orkney, KW16 3BH
Tel: 0845 6000 449 (Reservations)
Fax: 01856 851795
Email: info@northlinkferries.co.uk
Web: www.northlinkferries.co.uk

NorthLink Orkney and Shetland Freight also run two Class 1A Ro-Ro freight ferries from Aberdeen to the islands, the 7,606-GT sisters *Hildasay* (IMO 9119426) and the *Helliar* (IMO 9119397). Both are of 122.32 m overall length, with a 19.8 m beam and a draught of 6.21 m. Their engines are a pair of Wärtsilä 9R32 diesels, each developing 3,700 kW at 5,000 bhp for a speed of 14.2 knots. They have a capacity of 12 passengers and 63 trailers of 266 TEU on 1,055 m of deck lanes.

The Aberdeen Matthews Quay has a 220 tonnes maximum gross weight limit and Jamieson's Quay 186 tonnes. At Lerwick the Linkspan has a 100 tonnes passenger and 110 tonnes static and 60 tonnes moving mgw.

Contact Details
NorthLink Orkney & Shetland Freight, Stromness Ferry Terminal, Ferry Road, Stromness, Orkney, KW16 3BH
Reservations: 0845 6000 449
Freight: 0845 6060 449
Fax: 01856 851795
Email: info@northlinkferries.co.uk
Web: www.northlinkferries.co.uk

Aberdeen ferry terminal is at Jamieson's Quay, AB11 5NP. Car access is via the A93, A956 and Regent Road. At the terminal there is a ticket sales and enquiries desk, payphones, hot and cold drink vending machines, a left luggage counter, lift, disabled access and disabled toilets. Payable car parking is available at Apcoa Parking UK Ltd, Commercial Quay, close to the terminal; at Union Square a short distance away; and at NCP Ship Row a 15 minute walk away. Opening hours are from 06.45 to 17.00 with some variations according to time of year with some 19.00 closing times in winter months. Check before arrival.

Lerwick ferry terminal is located at Holmsgarth Terminal, Holmsgarth, Lerwick, ZE1 0PR, which is reached by car via either Gremista Road from the north or North Lochside from the south and is 2 miles from the town centre. The terminal houses a tourist information display

The Northlink ferry *Hildasay* arriving in Lerwick. (© Northlink Ferries)

with a bus stop to the town and there is also a ticket sales and enquiries desk, payphone, lift, left-luggage desk, disabled access and disabled toilets. There is very limited free car parking for both long and short-stay.

Scrabster ferry terminal is located at the Queen Elizabeth Pier, Scrabster, Caithness, KW14 7UT, approximately 1.5 miles from Thurston, and 22.5 miles from Wick. At the terminal can be found a ticket sales and enquiries desk, a snack bar, payphone, disabled access and disabled toilets. There is a long-stay car park in Scrabster operated by Scrabster Harbour Trust, and a pay and display facility. There is *no* left luggage facility. The terminal is open from 07.00 to 09.00 and 11.00 to 13.30 Monday to Friday, and 09.30 to 12,30 and 17.00 to 19.00 weekends, with varying times during Festivals. Times should be carefully checked prior to travelling.

The ferry terminal at Stromness is to be found at Ferry Road, KW16 3BH, and is 16 miles from Kirkwall, with a connecting bus service. At the terminal is a ticket sales and enquiries desk, a tourist information centre, luggage lockers, hot and cold drink vending machines, a lift, disabled access and disabled toilets. There is limited short-term only paid parking at the terminal with long-stay at Ferry Road.

Kirkwall ferry terminal is located at Hatston Quay, KW15 1RQ, about 3 miles from the town centre, but NorthLink operate a bus service to connect with the ferries. The terminal is reached via the A965 or Junction Road, and is approximately 16 miles from Stromness, 7 miles from Finstown and 15 miles from St. Margaret's Hope. There are connecting inter-island ferries to Shapinsay, Stronsay, Sanday, Eday, Westray, Papa Westray and North Ronaldsay. At the terminal itself is a ticket sales office and enquiry desk; hot and cold drink vending machines; a lift; disabled access and disabled toilet, but *no l*eft-luggage facility. There is a paying long stay car park 200 metres from the terminal.

Pentland Ferries
Pentland Ferries currently operate the 2,382-GT EU 98/10 Group B catamaran *Pentalina* (IMO 9437969). She was designed by Sea Transport Solutions, Australia, and built at the FBMA Marine Yard at Cebu in the Philippines at an estimated cost of £15 million. She is 70 m overall length, with a beam of 20 m and a 2.2 m draught. She is steel-hulled with an aluminium superstructure and was claimed to have been specially designed to cope for the notorious sea conditions on the Firth.

She has the capacity for carrying 350 passengers, between 32 and 58 cars, 9 lorries and has a maximum speed of 19.8 knots and a service speed of 15 knots for an average 1-hour passage. She has been known to make the journey in as little time as 45 minutes, and because the journey time is so short there is no cabin accommodation and the facilities aboard are limited to a cafeteria service and toilets; there is also a limited area of sun decking.

The timetable varies according to season with up to six crossings most, but by no means all, days, and these should be carefully checked prior departure as they are highly dependent upon weather and tidal conditions. There are no crossings on Christmas Day or New Year's Day. Special conditions include nobody under sixteen years of age is allowed unless accompanied by an adult, and pets (other than guide dogs) have to stay inside the vehicles *en route*. The St. Margaret's Hope office is staffed between 07.00 and 17.00.

Contact Details
Pentland Ferries, Pier Road, St. Margaret's Hope, Orkney, KW17 2SW
Reservations: 0800 688 8998
Head Office: 01866 831 226
Gill's Bay: 01955 611773
Fax: 01856 831697
Email: info@pentlandferries.co.uk
Web: www.pentlandferries.co.uk

Offshore Ferry Services

The *Pentalina* of Pentland Ferries crosses at high speed from Caithness to South Ronaldsay. (© Pentland Ferries Ltd)

Gill's Bay Terminal is reached by car via the A836. Facilities are minimal, just a booking office and basic toilets. The St. Margaret's Hope Terminal is reached by car via the A961 or the B9021. Facilities are equally sparse with just a booking office.

John O' Groats to Orkney Ferry
The 186-GT ferry *Pentland Venture* (IMO 8834122) was built by Hepworth Shipyard, Hull in 1986, and runs a passenger-only service between John O'Groats itself and Burwick, South Ronaldsay, in the Orkney Islands twice a day, and in 2012 three times daily between 1 May and 2 September. The crossing takes about 40 minutes. She was later extended in length by 6.6 m at Hepworth's, and is now 29.6 m overall, with a beam of 6.5 m and a 1.5 m draught, giving her a capacity for 250 passengers. She is powered by two CAT 3406 engines developing 480 bhp each. She is equipped with toilets.

The ferry terminal is open between 08.00 and 18.00 with a 15-minute pre-sailing check-in time. There is a large free car park at John O'Groats. In Orkney there is a connecting 45-minute coach service to Kirkwall.

25: Aberdeen – Shetland Isles – Scrabster – Orkney Islands

Contact Details
Office
John O'Groats Ferries Limited, The Ferry Office, John O'Groats, Caithness, KW1 4YR
Tel: 01955 611353; 01955 611342
Fax: 01955 611301
Email: office@jogferry.co.uk
Web: www.jogferry.co.uk

Inter-Island Services – Shetlands
The ferry from the Mainland to Yell, Ulsta, operates between Toft on the Mainland, and Ulsta on Yell, the route being between the island of Samphrey to the east and Bigga to the north. You can then travel overland on to ferries for Unst and Fetlar.

The 1,861-GT *Daggri* (IMO 9291614) and *Dagalien* (IMO 9291626) are Ro-Ro ferries that have been operated since 2004 by Shetland Islands Council. Built by Stoeznia Polnocna at Gdansk, Poland, they are each 65.36 m long overall, with a beam of 13.8 m and a 3.7 m draught. They

The John O'Groats Ferry's *Pentland Venture* alongside the Mole.
(© Fred Fermor, John O'Groats Ferries Ltd)

Among the newest vessels of the Shetland fleet the 2004-built *Daggri* operates between the Mainland and Yell Sound. (© Shetland Islands Council)

Offshore Ferry Services

Shetland ferry *Dagalien*. (© Shetland Islands Council)

Spacious three-lane car deck in the *Dagalien*. (© Shetland Islands Council)

have a capacity of 95 to 144 passengers, have a crew of 4–5 and can carry 31 cars or 4 trucks on their 52.6 m long car decks. They have two MAK6M20 engines of 1,200 kW at 1,000 rpm. The *Daggri* (Norse – Dag-gry) replaced the *Bigga* on the Yell Sound crossing in June 2004, while the *Dagalien* (Norse – Daga-liòr) replaced the *Hendra* the same year.

These boats operate an approximately 20-minute crossing at intervals of about 30 minutes. Facilities aboard the two ships are basic: there is a two-door passenger saloon (lounge) with fixed seating, tables, toilets, children's play area and vending machine.

Other than Lerwick, the numerous small local terminals are Belmont, Unst; Bressay; Grutness, which is the Fair Isle crossing terminal; Gutcher, Yell; Hamars Ness, Fetlar; Laxo; Papa Stour; Symbister, Whalsay; Toft; Ulsta, Yell; Vidlin and West Burrafirth. Most of these have only basic facilities and all are 24-hour operating, but none have any staff available to assist or any hearing loops and only a few have accessible toilets, these being Vidlin, Hamars Ness, West Burrafirth and Papa Stour. From Whalsay there is usually a 35-minute crossing, sailing up to seventeen times daily, six days a week with a more restricted Sunday service from Laxo, close to Voe, to Symbister, but under certain weather conditions the ship uses Vidlin. There are electronic road signs to indicate when this occurs. At Symbister there is a waiting room about 70 m from the non-segregated landing ramp up a steep slope or via eleven steps. There are toilets but they are unsuitable for wheelchairs.

At Laxo there is a waiting room about 90 m from the non-segregated loading ramp reached via a sloped car park. There are toilets but nothing is suitable for wheelchairs. There is also a telephone booth. At Vidlin there is a heated waiting room about 25 m from a non-segregated loading ramp. There are bench seats without arm rests, and a public payphone. There are heated toilets which are wheelchair suitable. At Maryfield, Bressay, the old stone-built pier is just 8 minutes across the water from bustling Lerwick. There are no bookings to be made as the service is continuous during the day, with approximately twenty crossings daily, with slightly fewer on Sundays and a late night service at high summer season. Adjacent to the terminal is a car park with public toilets which are not disabled friendly, and there is ramped access but no waiting room. Close by is the Bressay Heritage Centre.

The triangular Blumell Sound ferry route crosses between Belmont, Unst and Gutcher, Yell or to Hamars Ness, Fetlar is run by the *Fivla*, *Fylga* or *Thora* at approximately 30-minute intervals according to season, with the Fetlar passage taking abut 20 minutes or so, but they get very busy in the high summer season and booking is probably wise, as with everywhere in the Shetlands. At Belmont there is non-segregated access to the shore ramp with a heated waiting room approx 80 m distant, with bench seats without arm rests, payphone and basic toilets. Gutcher has an unheated waiting room with non-segregated access. There are bench seats with no arm-rests, with basic toilets, but the Wind Dog café near the pier offers tea and coffee, fresh home-bakes, homemade soups, sandwiches, burgers and a weekly specials menu, and there are wheelchair accessible toilet facilities. Nearby there is also a post office. At Hamars Ness there is a waiting room and a basic public toilet block. The passage between West Burrafirth and Papa Stour takes about 35 minutes. There is a heated waiting room and disabled access toilets at both the piers, with ramp access. The 20-minute ferry crossing is between Toft, close to Mossbank on the Mainland, and the pier at

Shetland ferry *Fivla* in Blumell sound. (© Shetland Islands Council)

Offshore Ferry Services

Ulsta on the south-west of Yell and runs at around 30-minute intervals during daylight. From Toft to the Belmont, Unst terminal is an approximately 10 minute journey. Toft terminal has segregated ferry ramp, with an unheated, stepped access waiting room approx 150 m away with bench seating without arm rests, payphone and internal toilet facilities. From the Grutness terminal, which is non-segregated, the Fair Isle ferry is run by the *Good Shepherd*. The terminal itself is close to Sumburgh Airport and has a basic unheated waiting room and a concrete toilet block and neither are disability friendly. Ulsta terminal building is approx 100 m from the segregated ferry ramp with an unsuited to disabled toilet block but no waiting room.

The various inter-island terminals operate at intermediate times according to seasonal demand.

For Whalsay the hours are: Mon–Thurs 08.30–13.00 and 13.30–16.00; Fri 08.30–13.00 and 13.30–15.00; Closed Sat and Sun.

For Bluemull and Yell: Mon–Sat 08.30–16.45; closed Sun.

Passengers intending to travel should always check before travelling via the Voicebank Service for up-to-date ferry information.

	Voicebank	*Bookings*
Bluemull (Unst/Fetlar/Yell)	01595 743971	01595 745804
Bressay	01595 743974	not bookable
Fair Isle	01595 743978	01595 760363
Papa Stour	01595 743977	01595 745804
Skerries	01595 743975	01806 515226
Whalsay	01595 743973	01806 566259
Yell	01595 743972	01595 745804

For general information on these inter-island routes the contact number is 01595 743970. At the time of going to press the booking offices do not currently have any online presence or email facilities. They hope to improve communications soon, but in the meantime booking queries can be emailed to ferries@shetland.gov.uk. It is also important to note that Shetland Island Ferry Services does not accept bookings where the travelling time through Yell, between Yell Sound terminal (Ulsta) and Bluemull Sound Terminal (Gutcher), is less than 25 minutes.

The little *Good Shepherd IV*, smallest of the Shetland Island fleet. (© Shetland Islands Council)

Contact Details
Shetland Islands Council, Town Hall, Upper Hillhead, Lerwick, Shetland, ZE1 0HB
Tel: 01595 693534
Fax: 01959 744509
Email: info@shetland.gov.uk
Web: www.shetland.gov.uk/ferries

Atlantic Ferries
This company leases the *New Advance* for services from the Shetland mainland to the most westerly island of the group, Foula, calling at the Ham Voe Pier on the twice-weekly, year-round service, to Walls, Mainland, subject to weather conditions, and the 20-mile journey takes approximately 2 hours. This crossing is supplemented by extra sailings in the summer months with a once a fortnight passage to Scalloway, which takes 3.5 hours. The 21.35-GT *New Advance* was constructed at Penryn, Cornwall and based on the Cygnus GM38 hull design. She was subsequently fitted out at Richardson's Boatyard, Stromness in the Orkney Islands, to replace the unsuitable *Westering Homewards II*, and has an overall length of 9.75 m, a beam of 4.05 m and a 1.72 m maximum draught. First entering service on 12 November 1996, this ferry has a top speed of 8.7 knots, a passenger capacity of 12, plus room for a single car (for island residents only), and is launched from Foula by being winched down by a pair of cranes. She was taken under a competitive tender lease from Shetland Islands Council on 20 November 2006.

Contact Details
Atlantic Ferries, Gronnack, Whiteness, Shetland ZE2 9LL
Tel: 01595 743976
Fax: 01595 840880
Email: bookings@atlanticferries.co.uk
Web: www.atlanticferries.co.uk

Inter-Island Services – Orkney
Orkney Ferries run a fleet of ships to the various islands but the timings and number of sailings is highly varied; some crossings take in some islands, other do not and the crossing times obviously vary enormously. Great care should be taken in checking prior to travelling which services are available and when. The Westray, North Ronaldsay, Stronsay, Sanday and Eday services are still operated with the *Varagen* (IMO 8818154), the *Earl Sigurd* (IMO 8902711) and the *Earl Thorfinn* (IMO 8902723) although these ladies are now getting rather long in the tooth. On-board facilities are rather basic as the journey times are only of approximately 90 minutes duration. The *Earl* duo have an upper

Earl Sigurd runs inter-island services for Orkney Ferries. (© Dave Greer)

Earl Thorfinn is a sister vessel to *Earl Sigurd*. (© Dave Greer)

lounge with bench seating, TV and vending machines, while there is a cafeteria with limited opening times on the vehicle deck for hot snacks and drinks. There are also several small shelter deck areas. The *Varagen* likewise has a passenger lounge with a sun deck abaft it, with another a much smaller lounge on one side of the lower deck with a cafeteria opposite. All ships have toilet facilities.

For the smaller islands a flotilla of little ships is also employed, which are rated as Small Passenger Ferries. All the terminals on the islands have just basic facilities with small waiting rooms with perhaps one toilet, but little else, and the timetables are varied, with summer and winter schedules and varying routes. Houton Pier is mid-way between Kirkwall and Stromness, and is accessed via the A964. The toilets at the ticket office have disabled facilities and there is a pay phone. Tingwall Pier is about 20 minutes drive from Kirkwall and is accessed via the A966. There are disabled facilities at the pier toilets. Car loading for ferries that visit several destinations is all done according to a disembarkation plan and is handled efficiently in the main. Shapinsay ferry terminal is reached via the A965 to the town centre and has disabled facilities at the toilet. Rousay Pier is accessed via the B9065 and the waiting room has disabled facilities and a pay phone nearby. The Loth Pier waiting room at the southern tip of Sanday has disabled facilities and a bus service close by. Scrabster terminal has a ticket sales office, payphone, snack bar, disabled facilities and toilets. The fare structures on the southern and northern routes are different and other factors make it quite a complex affair and it all requires very careful checking with the OIC Ferry Company well in advance of actual travel. All these little ships either have been, like the *Varagen*, or soon will be, adapted to make them disabled friendly with special toilets and seating, but their small size and oldish layout means there is a limit to just what can be done even with the best intentions. There are no refreshment facilities aboard these vessels.

For short crossing from the Gill Pier, Pierowall, Westray to the Moclett Pier, on the Papa Westray feeder service there is the 32.88-GT *Golden Mariana* (IMO 365680), which was built in 1973 at Bideford Shipyard, Devon and has an overall length of 15.24 m, a beam of 4.87 m and a 1.67 m draught. She is powered by a single Gardner engine for 9.5 knots and can carry 34/40 passengers with a crew of 2–3. There is only a small seating area for passengers. She has a single crane so that claims she can ship a 15-tonne lorry have been met with some wry scepticism in the islands themselves. Westray terminal is at Rapness Pier, a few miles south of Pierowall with a bus connection.

The South Isles to Graemsay and North of Hoy crossing from Stromness, Orkney to Moness Pier, Hoy, takes about 25 minutes direct or 30 minutes via a call at Graemsay, and is provided by the 81.87-GT *Graemsay* (IMO 728892). She was built in 1996 at the Ailsa Troon Ltd shipyard, and is 16.17 m overall, with a 6.08 m beam and a draught of 1.95 m. She is driven by a pair of Mermaid Marine engines which give her a speed of 9.5 knots and her capacity is 73 passengers with a crew of 2 and she is also capable of carrying 2 cars. She has a very limited passenger seating area below and some open decking space.

The 25-minute Shapinsay route between the west side of Kirkwall harbour basin and the Balfour Village Pier is covered by the 199-GT Ro-Ro ferry *Shapinsay* (IMO 8814184) herself. She was built in the Yorkshire Drydock in 1988 and is 26.602 m long overall, with a beam of 8.8 m and a 1.45 m draught. Her new engines are two of the Volvo-Penta type and they give her a top speed of 9.5 knots. Recently lengthened by 6 m and fitted with new electrical and bridge equipment, she can carry 91 passengers, with a crew of 4 and now has an increased capacity for up to 16 cars which have to reverse-load onto the ship. She has a large lounge with basic seating with two open deck viewing areas.

To provide links from Tingwall, Orkney to the islands of Rousay, Egilsay and Wyre, Orkney Islands Council have the 104-GT Ro-Ro unit *Eynhallow* (IMO 8960880), which was built in 1987 by David Abels, at Bristol. Of 28.8 m overall length, she has a 7 m beam and a 1.5 m draught and is powered by two Volvo engines generating 220.5 kW apiece for a speed of 10.5 knots. Since being lengthened by 5 m at Buckie in 1991 due to the demand she herself generated, her capacity is now 95 passengers, with a crew of 3–5, and 10 cars, which again have to reverse on board. She has a passenger lounge below the bridge and limited deck space. The Rousay terminal is at Trumland (Brinian) with a waiting room and toilets some distance from the loading slip.

The fourth *Hoy Head* (IMO 9081722) is a Ro-Ro vehicle and passenger ferry with both bow and stern ramps, built in 1994 by Appledore Shipbuilders, North Devon. She has an overall length of 39.5 m, a 9.8 m

The tiny *Graemsay* carries two cars and up to seventy-two passengers. (© Dave Greer)

beam and a draught of 2.5 m and can carry up to 125 passengers, with a crew of 5 and has a capacity for up to 18 cars. She is powered by two Volvo engines, is equipped with two 370 kW Schottel azimuth stern drive units and has a best speed of 11 knots. She has two windowless passenger lounges and for the claustrophobic among her passengers

Offshore Ferry Services

Shapinsay runs a short route intra-island route between Kirkwall harbour and Balfour village. (© Dave Greer)

space for 16 cars. The *Thorsvoe* has a lounge below the vehicle deck, and some open deck space abaft her bridge structure.

Contact Details
Orkney Ferries Limited, Shore Street, Kirkwall, Orkney, KW15 1LG
Tel: 01856 872044
Fax: 01856 872921
Email: info@orkneyferries.co.uk
Web: www.orkneyferries.co.uk

there is a limited amount of open deck space to port and starboard of the car deck. Her 30-minute route is between the Linkspan at Houton, Orphir, and Lyness, Hoy, with additional calls at the Gibraltar Pier Linkspan at Flotta.

The *Thorsvoe* (IMO 9014743) currently acts as a summer relief ship on the inter-island routes including the Hoy crossing. She is a 385-GT vessel built in 1991 at the Campbeltown Shipyard and is 35 m overall length, with a beam of 9.5 m and a draught of 1.8 m. Engined by two Volvo units developing 346 kW apiece she is good for almost 11 knots speed. Her capacity is 121 passengers and she has a crew of 4–5 and

26: Ullapool – Stornoway, Isle of Lewis

Background

From August 1870 there was a paddle steamer service with the *Ondine* working this crossing regularly three days per week. This was in conjunction with the opening up of the railways into the Highlands which acted as feeders. In 1881 the route was taken over by a new company but their operational period was brief, for in 1885 Ullapool terminus was changed to Strome Ferry, which at that time was at the head of the rail link to Inverness.

Stornoway sailings were made from Loch Seaforth, via the Kyle of Lochalsh to Mallaig for the next century. The impending arrival of the Ro-Ro ferries meant that the shorter crossing to Ullapool was again deemed to be practical. In preparation for the re-instated crossing much work had to be done and it was not until 1 May 1972 that the direct service between Ullapool and Stornoway was finally re-instated.

The first ferry to be employed was the *Iona*, but with no Linkspans at the terminal, side ramps and hoists had to be employed which made for a slow process. The *Iona* was a 1,324-GT; Steel DSMV Ro-Ro ship built by Ailsa Shipbuilding at Troon, the first such to be built for the David MacBrayne Company. She featured bridge-controlled engines and twin rudders, which helped her stern-load her cargo at Ullapool and bow-load it at Stornoway. She suffered from frequent break-downs, particularly caused by her highly temperamental and unreliable gearboxes. This unseamanlike arrangement continued until March 1973 when *Iona* was replaced with the arrival of the reconstructed Ro-Ro ship *Clansman* and the completion of both the Linkspans in May, the whole loading process was vastly speeded up and simplified and the route gained in popularity. However, the change-over was not a smooth one and due to technical problems with both ferries and the new spans, *Iona* had to be re-instated for another short period until the modified *Clansman* could settle down on the route.

The *Clansman* was another hoist-loading car ferry built by Hall, Russell & Co at Aberdeen, which had operated for a decade on the Mallaig to Armadale crossing before being converted to Ro-Ro operations as a drive-through ship in October 1972. Of 1,420-GT and as prone to mechanical failures as the *Iona*, she also proved slow and inadequate for the task and the Minches' weather and was soon withdrawn.

In 1973/74 the *Suilven* took over the crossing. The *Suilven* was built in Norway by Moss Rosenberg in 1974 and originally intended for service in Oslofjord. She had a 1,980-GT was powered by three 7-cylinder Wichmann diesel engines which made her good for 14 knots, and had a pair of variable pitch propellers and was fitted with bow thrusters. She had a passenger capacity of 408, a crew of 25 and space for 120 vehicles on a pair of mezzanine car decks. While she was still building she was bought outright by Caledonian MacBrayne and converted for the Isle of Lewis Lifeline route. She proved far more reliable and successful and, although her car capacity was reduced to 85 later in her career, she was fitted with stabilizers and proved capable of coping with inclement weather conditions on the route far more easily than the rest of the fleet. Unlike her two predecessors, *Suilven* was a popular ship and remained until she was replaced twenty-two years later by the *Isle of Lewis*.

Current Operators, Ships and Details

Isle of Lewis (IMO 9085974) is a well-planned 6,753-GT, Steel DSMV, passenger/vehicle ferry with a speed of 18 knots and is 101.25 m overall

Offshore Ferry Services

Isle of Lewis loading with her bow visor open. (© Dave Greer)

length, with a 18.52 m beam and a draught of 4.19 m. Her two passenger decks have a capacity of 680 passengers and her 32-strong crew. Her fully-enclosed, five-lane car deck can contain 123 cars and 10 trucks with full quiet lounge facilities for their drivers. The stern ramp was off-centred to port in order for her to access the Linkspan at Ullapool while her central bow ramp had to have its forward section skewed over to starboard to offload at the Stornoway Linkspan. She is fitted with electrically-hoisted adjustable mezzanine decks to increase or decrease her vehicle capacity according to demand. One of the largest vessels in the CalMac ferry fleet, she was built by Ferguson Shipbuilders Ltd, at Port Glasgow on the Clyde, especially to serve the Ullapool to Stornoway route previously served by the smaller and slower *Suilven*. She was launched by HRH Princess Alexandra on 18 April 1995. Her two K6 Major Diesel engines were supplied by Mirrlees Blackstone Ltd, of Stockport, Cheshire, and give her an operating speed of 18 knots.

The facilities aboard this fine vessel are among the finest in the fleet and include on Deck 4, the information desk, the large Mariners cafeteria, Shop@CalMac, the Still Bar which stocks an enviable range of fine whisky and other spirits and beverages, the teenage video-game Mecca of Game-On, along with toilets, mobility impaired facilities, baby-changing unit and a dedicated area for pets. On Deck 5 there is Cub Club for younger passengers and the Coffee Cabin, also a TV lounge, and observation lounge and recliner lounge. Even though the weather is not always accommodating, there is ample open-air seating for viewing on Decks 5 and 6. She is equipped with two rigid boats, a single RIB fast rescue craft and inflatable life-rafts.

The *Isle of Lewis* (Gaelic – *Eilean Leodhais*) entered service on 31 July 1995 and currently operates the northernmost CalMac timetable, across the intemperate and unpredictable waters of The Minch on the Ullapool (Loch Broom, Ross-shire) to Stornoway, Isle of Lewis, crossing, making the journey in approximately 2 hours 45 minutes. Service times precluded Sundays in deference to local religious susceptibilities but from 19 July 2009 a seven-day timetable became an actuality. Currently the summer service provides two sailings daily in each direction, with a single sailing on Sundays, but on certain select weekdays and Sundays there are extra sailings, all of which need careful checking before travelling. There is a 45-minute latest check in time for this service and the terminal has dedicated parking spaces in the vehicle queuing area, and wheelchair access. There is a 78-seat waiting room with toilets and disabled toilets and baby-changing.

Traffic on this route has steadily increased, necessitating the use of the *Muirneag* freight ferry to ease the load at peak periods. There are currently about 92,000 passengers a year using this link and between 2008 and 2011 a detailed Scottish Transport Appraisal Guidance (STAG) has been held to review provision on this route and report to the Lewis and Harris communities.

Contact Details
Caledonian MacBrayne, Shore Street, Ullapool, IV26 2UR
Tel: 01854 612358
Fax: 01854 612433
Email: david.cannon@calmac.co.uk
Web: www.calmac.co.uk.

BAI (UK) Ltd, Millbay Docks, Plymouth, Devon, PL1 3EW
Tel: 0871 244 0744
Email: customer.feedback@brittanyferries.com
Web: www.brittanyferries.com

The ferry terminal at Ullapool is at Shore Street, has a 78-seat waiting room with toilets and full disabled toilet, and baby-changing facilities. There is a latest check in time of 45 minutes prior departure. It is usually open between 09.00 and 17.30 and has disabled parking space in the assembly area and a bus stop within 10 metres.

27: Hull – Zeebrugge – Rotterdam

Background

The port at Kingston-upon-Hull on the Humber Estuary has a long and distinguished history dating back to the twelfth century, when seaborne trade from Wyke flourished, and carried on by the wool trade, the growth of new docks in the eighteenth century and the emergence of shipping companies like Wilson Ellerman Line and Associated Humber Lines. However, the Hull to Rotterdam Europoort and Zeebrugge crossings as we know them today are a relatively new route which was first inaugurated on 17 November 1965 by the joint Anglo–Dutch company of P&O North Sea Ferries and Noordzee Veerdiensten, AV, Rotterdam. This company later became North Sea Ferries and then P&O Ferries and currently is just P&O.

The first ships employed were the 3,692-GT *Norwind* and *Norwave*. Built in 1965 and 1966 respectively by Weser AG Werk, Seebeckwerft, Bremerhaven, they had an overall length of 108.8 m, beam of 18.95 m and a 5.40 m draught. They were powered by two Smit & Bolnes 14-cylinder diesel engines which made them good for 15 knots. Their final capacity was 249 passengers and 70 cars and 47 trailers. They were operated by North Sea Ferries 1965–1975 on Hull to Rotterdam and then replaced and switched to the Hull to Zeebrugge route until 1987. The *Norwind* was replaced by *Norstar* and became the *Grecia Express* and sank in 1993. *Norwave* was replaced by the *Norland* and became the *Italia Express* and was destroyed in a shipyard explosion in 1988.

In December 1970 the *Norcape*, originally built as the *Rhonetal*, was chartered to North Sea Ferries for work on the Hull to Zeebrugge and Rotterdam crossings. She was withdrawn in May 1974 and later sold as the *Rhone*. The *Norland* and *Norstar* were 27,000-GT Ro-Ro ferries built in 1974 by AG Weser Seebeck-Werft at Bremerhaven for Noordzee Veerdiensten, AV, Rotterdam. They were 153.02 m overall length, with a 25.20 m beam and a draught of 6.22 m. Their engines were two 16-cylinder Stork-Werkspoor diesels driving two controllable-pitch propellers for a speed of 18.5 knots. They could carry 1,243 passengers and had space for 134 trailers (of 12.19 m). Both serviced the North Sea Ferries Hull to Rotterdam passage until 1987, with *Norland* seeing intervening war service in the Falklands in 1982 followed by an extensive refit. *Norland* ran aground at Maasvlakte while trying to avoid a German ship on 7 June 1985 and was replaced by the chartered *Viking V*. *Norland* was under repair for ten weeks. Both ships were lengthened by their original builders to 173.29 m, and then switched to the Hull to Zeebrugge crossing, being taken over by P&O North Sea Ferries in 1996 and being sold in 2002 to become the *SNAV Sicilia* and the *SNAV Campania* respectively. Both ships were finally scrapped in 2010.

The first *Norsky* was built for the Stena Line in South Korea in 1977 by Hyundai Shipbuilders & Heavy Industries, Ulsan, and they chartered her out to North Sea Ferries in 1977 and she served in the North Sea for three years. A second *Norcape*, built in Tamano, Japan by Mitsui Engineering and Shipbuilding for P&O Ferries in 1979 as the *Tipperary*, was purchased in 1988 and briefly employed on the Hull to Zeebrugge route in 1995 and after a number of years elsewhere, returned to that crossing in 2008.

In 1987 the second *Norsea* arrived on the scene. She was built for P&O's North Sea Ferries by Govan Shipbuilders at Govan. She had an

27: Hull – Zeebrugge – Rotterdam

The big new P&O ship *Pride of Hull*. (© P&O)

overall length of 170.078 m, a beam of 25 m and a 6.096 m draught and was powered by four Sulzer diesel engines. and used on the Hull to Rotterdam route, moving over to the Zeebrugge route in 2002 and being renamed as *Pride of York* in 2003. Similarly the *Norsun*, a near sister, was constructed in Japan by NKK at Tsurumi and ran the same passages, and was, in turn, renamed as *Pride of Bruges* in 2003. The 1989-built *Norcape* was originally built as the *Puma* by Mitsui Engineering and Shipbuilding Company Limited at Tamano, was of 6,310-GT, with a length overall of 150.85 m, with a 20.73 m beam and a draught of 5.12 m. She was powered by two Mitsui 12-cylinder diesel engines driving twin screws for 19.5 knots. Her capacity was 12 passengers and 125 vehicles. She served on the Zeebrugge to Hull route from 1995 onward.

In 1991, two sister Ro-Ro cargo ships, the 17,884 *Norqueen* and *Norking*, originally built by Rauma Repola Oy, in Finland, as the *Bore Queen* and *Bore King*, were placed under long-term charter to North Sea Ferries, *Norking* later being moved to the Tilbury to Zeebrugge crossing. Their dimensions were 170.90 m overall length, 23.05 beam and 7.60 m draught. They were engined by two MaK 8M552C, developing 12,000 kW for 17.5 knots. They had a car capacity of 920 using all decks and had side and stern ramps. Later two more sisters, the *Norbank* and *Norbay*, built in 1993 and 1994 respectively by Van der Giessen-De Noord, in the Netherlands, worked on the Hull to Rotterdam service until 2002 when they were switched to the Irish Sea.

Since 1999 the third *Norsky*, built in Finland by Aker Finnyards at Rauma for Bore Sky AV, has been chartered to run a freight-only service between Middlesbrough, Teeside and Zeebrugge, while the 19,992-GT *Norstream* and the 8,007-GT *European Trader* operated similar freight-only traffic between that port and Zeebrugge. The former was built at Aker Finnyards, Rauma and was 180 m overall length, with a beam of 29.25 m and a 6 m draught. Powered by two Wärtsilä 9-cylinder diesels driving two screws she had a best speed of 21 knots. Her capacity was 12 passengers and 210 vehicles. The latter vessel had original been built in 1975 by Schichau-Unterwesere, Bremerhaven for Townsend Thoresen, and had an overall length of 117.85 m, a beam of 20.3 m and a 5.09 m draught. Her engines were two Stork Werkspoor which gave her 18 knots and she could carry 132 passengers. She was taken over by P&O European in 1987 and eventually sold in 2001, becoming the *TagranTrader* and then the *Lina Trader* before being scrapped in 2006.

Current Operator, Ships and Details

P&O run seven sailings per week on a 10 hour 15 minutes crossing from Kingston-upon-Hull to Rotterdam, the majority of overnight services leaving at 21.00 with a 90-minute check-in time, and arrive at 08.15; although on certain dates in January the times change to 19.00 departure and 09.00 arrival. Care should be taken when booking. The reverse route leaves Rotterdam at 21.00 and arrives at Hull at 08.00,

P&O's new ship *Pride of Rotterdam* makes her debut. (© P&O)

again certain dates vary with 20.00 departures and should be checked. There are no sailings at all on the 24, 25, 30 and 31 December.

The two ships employed on this crossing are the 59,925-GT sister ships *Pride of Hull* (IMO 9208629) and the *Pride of Rotterdam* (IMO 9208617), built in Italy in 2001 and 2000 respectively by Fincantieri-Cantieri Navali Italiani S.p.A. at Marghera, Venice. They have twelve decks, took fourteen months to build and cost £90 million apiece. The *Pride of Hull* was originally built for North Sea Ferries. The *Pride of Rotterdam* was originally laid down as the *Pride of Hull* but the name was changed when she was launched. In 2006 she was sold to P&O. They are of 215.45 m overall length, have a beam of 31.5 m and a 6.05 m draught. They each have four Wärtsilä NSD 9L46C engines, with 37,800 kW output at 500 rpm, driving two 4.9 m diameter propellers, and they also have two auxiliary Wärtsilä 9L32 engines for back up. Each ship has a service speed of 22 knots. They are fitted with two Fincantieri 2,000 kW bow thrusters

Each of these magnificent ships, among the largest ferries in the world, can carry 1,360 passengers, with 546 cabins and 1,376 berths, (on Decks 7, 8, 9 & 10) with a crew of 141 (accommodated on Deck 11), 250 cars or 400 lorries on 3,255 lane meters of 2.7 m high vehicle deck. They were too large for existing facilities at their ports of call and new multi-million pound terminals had to be constructed for them at Hull and Rotterdam.

Facilities aboard have all cabins being fitted with *en suite* shower room and toilets, with towels and bed linen and clothes storage space. Premier cabins, either inside or external, are either two, four or five bunks, while Club cabins have a sea view, colour television, tea and coffee making facilities. Standard cabins are either two or four bunked, internal or external. Both ships are well-designed for disabled and wheelchair access and have disabled toilet facilities.

Deck 7 has the main side loading car entrance and aft of that has 14 single and 39 double cabins reserved exclusively for freight drivers. Decks 8 (Red Deck) and 9 (Blue Deck) feature most of the enormous range of passenger facilities. Deck 8 features the Four Seasons buffet restaurant; two shops; reception; the information desk and *bureau de change*; toilets and disabled toilets; wine bar; and the double-deck Sunset Show Lounge which features inbuilt stage, sound and light system. There is a cyber café and the casino. Deck 9 has Lagan's Brasserie; the business centre; a wine bar; the quiet room; the exclusive Freight Driver's restaurant and lounge; the Continental café; a shop; Children's World play zone; the Irish Bar; a video arcade and two cinemas. The Sky Lounge with piano bar and breakfast area is on Deck 12 which also has the sun decks with teak planking.

27: Hull – Zeebrugge – Rotterdam

P&O Ferries run seven sailings per week on a 12 hour 15 minutes overnight crossing to and from Hull and Zeebrugge, normally sailing at 18.30.

The two vessels used on this route are the near sisters *Pride of Bruges* (IMO 8503797) and the *Pride of York* (IMO 8501957), the former *Norsun* and *Norsea* respectively. This duo were built in 1987 at widely separated shipyards, the former by NKK (Nippon Kaiji Kyokai), at Tsurumi, Japan and the latter by Kvaerner Govan Shipbuilders, Glasgow, for the North Sea Ferries company, which at the time were jointly owned by P&O and The Royal Nedlloyd Group.

The 31,598-GT *Pride of Bruges* has an overall length of 179.03 m, a beam of 25.35 m and a 6.19 m draught. She is powered by four Wärtsilä Sulzer engines for a speed of 19 knots. Her capacity is approximately 1,000 passengers and she can carry 850 cars or 180 lorries on 2,250 lane meters of vehicle deck. She originally operated between 1987 and 1996 as the *Norsun* for Nedlloyd, as one-half of a jointly-owned venture with P&O known as Noordzee Veerdiensten (North Sea Ferries). In 1996 this became wholly P&O owned and continued operations under their flag until 2001.

The 31,785-GT *Pride of York* has an overall length of 179.41 m, a beam of 25.35 m and a 6.13 m draught. She has four Stork-Werkspoor 16TM410 diesel engines which give her a speed of 19 knots. Her capacity is around 1,000 passengers, and she can convey 850 cars or 180 lorries on 2,250 lane meters of vehicle deck. From 1996–2002 she was operated by P&O North Sea Ferries and from 2002 by P&O. Both ships have two controllable-pitch propellers and two bow-thrusters. Both initially conducted the Hull to Rotterdam crossing between them, and

The *Pride of York* working out of Hull. (© P&O)

The *Pride of Bruges*, part of the PO Ferries fleet. (© P&O)

in 2002, after a complete refurbishment, were moved to the Hull to Zeebrugge passage

Facilities aboard both vessels are basically the same, with all cabins being fitted with *en suite* shower room and toilets, with towels and bed linen and clothes storage space. Premier cabins, either inside or external, are either two, four or five bunks while Club cabins have a sea view, colour television, tea and coffee making facilities. Standard cabins, are either two or four bunked, internal or external.

For fine dining there is the Langan's Brasserie with a large wine list in the evening and a breakfast menu in the morning. Other facilities include the Four Seasons carvery and 'Eat-as-much-as-you-like buffet' and the wine bar; there is also a quiet room and the children's playroom with the Kids Club and the Junior Crew Club on Deck 4. Entertainment is at the Sunset Show Bar with the Continental Café and Boulevards Bar and the Offshore Shopping Zone, there is also a *bureau de change*, all on Deck 5. The Moonlight Lounge on Deck 6 has bingo, dancing and quiz shows among its entertainments and there is a cinema. In addition drinks are served at the Piano bar and there is a Costa Coffee outlet.

The ships both have limited-mobility and wheelchair access, with lifts at the terminals and from the car decks and embarkation walkways. There are a limited number of specially-modified wide-door cabins which can be pre-booked.

The ferry terminal at Hull is located at the King George Dock, Hedon Road, Kingston-upon-Hull, HU9 5QA. It is car accessed via the M62 or the A1079 to the A63 and the A1033, and is signed to King George Dock & Ferries. All vehicles should check in at the Rotterdam terminal. The Europort has a multi-storey car park, while the Hedon Road Zeebrugge service has three open-air car parks near the terminal. All are paid car parking. There is a connecting bus to the Paragon rail station for trains that connect to Kings Cross. There is a 90-minute pre departure check-in limit.

The ferry terminal at Rotterdam, the Europort, is at Luxembourg Weg No. 2, 3198 LG Europort, The Netherlands. It is some 24 miles from Rotterdam central accessed by car via the N15 and is signed to Europort and P&O Ferries, with the Havennummer 5805 as the PO dock. The central rail station is connected by Eurolines bus service.

The ferry terminal at Zeebrugge, in the Buitenhaven is at Leopold II Dam 13 (Havendam) B8380, Belgium, and is car accessed via the N31, N300 N34a and is signed Zone 1, P&O Ferries. A bus connects to Bruges central rail station, and there are bus services from Minnewater/Bargeplein.

Contact Details
Kingston-upon-Hull Office
P&O, King George V Dock, Hull, East Yorks, HU9 5QA
Tel: 01482 708200
Fax: 01482 708269
Email: freight.hill@poferries.com
Web: www.poferries.com

Zeebrugge Office
P&O Beneluxhaven Luxemburngweg 2, Havennummer 5805,
3198 LG Europoort (Rotterdam), The Netherlands
Tel: (031) (0) 181 256156
Fax: (031) (0) 181 263022
Email: freight.bookings.europoort@poferries.com
Web: www.poferries.com

Rotterdam Europoort Office
P&O NV Leopold II Dam 13, Havendam, B8380, Zeebrugge, Belgium
Tel: (032) (0) 5055 9200
Fax: (032) (0) 5055 9274
Email: freight.bookings.zeebrugge@poferries.com
Web: www.poferries.com

28: Killingholme – Hoek van Holland – Rotterdam Europoort

Background

One of the new ferry routes Stena, had trialled its practicability with the *Stena Searider* built in 1969, and the 6,209-GT *Stena Seatrader* built in 1973. The *Stena Searider* was built in Finland by Oy Wärtsilä AB and Helsingfors as the *Finncarrier*, and had an overall length of 178.70 m, a 24.6 m beam and a 5.5 m draught. She had two 12-cylinder Wärtsilä-Pielstick diesel engines driving two screws for an 18 knot speed. Her capacity was 120 passengers and she had 2,390 lane meters of car parking. After over three decades of service with numerous ownership and name changes she was sold to Stena Line UK in 1998 for use on the Hoek van Holland to Harwich service, later switching to Killingholme.

The 17,991-GT *Stena Seatrader* was the former *Svealand*, a 1973-built vessel constructed in Denmark by Nakskov Sibsvaerft for Lion Ferry AB. She was taken over in 1990 and served with Stena Line for eighteen years. She was of 148.01 m overall length, with a 21.64 m beam and a 5.54 m draught. She could carry 221 passengers and 210 cars on 2,100 lane meters of vehicle deck. The *Stena Searider* served between 8 October 2000 and 18 June 2007 while *Stena Seatrader* worked the crossing from 14 March 2001 to 11 August 2006.

The experience was sufficiently encouraging to expand the service and €200 million was invested to bring in new Ro-Ro ships. Another vessel employed was the 13,867-GT *Rosebay*. She was the former *Transgermania*, originally built in Germany in 1976 by J.J. Sietas Werft for Poseidon Schiffahrt AG, and which was taken over by Stena between 1993 and 1997. She was 135.75 m overall length, with a beam of 23,72 m and a 6.05 draught. She had two MAN 6-52/55A engines for 17 knots speed and could carry 165 passengers with 104 berths, and had 1,270 lane meters of car deck. She inaugurated the route from 8 October 2000 and plied it until 9 March the following year before becoming the Sally Line *Eurostar*.

Also in 2006, Norfolkline announced that from June they were commencing their own daily service from Killingholme HST to Vlaardingen in the Netherlands where they had opened a brand-new ferry terminal. The line was already operating a once a week weekend Killingholme to Scheveningen crossing.

This pair was eventually replaced by two new-builds, the 25,900-GT sisters *Stena Trader* and the *Stena Traveller* respectively which were mainly assembled in Russia, and finished off in Norway, a new concept at the time, initial construction taking place at the Baltijsky Zavod Shipyard and completion work being done by Fosen Mekaniker Verksted, at Rissa. They were of 212 m overall length, with a 26 m beam and a draught of 6.3 m. They had MAN diesel engines and a speed of 22 knots and could accommodate 200 passengers. The *Stena Trader* and *Stena Traveller* served with Stena Line on the route from 12 August 2006 and 20 June 2007 respectively but both were transferred to the Canadian Government in 2011. They were both shortened at Lloyds Werft shipyard in order to fit the Canadian east-coast ports and were chartered for five years to the Marine Atlantic Company to take over the Nova Scotia and Newfoundland passage. They were renamed as *Highlanders* and *Blue Puttees* respectively, after Canadian army regiments.

A pair of huge modern ships, the *Stena Transporter* and *Stena Transit*, were ordered from the South Korean shipyard of Samsung in South

Korea to drive the success onward. To cover the gap until this brace could be completed, two substantial vessels were taken under charter, the first of these being the 25,996-GT *Finnarrow*, which was originally built as the *Gotland* in 1996 by P.T. Pelita Bahari in Indonesia for Rederi Ab Gotland as Tor Line, for use on the Malmö to Travemunde crossing. *Finnarrow* has an overall length of 168.15 m, a beam of 27.7 m and a draught of 6 m and is powered by four Sulzer 6ZA40S engines, giving her a speed of 21 knots. Her capacity is 200 passengers, with 1,888 berths, and she can carry 800 cars on her 2,400 lane meters of vehicle deck. She had seen service with a variety of owners, Seawind, Nordo Link, Finnink and Scandlines GmbH in the intervening years but in Stena colours she commenced service on the passage in December 2010 and was replaced at the end of February 2011. The second chartered ship was the 23,000-GT *Coraggio* which had been built in Italy in 2007 by Nuovi Canterie Apuani for Grimaldi Holdings S.p.A. as *Grandi Navi Veloci*. She had an overall length of 199.14 m, a beam of 26.6 m and a 6.4 m draught. Her engines were two Wärtsilä 12V46 diesels for a speed of 24 knots. Her capacity was 500 passengers with 268 berths and she had 2,623 lane meters of vehicle deck. She served from September 2010 until October 2011.

The first of the new vessels, the *Stena Transporter*, took over from the *Finnarrow* on 1st March 2011. The second vessel, the *Stena Transit*, arrived in October 2011.

By this time other operators had moved on, in the summer of 2010 it was announced by DFDS Seaways (the former Norfolkline), that the Killingholme to Vlaardingen service which ran from the Humber Sea terminal, were to be transferred to DFDS's existing terminal at Immingham, with the last Killingholme sailing being made on 31 July. This meant that some Ro-Ro ships like the 29,004-GT *Humber Viking*, which had been built at Odense, Denmark in 2009, and had operated briefly between Killingholme and Vlaardingen, were moved to the new route.

Current Operators, Ships and Details

Stena RoRo AB operates a daily crossing to and from Rotterdam-Europort.

Stena has the 33,690-GT sisters *Stena Transporter* (IMO 9469376) and *Stena Transit* (IMO 9469388) in service. Built by Samsung Heavy Company Industries in their Geoje Shipyard, South Korea for Stena RoRo AB, and owned by Katrine Leasing Limited, these are 33,690-GT Seabridger Mk. II type vessels, with an overall length of 212 m, a beam of 40 m and a 6.3 m draught. They are powered by two 10,800 kW STX-MAN 9L 48/60 B engines, with two 1,450 kW STX-MAN 7L 21/31 auxiliaries, developing 21,600 kW for a speed of 23 knots, can carry 300 passengers and have space for 260 lorries on 4,057 lane meters of vehicle deck. Onboard facilities on these ships will include a restaurant, a shop and lounges for the drivers.

Cobelfret Ferries NV in conjunctions with Compagnie Luxembourgeoise de Navigation SA (CLdN) operate a crossing most days of the week between Killingholme HST terminal and either CdMR Botlek, Rotterdam or Sea-Ro Zweedse kaai, Zeebrugge, but weekend services are subject to cargo availability and customer requirements and should be carefully checked. The two 49,166-GT Ro-Ro cargo ships currently in use on these routes are the sisters *Pauline* (IMO 9324473) and *Yasmine* (IMO 9337353). The schedule is for a ship to leave Rotterdam and Killingholme at 19.00 each day and arrive at 08.00/08.30 the next morning Monday to Friday, with the Saturday sailing leaving at 16.00 and 17.30 respectively, with next day discharge only, while Sundays are not scheduled but depend on customer requirements.

Built by Flensburger Schiffbau Gesellschaft mbH & Co, KG, Germany for Conway S.A. and operated by Cobelfret Ferries, these two modern 'Humbermax' cargo vessels are state of the art and have an overall length of 202 m, a beam of 31 m and a 6.6 m draught and are powered by two MaK 12M43 engines, giving a speed of 21.7 knots. They have

28: Killingholme – Hoek van Holland – Rotterdam Europoort

The *Stena Transporter* freight ferry in the Orwell. (© Harwich International Port)

five decks, can carry 12 passengers in twelve berths and a total of 1,358 cars or 251 trailers and 650 cars on two dedicated car decks, with a total 4,600 lane meters of vehicle decks.

The Humber Sea terminal at Killingholme is on the south bank of the Humber Estuary and is accessed via the M180, A180 and A160, being signed for Immingham Dock West Gate and then Humber Sea terminal. The terminal has six purpose-built berths with 24 hour access, digital CCTV monitoring and perimeter fencing. Accompanied vehicles are allowed a 12-hour pre-sailing check-in period and there is a maximum of three-day uncharged parking. Facilities for truck drivers include a lounge, showers and a snack bar with toilets.

Hoek van Holland ferry terminal at Stationsweg 10, 3151 Hoek van Holland, is located on the north bank of the Nieuwe Waterweg shipping canal and is accessed by road via the A20/N20 then the E19/E30 and is signed 'Engerland' and 'Hook van Holland' to the dock. There are both long- and short-stay paid car parks with some disabled parking spaces. The Hoek van Holland Haven rail station is next door to the ferry terminal and connects with the NS rail system to The Hague and Rotterdam in under an hour as well as the Amsterdam Express. Facilities include the ticket office and check-in, a café/bar, ATM and full disabled facilities.

Contact Details

Killingholme Office
Stena Line, Humber Sea Terminal, Haven Road, North Killingholme, North Lincolnshire, DN40 3JP
Tel: 01469 542 170
Fax: 01469 542 179
Email: freightbooking.uk@stenaline.com
Web: www.stenaline.co.uk

Colbelfret Humber Sea Terminal, Clough Lane, North Killingholme, North Lincolnshire, DN40 3JS
Tel: 01469 573115
Tel: 01469 573739
Fax: 01469 573739
Email: ukbookings@cldn.com
Web: www.cobelfret.com

Hoek van Holland Office
Stena Line, Postbus 2, 3150 AA Hoek van Holland, The Netherlands
Tel: +31 (0) 174 389333
Fax: +31 (0) 174 389459
Email: nell.eichhorn@stenaline.com
Web: www.stenaline.com

Zeebrugge Office
Colbelfret Ferries NV, Hendrik van Minderhoutstraat 50, Brittannia Dok, B-8380 Zeebrugge, Belgium
Tel: +32 (0) 5050 2245; +32 (0) 5050 2248
Fax: +32 (0) 5050 2249
Email: freight.irl@colbelfret.com
Web: www.cobelfret.com

29: Other Offshore Operators

Bere Island Ferries
Bere Island Ferries, operated by Colin and Ann Harrington, run a three-ship, year-round, passenger and vehicle ferry service from Castletownbere, County Cork across Bantry Bay to Bere Island. The normal journey time is approximately 10 minutes. There is normally a summer schedule between 21 June and 21 September with 8 daily (5 only on Sundays) sailings and a winter schedule between 22 September and 20 June offering 7 daily (3 only on Sundays) sailing. The company has a fleet of three ships.

Morvern, of 64-GT, has an overall length of 23.7 m, a beam of 6.66 m, and a 1.33 m draught, with a best speed of 8 knots. She was built in 1973 as one of a class of eight such vessels by James Lamont & Company at Port Glasgow (Yard No. 417), and engined by English Electric Kelvin Division, Glasgow, for service with Caledonian MacBrayne. After twenty years service on various routes she was leased out for six weeks in 1995 to Aranmore Ireland Ferry Services, Portrush, and shortly afterward purchased outright by that company. In 2001 she was again sold, this time to Bere Island. She had a passenger capacity of 12 and 6 cars, and recently operated solely as a freight-only vessel but is currently reported to be out of service.

Oilean Na H-Oighe, (Island of Youth), the former *Loch Bhrusda*, is a 18.6 m overall, 69-GT bow-loading ferry built in 1980 by Lewis Offshore Ltd, Stornoway for the Western Isles Council, under the name *Eilean Na H-Oige*. She was credited with being the first Ro-Ro vehicular ferry on the service between Eriskay and Ludaig and served for over twenty years on that route until the opening of the causeway in July 2001 ended this part of her long career. After a period laid-up she re-entered service between Ceann a Gharaidh and Aird Mhór over the Sound of Barra from March 2002 until April 2003. She was later purchased by Bere Island and left Eriskay for that port on 14 August 2003. Her initial task was to service US Navy vessels attending the re-opening of an old Martello Tower there, and then commenced work on the Castletownbere to Bere Island route. Currently she is capable of 7 knots, and she can carry 4 cars and up to 35 passengers.

Sancta Maria was completed in 1983 and has the same car/passenger capacity as her sister. She was built by George Brown and Company, Greenock (Yard No. 283) and engined by Volvo Penta (UK) Ltd, Watford as the *Eilean Bhearnaraigh*. She is of 68-GT with an overall length of 15.9 m, a beam of 7 m and a 1.65 m draught, and has a maximum speed of 7.3 knots, powered by twin diesel engines. She was built for the Scottish Western Islands Council (*Comhairle nan Eilean Siar*), Stornoway, being designed to ply between Berneray and Otternish on North Uist, which she did for fourteen years, the latter period from 1996 to 1998 with Caledonian MacBrayne, until the construction of a causeway rendered her services null-and-void. She then served at Eriskay, carrying cattle across the Sound of Harris to Berneray, and also worked the Sound of Barra before being bought by the *Transalpine Redemptorists Inc* monks at Papa Stronsay, Orkney, as a supply ship for the monastery there. She was docked in 2002 and in 2008 she was purchased by Bere Island who renamed her in 2009.

Offshore Ferry Services

The Fastnet Ferry *Julia* passing Blackrock Castle. (© Fastnet Lines)

Contact Details
Ferry Lodge, West End, Bere Island, County Cork, Irish Republic
Tel: (353) (0)27 75009
Fax: (353) (0)27 75000
Email: biferry@eircom.net
Web: www.bereislandferries.com

Doolin Ferries
From Doolin, County Clare, in the Irish Republic, Doolin Ferries operates the 1989-built, MV *Happy Hooker* for services to Inisheer and Inishmor between April and September although services and times are subject to weather conditions. This vessel is a 77-tonner, with a 96-passenger accommodation. There is also the older 113-ton *Rose of Aran*, built in 1976, with identical capacity.

29: Other Offshore Operators

The *Julia* of Fastnet Lines passing Roches Point. (© Fastnet Lines)

Offshore Ferry Services

Contact Details
Doolin Pier, Doolin, Co. Clare, Irish Republic
Tel: (353) (0)65 7074 455
Fax: (353) (0)65 7974 914
Email: info@doolinferries.com.
Web: www.doolinferries.com

Inis Mor Ferries
Inis Mor Ferries, Galway, Irish Republic, had a new vessel constructed in France which was launched in June 2001 as the *Queen of Aran II*. She was at Rossaveal, with the Island Ferries log painted on her side.

Contact Details
Kiosk C, Āras Fāillte, Tourist Office, Forster Street, Galway
Tel: 091 566535
Fax: 091 534315
Email: info@queenofaran2.com
Web: www.galwaylive.com/InisMorFerries

Fastnet Ferry
The recession has claimed many victims, one of which was the Fastnet Ferry Company which operated a rump Swansea to Cork ferry service. The company went into receivership in November 2011 and the MV *Julia* is, at the time of writing, at Cork and up for sale.

Kintyre Express
This company, owned by West Coast Motors, and under Managing Director Colin Craig, runs the *Kintyre Express*, with services between Campbeltown and Troon, utilizing a 10.9 m Redbay *Stormforce* 11-metre RIB (Rigid Inflatable Boat), which has centrally-heated fully-enclosed cabins, is coded to the M.C.A. required standard and is crewed by fully qualified, experienced skippers. The Redbay Company of Cushendall, County Antrim, Northern Ireland, has a strong track record in this type of build.

The company also has plans to run a ferry service from Campbeltown on the Kintyre peninsular to Ballycastle in Northern Ireland from the summer of 2012. The intention is to use the Redbay RIB with a passenger capacity of 12, to run two passenger-only return journeys each day for a 90-minute crossing time during an operating period from 27 May to 26 September, with sailings on Friday, Saturday, Sunday and Monday. There are plans for extra journeys according to demand. The planned single journey time at 37 knots would be 1 hour 15 minutes. Visitor attractions include famous golf courses, distilleries and the Giant's Causeway which could generate sufficient traffic to make the service viable.

If subsidies were forthcoming, (which with the current Government's obsession with cuts seems problematical), then it would be a welcome return of this route, which Sea Containers ran as a passenger and car operation between 1997 and 1999 before pulling out.

Contact Details
Kintyre Express, Benmhor House, Saddell Street, Campbelltown, PA28 6DN
Tel: 01586 552319
Email: info@kintyreexpress.com
Web: www.kintyreexpress.com

Murphys Ferry
Murphys Ferry Service, owner Carol Murphy, runs an almost daily all-year round service with the *Ikom K* to Bere Island, Castletownbere, Bantry Bay, Eire every day except Christmas Day, utilizing. The winter service has first departure from Bere Island at 07.30, and from the

Pontoon at 08.00 (weekdays) and 09.15 and 10.00 (weekends). The final service from Bere Island is 18.30 in September and May only and 20.00 Friday only, and the last sailing from the Pontoon is 19.00 September to May only and 20.30 Friday only.

The summer timetable for June/July and August 2012 began at 08.00 (excluding Sunday) from the Pontoon and 07.30 (excluding Sunday) from Bere Island, with final services at 20.30 and 20.00 respectively.

Contact Details
Murphys Ferry Service, Lawrence Cove, Bere Island, Co. Cork, Ireland
Tel: 00 353 27 75014
Mobile: 00 353 87 2386095
Email: info@murphysferry.com
Web: www.murphysferry.com

O'Brien Line

O'Brien Line, the former Doolin Ferry Company, had their origins in 1970 when Bill O'Brien commenced operations with a small speed boat from Doolin, County Clare, Irish Republic, then gradually increased in size and scope. With the introduction of new Irish Department of Transport regulations in 1987 a new standard was required and this resulted in the introduction of the *Tranquility*, a steel-built vessel conforming to European Class 2A standards in 1988. She had accommodation for 48 passengers. In 2002, with the company now jointly run by Bill and his son Liam, the *Tranquility* was lengthened by almost 8 m and new passenger accommodation and wheelhouse was built into her, raising her external and internal passenger capacity to 100 and her tonnage to 62. Other facilities include a bar/shop, panoramic windows, toilet facilities, plasma screen televisions, air conditioning, heating and a sun deck.

The MV *Tranquility* is operated by Doolin Ferry Company to the Cliffs of Moher and Inisheer and the Aran Islands. (© Doolin Ferry Company)

A sister ship, *Queen of Aran*, (IMO 7527928) was originally built in 1976 and she was given a refurbishment in 2008, giving her a tonnage of 113 and a length of 20.1 m. She has external and internal seating for 110 passengers but is self-limited to 100. There are toilet facilities and heating.

Services include the basic Doolin Inishmore, Doolin to Inisheer routes and in 2007 a cruise to the Cliffs of Moher was introduced.

Contact Details
Ticket Office, Doolin Pier, Doolin, C. Clare, Irish Republic
Tel: (353) 065 707 5555; 065 707 5618; 0879 581465
Email: info@obrienline.com
Web: www.obrienline.com

Glossary

AB – Aktiebola G.
A.G.O – Aktiengellschaft.
AIS – Automatic Identification System.
A/S – Aktieselskab.
ATM – Automatic Teller Machine.
B+I – British and Irish.
CCTV – Closed-circuit Television.
CinVen – Coal Investment Nominees for Venture Capital.
DDC – Display Data Channel.
DFDS – Det Forenede Damskibs-Selskab.
DG – Dangerous Goods.
DSMN – Device Session Monitoring Protocol.
DSMV – Double-screw Motor Vessel.
DSC – Digital Selective Calling.
FBMA – Fairey Babcock Marine Abolitz (formerly Cowes, IoW and Cebu, Philippines).
FF – Fast Ferry generally high-speed craft with speed of 30 knots or more, normally a catamaran type, either aluminium or steel hulled and generally passenger carrying.
GEC – General Electrics Company.
GER – Great Eastern Railway.
GPS – Global Positioning System.
GT – Gross Tonnage. (Formerly GRT – Gross Registered Tonnage).
HIAB – Hyrauliska Industri AB.
HSC – High-Speed Craft.
HSS – High-Speed Sealift.
HST – Humber Sea Terminal.
ICOM – Aikomu Kabushiki-Gaisha.
IESM – Industrial Engineering Systems Management.
IMO – International Maritime Organization registration number, assigned to every ship over 100-GT and which stays with the ship regardless of change of ownership and name. Registered at Lloyd's, London on their Fairplay Index.
INTERFET – International Force in East Timor.
ISO – International Standards Organization.
ISSSco – Integrated Software Systems Corporation.
LCS – Liquid Cooling System.
Linkspan – A hinged bridge on the quay at a port or ferry terminal which can be connected with a ramp on a vessel to allow loading or unloading.
LNER – London & North-Eastern Railway.
Lo-Lo – Lift-On, Lift-Off.
MAK or MaK – Maschinenbau Kiel.
MCA – Maritime & Coastguard Agency.
MDS – Motion De System.
MES – Marine Evacuation System.
MOB – Man Overboard.
MS – Motor Ship.
MTU – Maximum Transmission Unit.
M/V – Motor Vessel.
NKK – Nippon Kaiji Kyokai.
NSW – New South Wales.

Glossary

OIC – Orkney Islands Council.
P&O – Peninsular & Orient.
Pax – Passengers.
PS – Paddle Steamer.
RFD – Reginald Foster Dagnell. (Beaufort, now part of SURVITEC).
RIB – Rigid-Inflatable Boat.
RMS – Royal Mail Steamer.
RMT – Regie voor Martiem.
Ro-Pax – Vehicles plus passenger ferries, some of the larger modern type now approach cruise ships in both size and luxury.
Ro-Ro – Roll-on-Roll-off, applied to vehicle carrying ferries.
S.A. – Sociedad Anónima.
SART – Search and Rescue Transponder.
S.E.M.T. – Societe D'Etudes de Machines Thermiques.
SMZ – Stoomvaart Maatschappij Zeeland.

SNAT – Secure Network Address Translation.
SNAV – Societa Navigazione Alta Velocita.
SNCF – Société Nationale de fur Français.
SOLAS – Search and Rescue Transponder.
S.p.A. – Società fur Azioni.
SSC – Steam Ship Company.
STAG – Scottish Transport Appraisal Guidance.
TAMD – Turbocharged Aftercooled Marine Diesel.
TGV – Train à Grande Vitesse.
TRIS – Transportation Research Information Service.
TRS – Tariff Rate Subsidy.
TT Line – Travemünde to Trelleborg.
VHF – Very High Frequency.
WiFi – Wireless Fidelity.
WPC – Wave-piercing Catamaran.